QUALITATIVE DATA ANALYSIS

from **START** *to* **FINISH**

SAGE has been part of the global academic community since 1965, supporting high quality research and learning that transforms society and our understanding of individuals, groups, and cultures. SAGE is the independent, innovative, natural home for authors, editors and societies who share our commitment and passion for the social sciences.

Find out more at: **www.sagepublications.com**

Connect, Debate, Engage on Methodspace

 **Connect with other researchers and discuss your research interests**

Keep up with announcements in the field, for example calls for papers and jobs

Discover and review resources

Engage with featured content such as key articles, podcasts and videos

Find out about relevant conferences and events

Methodspace
Connecting the Research Community

www.methodspace.com

brought to you by

⑤SAGE

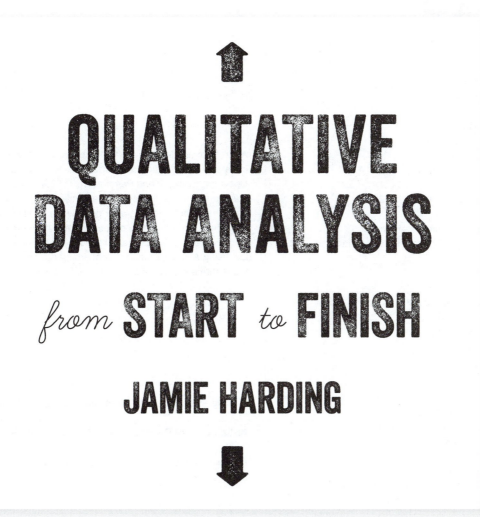

QUALITATIVE DATA ANALYSIS

from **START** *to* **FINISH**

JAMIE HARDING

Los Angeles | London | New Delhi
Singapore | Washington DC

Los Angeles | London | New Delhi
Singapore | Washington DC

SAGE Publications Ltd
1 Oliver's Yard
55 City Road
London EC1Y 1SP

SAGE Publications Inc.
2455 Teller Road
Thousand Oaks, California 91320

SAGE Publications India Pvt Ltd
B 1/I 1 Mohan Cooperative Industrial Area
Mathura Road
New Delhi 110 044

SAGE Publications Asia-Pacific Pte Ltd
3 Church Street
#10-04 Samsung Hub
Singapore 049483

Editor: Katie Metzler
Assistant editor: Anna Horvai
Production editor: Ian Antcliff
Copyeditor: Rosemary Morlin
Proofreader: Louise Harnby
Marketing manager: Ben Griffin-Sherwood
Cover design: Francis Kenney
Typeset by: C&M Digitals (P) Ltd, Chennai, India
Printed by: MPG Printgroup, UK

Library of Congress Control Number: 2012942966

British Library Cataloguing in Publication data

A catalogue record for this book is available from
the British Library

ISBN 978-0-85702-138-0
ISBN 978-0-85702-139-7 (pbk)

This book is dedicated to my wife Allison, with heartfelt thanks for her constant encouragement and love.

Contents

About the author

Jamie Harding received his PhD from the Department of Sociology and Social Policy at the University of Newcastle upon Tyne. He has been employed at Northumbria University since 1995, first as a Lecturer in Housing Studies and more recently as a Senior Lecturer in Research Methods in the Department of Social Sciences. Before moving into higher education he worked for a number of social housing organisations.

Jamie's main area of teaching is qualitative and quantitative research methods, which he teaches at undergraduate, postgraduate and doctoral level. He also lectures on criminal justice and is a Director of the Centre for Offenders and Offending. A key area of interest is homelessness, a subject on which he has published a book and several journal articles and also teaches a specialist module. He and his colleagues work in partnership with the local authority and voluntary organisations dealing with homelessness to undertake research, develop policy and provide student placements. Jamie has also published journal articles about higher education; his publications report on qualitative and quantitative data analysed by a range of methods.

Jamie is married with two adult children and a grandson; he is an enthusiastic but slow marathon runner.

Acknowledgements

Thank you to all the anonymous interviewees who generously gave up their time to support this project and for others at the case study university who made me feel so welcome.

I am very grateful to the young man in the temporary accommodation project who agreed to be quoted at length and to Misha Kennedy for the role that she played.

Thanks are also due to the focus group members, who provided such a lively discussion with so many examples to draw on.

Thank you to all my colleagues at Northumbria University who have offered valuable support and advice, particularly Matt Baillie Smith, Pam Davies, Karen Williamson and Carol Stephenson.

I am also grateful to all the staff at Sage who have advised me so well: Patrick Brindle, Katie Metzler, Anna Horvai and David Hodge.

1

Introduction

This book was written largely because I have worked with many students, at both undergraduate and postgraduate level, who have wanted guidance as to how to analyse qualitative data. Being confronted with a set of transcripts from interviews, or the record of one or more focus groups, can create great uncertainty as to what to do next. While acknowledging that there are no 'correct' answers, this book will make suggestions as to how the analysis can be undertaken, using real data to provide examples and exercises.

Structure of the book

Data analysis is never the first task of any research project, so Chapter 2 discusses briefly many of the factors and decisions that affect the earlier stages of the research process. The researcher must decide, for example, whether to use a primarily inductive or a primarily deductive approach, how to collect data and how to ensure that the research is conducted in an ethical manner.

Not all qualitative research involves collecting data directly from humans; some important studies use documents or other materials (such as television programmes) as their data. However, most qualitative studies involve a large element of interaction with people; interviews and focus groups are the most popular methods by which data is collected. Accordingly, Chapter 3 discusses these two forms of data collection, identifying the opportunities that each provides and some of the skills that are required by the researcher in each case.

Chapters 4–6 demonstrate the process of analysing interview data, from the moment when the researcher first looks at their transcripts to the point at which they can identify the key findings of the research. Each of these chapters discusses techniques that may be helpful at different stages of the analysis, shows how I put these techniques into practice with some of my data and presents exercises in which you are invited to do the same. Chapter 7 discusses a range of alternative approaches that could have been taken.

Some of the skills and techniques used to analyse focus group data are the same as those that can be employed in the case of interviews, but the interaction that takes place between focus group members provides extra opportunities for analysis to explore further the views of individuals and of the group. Chapter 8 shows how these opportunities were exploited in the case of one focus group discussion.

Once the analysis is complete and the researcher has identified the findings from the interviews or the focus group(s), the final stage of most research projects is to communicate these findings in the form of written output. The output is the subject matter of the last two chapters. Chapter 9 demonstrates how the researcher can write about their methods and findings, covering questions such as when to include quotations. Chapter 10 considers how to write about the existing literature and how to tie together the findings and the literature in a conclusion.

The interviews and the focus group

The interviews which are analysed in Chapters 4–7, and the focus group discussion which is the subject of Chapter 8, require some introduction. The interview data was collected by an interviewer, under my supervision, in the Faculty of Social Sciences at a case study university. This was primarily an inductive piece of research, which meant, as will be discussed in Chapter 2, that there was no theory to test and no research questions to answer. However, there were a number of research objectives that arose from my experience of working in higher education and of current debates within the field. These objectives were:

1 to identify the motivation of lecturers for their choice of career;
2 to identify feelings about, and practical difficulties associated with, different elements of the job;
3 to discuss different types of students and the experience of teaching them;
4 to identify feelings about reflective practice and methods by which it was put into practice; and
5 to discuss changes with time in relation to the above factors.

Confidentiality is normally a key ethical requirement of any research project, but in this case the interviewees agreed that material could be included that would enable them to be identified. However, I have sought to avoid this and so, in addition to referring to each lecturer by a pseudonym, have taken out of the transcripts some of the more specific details that would have made identification possible. All the interviewees have read what has been written about them and agree that it reflects fairly the comments that they made. A brief description of each of them appears below:

- Fern was a senior member of staff who had been employed continuously at the case study university for a substantial period of time.
- Susan was a lecturer who had experience of working for other universities before moving to the case study university.
- Rachel was also a lecturer who had experience from other universities; in addition she had worked outside higher education. She had recently moved to the case study university.
- Laura was a lecturer whose previous experience had been in research. She had been at the case study university for a short period of time.
- Lewis had a management position within the Faculty of Social Sciences although he continued to teach and research. He had been employed at the case study university for a substantial period of time.
- Paula was newly appointed to a management role but also retained teaching and research responsibilities. She had been employed at the case study university for a number of years.
- Thomas was a lecturer with previous work experience in industry. He had been employed at the university for a substantial period of time.

Introduction to data analysis

Discussions of the process of qualitative data analysis can sometimes be confusing. Trying to characterise the process discussed in Chapters 4–6 proved surprisingly difficult. As Boeije (2010: 76–77) notes, qualitative analysis consists of cutting data up in order to put it together again in a manner that seems relevant and meaningful. However, Bryman and Burgess (1994: 6) point out that many discussions of qualitative methods fail to address the choices that are available to the researcher in terms of how exactly such analysis can be conducted. Indeed, books on qualitative methods often launch into the process of analysis without discussing the options that are available. To make matters more difficult, where books discuss possible approaches, the terms used can vary quite widely. The most helpful list of options for the new researcher to choose from is, in my opinion, the one provided by Dawson (2009: 119–125):

- Thematic analysis, which is particularly associated with inductive approaches (see Chapter 2) and involves identifying themes that emerge from the data.
- Comparative analysis, which involves comparing and contrasting data collected from different respondents until no more new themes or issues arise.
- Content analysis, where the researcher works systematically through each transcript, looking to see how often certain factors (which are recorded by codes) arise. A similar process of content analysis is associated with the analysis of documents, as will be discussed in Chapter 2.
- Discourse analysis, which focuses on patterns of speech and the way that language is used to convey meaning.

Dawson (2009: 120) acknowledges that these approaches are related and may be used within the same research project. Discourse analysis is not used in the process of analysis which is covered in Chapters 4–6, but is discussed as one of a number of alternative approaches in Chapter 7. However, elements of all the other three approaches are used in Chapters 4–6. Comparative analysis is particularly important when discussing the constant comparative method in Chapter 4 and there are elements throughout of counting the occurrences of different factors, as required by content analysis. However, the approach used draws most heavily on thematic analysis, as the search for themes is a central concern of these chapters.

Thematic analysis has been criticised on the grounds that, by looking for broad areas of similarity and difference, it removes much of the detail and produces accounts that can be quite distant from the experience of any one individual (Gibson and Brown, 2009: 129). However, Gibson and Brown (2009: 129) reject these criticisms on the grounds that thematic analysis:

> … provides a way of linking diverse experiences or ideas together, and of juxtaposing and interrelating different examples and features of the data. The themes do re-present and re-contextualise the data to which they relate, but this can be of value in creating new readings and renderings of that data.

Gibson and Brown (2009: 128–129) suggest that there are three sets of aims of thematic analysis:

1 Examining commonality – pooling together all the material across a dataset that has something in common. Commonalities which are discovered can then be analysed further, which may mean that subdivisions are found within them.

2 Examining differences – the researcher should also identify differences across the dataset and examine the relevance of them to the issues and themes that are being examined.

3 Examining relationships – the researcher should examine how different parts of their analysis fit together and contribute to an understanding of different issues and themes.

A commonality can be any feature that two or more cases have in common, including

- a common characteristic such as being female;
- a common experience such as enjoying giving lectures; or
- a common opinion such as believing that the costs of higher education are causing difficulties to students.

The focus group data discussed in Chapter 8 again involved social science lecturers, one of whom (Nick) was in a senior position while the others – Amy, Eric, Evan, Ian, Kevin, Leanne, Melissa, Neil and Yvette – were lecturers or senior lecturers. I moderated the focus group discussion, which was part of a broader educational project where one objective was to 'Research, identify and disseminate good practice in the organisation and delivery of seminars'. It took place alongside a focus group of students, who also considered the characteristics of effective seminars, and was followed by a joint event where a good practice guide was agreed.

Validity

Auerbach and Silverstein (2003: 32) argue that there is no single 'right way' to analyse a dataset and that the decisions taken are inevitably subjective. This point is made frequently in the forthcoming chapters, particularly where I set exercises and then show you how I would have completed them: it should not be assumed that my way is the only useful or correct way, or that your outcome is not valuable simply because it differs from mine.

However, this does not mean that the qualitative researcher has a free reign to analyse in any manner that they choose; they should be guided by the key principle of validity. Validity is defined by Jupp (2006a: 311) as:

The extent to which conclusions drawn from research provide an accurate description of what happened or a correct explanation of what happens and why.

Quantitative studies have some widely agreed methods of measuring validity – for example, to establish the validity of measures used for different phenomena (De Vaus, 2002: 53–54) – but there is no such consensus with regard to qualitative approaches (Steinke, 2004). However, as Steinke (2004: 185) notes, to decide that the quality of qualitative research cannot be assessed would mean that such research was conducted in random and arbitrary fashion. There are some simple techniques that can be used to enhance the validity of qualitative studies, such as reading thoroughly through interview transcripts before beginning analysis (Schmidt, 2004: 255). Chapter 9 considers a number of further measures that can be taken when the researcher has produced their findings, but wants to check that they are valid before writing them into their research output.

One particularly important concept associated with enhancing the validity of qualitative research is reflexivity. The following definition is offered by Heaton (2004: 104):

> Reflexivity in primary qualitative research generally involves the self-examination of how research findings were produced and, particularly, the role of the researcher(s) in their construction.

It is very important that the researcher is aware of the choices that they make when analysing data; they may keep an account of such decisions in order to later consider the implications of their approach (Jupp, 2006b: 258). Gibson and Brown (2009: 195) suggest that keeping a research diary of thoughts and decisions may be a helpful way of showing how analysis has developed before key decisions are forgotten or the reasons for them become less clear with time. An alternative approach, and the one used in Chapters 4–6, is to record key decisions through methodological memos, which should be referred back to when writing the methodology section of the research output (discussed in Chapter 9).

Definitions

It is important to be aware of the definitions of some of the key terms that are used in later chapters, many of which could easily be confused:

- An issue – a specific question or subject to be examined such as student non-attendance at teaching sessions.
- A theme – an idea that can be seen running through several responses such as the danger of students taking assessments without having attended teaching sessions.
- A concept – an underlying idea that is not necessarily referred to directly by respondents such as responsibility for learning (see Chapter 6).
- A category – a heading under which different sections of data can be placed for the purpose of analysis such as the debate over student employment.
- A respondent – someone who contributes data to a research project by, for example, being interviewed or taking part in a focus group discussion.

It is hoped that, when you have read this book, you will feel more confident to undertake a qualitative research project and, in particular, that the analysis of the data will seem a less daunting task.

2

Beginning the study

Introduction

The majority of this book is concerned with the analysis of data and the presentation of findings. However, it is critical that the researcher considers carefully every stage of the research project that precedes the analysis. It is assumed, because you are reading this book, that you have decided to collect, or are at least considering collecting, qualitative data. This chapter will consider some of the reasons for choosing a qualitative approach rather than a quantitative one. It will also discuss the differences between deductive and inductive approaches, with particular reference to the role that they ascribe to theory and literature. It will be shown that the plan or design for a research project is likely to be affected by decisions about quantitative, qualitative, inductive and deductive methodology.

It is worth mentioning briefly here the distinction between methodology and methods. As Clough and Nutbrown (2012: 36) note, these are difficult concepts to define, with different writers often providing different definitions. Sapsford (2006: 175) argues that 'Methodology is the philosophy of methods'. Clough and Nutbrown (2012: 31) suggest that methodology is the purpose of the study while methods are the tools by which this purpose is achieved. This chapter will consider discussions about underlying principles of quantitative and qualitative approaches – and of induction and deduction – as methodological, while more practical issues will be described as methods. Discussions about methods will include the manner in which samples can be chosen and the situations in which different forms of data collection are most appropriately used.

Finally, in any research study it is important to take account of a wide range of ethical issues. Some of the most frequently occurring issues will be identified here, with suggestions as to how common difficulties and dilemmas may be overcome.

Qualitative and quantitative research

A very simple distinction between quantitative and qualitative methods is that quantitative studies tend to involve larger numbers of respondents while qualitative research involves collecting more detailed information from a smaller number of people. While there are innumerable difficulties with these definitions – for example, social science research does not always involve collecting data directly from people – they can be used as a starting point for identifying more subtle differences.

In many cases, the choice between quantitative and qualitative methodology is a pragmatic one. A good pragmatic reason for choosing a qualitative approach is that there are only a small number of people available to collect data from. A less good but very common reason is that the researcher feels more confident using qualitative methods than using quantitative ones. However, even when the choice is made on pragmatic grounds, it is important to be aware of some of the principles that underpin qualitative methodology.

Taking a step backwards, it is also useful to reflect briefly on some of the underpinning principles of quantitative methodology, because qualitative approaches were developed partly as a result of social scientists becoming dissatisfied with the rationale behind quantitative research. Early social research was dominated by quantitative studies with leading figures such as Durkheim seeking to reproduce the success of the natural sciences by using similar methodology. For example, Durkheim's classic study of suicide (discussed in Gilbert, 1994) sought to explain objectively different rates of suicide in different countries.

Some of the key principles associated with quantitative research are clearly related to those of the natural sciences, i.e.:

- Measurement – this reflects the idea that social phenomena can be measured in the same manner as natural phenomena such as heat. So people are asked to state on a scale of 1 to 10 how far they agree with certain statements or figures are produced by political opinion pollsters representing the percentage of people who say that they would vote for different political parties if there were a general election tomorrow.

- Causality – it is not possible for social scientists to produce the same sort of 'laws' as natural scientists: for example, that water always turns to steam when heated to 100 degrees Celsius at sea level. However, it is well established in the social world that some factors have an impact on others: for example, that an individual having a low income increases the risk of them smoking (see, for example, Hemingway, 2007). Quantitative researchers have developed a number of complex procedures such as regression analysis to examine the relative impact of different independent variables on a dependent variable.

- Generalisation – the quantitative researcher does not just want to find what is true for the people who are subjects of their research, but to generalise to others. So, if they cannot collect information from an entire population, they will tend to choose a random sample from which they can make statistical inferences about the population. In the United Kingdom, major social surveys such as the General Household Survey and the British Crime Survey take this approach.

(Bryman, 1988: 21–37, with my examples)

A critical examination of the above points suggests some limitations of quantitative research. For example, an opinion pollster can ask which candidate or party a respondent would vote for alongside further questions to explore whether they prefer a particular candidate or party's policies on health, defence, and so on. However, this will only provide a limited picture of the complicated set of factors that affect how people vote. A realisation that human behaviour is more complex and less rational than that of the inanimate subjects of research in the natural sciences was central to the development of qualitative methods, which began to flourish in the second part of the twentieth century (Flick, 2009: 57–59). Qualitative methodology has a very different set of underpinning principles and characteristics to those of the natural sciences, most notably:

- Naturalism – qualitative researchers believe that the research techniques of quantitative methods, such as giving questionnaires to respondents, create an artificial environment which is unlikely to reflect people's true behaviour. So, for example, people's alcohol consumption will be more accurately assessed by observing them socialising on a number of occasions than by approaching them once and asking them how much alcohol they typically drink, which may result in a cautious (or dishonest!) answer being given.

- A holistic approach – the qualitative researcher often wishes to consider the series of events that leads to the action that they are studying (ethogenics), to describe a scene in order to understand the human behaviour within it or to study every part of the life of a school, gang, sports club, and so on. This is in contrast to the quantitative researcher's concern with isolating some variables (e.g. income) and examining their impact on other variables (e.g. smoking).

- Seeing through the eyes of others – understanding the perspectives of respondents is often the key aim of the qualitative researcher. Methods such as observation and unstructured interviews allow respondents to demonstrate what is important to them, rather than data collection focusing on the concerns of the researcher. Quite often, qualitative studies will identify a range of different perspectives on one situation or issue.

(Bryman, 1988: 50–68, again with some of my examples)

Mixed methods

Given that quantitative and qualitative methods are based on such different methodologies, it is sometimes suggested that they cannot be combined within one research project (Spicer, 2012: 480). However, writers such as Moses and Knutsen (2007: 293–294) argue that the distinction between the two approaches is an unhelpful one and many studies will include elements of both quantitative and qualitative methods – a mixed methods approach. The methods are treated as being of equal status, in contrast to triangulation, where one is used to 'check' the other. Spicer (2012: 485) suggests that combining methods can facilitate asking a wider range of questions than would be the case if just one approach was used.

An example of a study that used mixed methods was the one conducted by Winchester (1999) into the experiences of lone fathers in Newcastle, Australia.

Qualitative interviews with a small number of respondents revealed that they experienced difficulties in the areas of access, custody and maintenance arrangements for children, with many discussing in some detail the frustration that they experienced with the legal system. Questions about these issues were included in questionnaires given to a much larger number of respondents, with the results showing that 89 per cent had experience of the legal system and that this experience had been almost universally painful. So the quantitative data indicated that legal difficulties were widespread, while the qualitative data provided details of these difficulties in a small number of cases, creating a comprehensive picture of the problems that lone fathers faced.

Critical research

Critical research rejects the principles underlying both quantitative and qualitative approaches and suggests that 'the aim of social research should be to change society for the better' (Henn et al., 2009: 27). Critical researchers believe that the dominant values of society are those of powerful groups and that research that does not address these values will inevitably reproduce power relations. So, for example, studies that examine methods of increasing political participation tend to be underpinned by the value that such participation is good, giving everybody a voice within the political system. A critical researcher who believed instead that the political system consolidates the power of the ruling classes, and that the participation of others only serves to create an illusion of democracy, might concentrate instead on exposing the lack of effect when people from lower social classes seek to become involved.

Critical researchers have sought to challenge structures of power exerted on the basis of gender, ethnicity, social class and disability (Henn et al., 2009: 29–38). The concern of critical approaches with empowerment has resonance with the principles of action research. Reason and Bradbury (2006: 1) acknowledge that action research is an ambiguous concept but offer their own definition: 'a participatory, democratic process concerned with developing practical knowing in the pursuit of worthwhile human purposes'. Participatory action research, sometimes referred to as participatory appraisal, is particularly concerned with changing the power relationships between researchers and respondents, reducing the distinction between the two roles (Lopes, 2006: 216–217). It may involve creating research outputs where participants make a substantial contribution. For example, the output from Pain and Francis' (2004: 100) study of the opinions that young homeless people held of police officers included a spider diagram with comments ranging from 'never had bad encounter' to 'do as they please' and 'perverts'.

Induction and deduction

In addition to choosing between quantitative, qualitative, mixed methods and critical approaches, a researcher will have to decide at the outset of their study whether they should use a methodology that is primarily deductive or inductive.

Deductive research and research questions

A deductive approach moves from the general to the particular. In practical terms, this is likely to mean the researcher undertaking a thorough search of a broad range of literature before choosing their own specific area of study. Deductive research is sometimes characterised as testing theory by creating specific hypotheses and then using research to determine whether they are correct (a process described by De Vaus, 2002: 13–15). However, in practice the process is often slightly different, involving setting a research question based on the existing literature.

Research questions are different from the general questions that most people have about the social world. Green (2008: 51–57) suggests that a researcher should begin with a broad (or general) question and then narrow it to one that fits the criteria for a research question. These criteria are that the question is:

- interesting – if the researcher is not interested in what they are doing, it is virtually guaranteed that they will not pursue the task with any enthusiasm;
- relevant – addressing the question should potentially contribute something useful to our understanding of social phenomena;
- feasible – boundaries should be placed around the research to ensure that there is a realistic prospect that it can be successfully completed;
- ethical – ethical issues are discussed later in this chapter;
- concise – the question should be as precisely worded as possible; and
- answerable – this is the most important difference between a general question and a research question; it must be a question that is capable of being answered by a piece of social research.

So a researcher might have a general question such as 'Have improvements in electronic communication affected patterns of work?' However, substantial refining would be needed to convert this into a question that fitted the above criteria, e.g. 'What effect have improvements in electronic communication had on types of workplace relationships, working hours and opportunities to work at home in selected public sector organisations in Seoul?' This is an example of an explanatory research question, because it seeks to explain the impact of improvements in communication. Explanatory research questions are well suited to quantitative approaches, because of the emphasis on causality.

An alternative it to ask a descriptive research questions; such questions are more commonly used in qualitative research studies. Some of the elements that De Vaus (2002: 23) suggests should be included in a descriptive research question are:

1 time frame,

2 geographical location,

3 whether the researcher is interested in comparing and specifying patterns for sub-groups, and

4 how abstract the researcher's interest is.

So an example of a descriptive research question might be: how do the feelings of men compare to those of women after watching a romantic film in a Mumbai cinema in January 2013?

Inductive research and research objectives

An inductive approach begins with the particular and moves to the general; the researcher does not start with what is already known about a subject but instead with data collection and analysis. It is only at a later point that efforts are made to build more general truths, by considering the relationship of the findings to existing knowledge (Moses and Knutsen, 2007: 22). So a substantial reading of the literature usually takes place after the researcher has reached findings based on their data.

One specific type of inductive approach that has been discussed substantially in the research methods literature is grounded theory. It should be emphasised that not all inductive studies do, or should, follow the grounded theory model and that some studies incorporate only certain elements of it. However, some of the principles of inductive research are better understood by considering grounded theory as an example.

Glaser and Strauss (1967: vii), who are considered the creators of grounded theory, argue that deductive approaches produce an 'embarrassing gap between theory and empirical research'. They suggest an alternative where the researcher approaches a subject without pre-determined ideas of what they are looking for and seeks to generate 'middle range' theory – somewhere between grand theory and a working hypothesis – based on their data. Once data analysis is complete, the researcher should decide which of a number of existing theories fits best with their new middle range theory (Harding, 2006: 131–132).

The relationship between data analysis, theory building and sampling is crucial when using a grounded theory approach. Theory building should begin as soon as there is sufficient data to analyse and cases should be chosen to add to the sample on the basis that they can contribute to the emerging theory. This sampling method is known as theoretical sampling (Harding, 2006: 131–132).

The collection of data without reference to existing literature and theory has led to the slightly cynical – but almost certainly accurate – criticism of Barbour

(2008: 197) that a grounded theory approach is sometimes used because the researcher is too lazy to read the relevant literature. At a more conceptual level, it could be questioned how far a researcher ever approaches their subject without any pre-conceived ideas. Researchers quite naturally and correctly choose to examine subjects where they have an interest and where they are motivated to find out more; this interest is often linked to having strong views about the subject.

So it may be difficult to conduct research in a manner that reflects entirely the principles envisaged by the grounded theory approach. This does not mean that inductive studies are impossible to conduct or that all research must involve theory testing. Identifying one or more research objectives for a qualitative study represents a middle way between testing a specific theory, or answering a specific research question, and approaching a subject with a completely open mind. Research objectives are less specific than research questions and are defined by Davies et al.(2011: 353) as:

> The purpose for which the research is being carried out. They can be basic (couched in terms of exploration, description, understanding, explanation or prediction) or they can be of an applied nature (e.g. to change, to evaluate or to assess social impacts).

The decision as to whether to use a primarily inductive or a primarily deductive approach has some links to other choices about methodology and methods. Quantitative research is usually primarily deductive, because the emphasis on causality means that it is well suited to testing theories or answering specific research questions. In contrast, qualitative research can be either primarily inductive or primarily deductive. An example of a qualitative study with a deductive orientation was Boyce's (2006) study of a low-income estate in the United Kingdom, which specifically sought to test the hypothesis that people no longer had close ties with their neighbours and others in their community. This contrasts with the inductive approach of Jackson et al. (2003) who had a research objective of developing indicators of community capacity in neighbourhoods of Toronto, Canada, but allowed questions about the neighbourhoods to develop as the research progressed.

In practice, the distinction between inductive and deductive research tends to be even less clear than the one between quantitative and qualitative methods. For example, a researcher may have a very clear research question for their study (a deductive characteristic) but may choose respondents for the later stages of data collection on the basis of their early data analysis (i.e. theoretical sampling, a feature of grounded theory). There is no need for the researcher to feel that a study must be based entirely on one set of principles or another: it is usually more helpful to consider where it is located on an inductive–deductive continuum.

Research designs

The theory to be tested, research question(s) to be answered or research objective(s) to be met by a study should be reflected in the research design. The design represents a practical plan for the methods to be used – incorporating areas such as sampling, data collection and data analysis – which is drawn up in accordance with the decisions that have been made about methodology (e.g. to use a qualitative approach). A good research design will ensure that credible conclusions are based on the evidence generated by the research (Davies, 2006: 265–266).

The extent to which the research design can be determined at the start of a project is affected by whether the research is primarily deductive or inductive. When using inductive methodology, and particularly grounded theory, it is important not to have a design that is too clearly prescribed, because the progress of the research should be driven by the analysis of the early data. It is here that the distinction made by Robson (2002, cited in Semmens, 2011: 58–59) between fixed and flexible designs is helpful. Fixed designs tend to involve working closely to a pre-determined format and following a set of rules and procedures. In contrast, flexible designs involve adopting an approach that can develop as the research progresses.

The tendency of quantitative research to be deductive and to be concerned with causality is linked to the existence of fixed research designs for quantitative studies such as classical experimental designs. These aim to measure the impact of specific changes (De Vaus, 2002, 30–37). In the case of qualitative studies, there are no such standard approaches, although this does not mean that research design is any less important.

There are two specific designs that will be considered briefly here – ethnography and case studies.

Ethnography

Ethnography is the study of a group or culture and is concerned with the ordinary, i.e. people's daily routines. Although ethnography can incorporate both quantitative and qualitative data collection, it is typically based on the qualitative principles of seeking to see the world as it looks to other people and examining multiple perspectives (Fetterman, 1989: 15).

Ethnography also satisfies the qualitative principle of naturalism, i.e. observing people in their 'natural' settings. It is an approach where there has been a historical emphasis on fieldwork. Classical anthropological studies of pre-industrial societies such as *Coming of Age in Samoa* (Mead, 1943) involved the researcher going to live among the people who were being studied, as did post-war studies of working class communities in the United Kingdom such as

Family and Kinship in East London (Young and Willmott, 1957). More recent forms of ethnography have tended to take a selective approach: for example a study of a workplace might involve attending full time, for two days each week or at selected key moments such as staff meetings. The most recent development in this field is the opportunity to conduct digital ethnography with people who are linked via electronic mediums – here the researcher may not be able to see the respondents at all (Murthy, 2008).

Case studies

For many students and researchers, resource implications mean that a case study (or a small number of case studies) is the only research design that is realistically available to them. The entity that is described as a 'case' can take any number of forms: a researcher may select for study one school, prison, political party, social club, and so on. This raises questions about generalisation, although it was noted above that this is predominantly the concern of the quantitative researcher. In addition, Yin (2003: 10) suggests that the aim of case studies should not be to generalise but to contribute to theory. So, for example, a piece of case study research might find that the introduction of a new transport link to an area encouraged businesses to locate there and local people to look further afield for jobs. However, the researcher should not use their findings to argue that these will always be the outcomes of creating new transport links but rather that they are possible impacts that may occur in some cases.

Case study research designs can be qualitative or quantitative or take a mixed methods or critical approach. Yin (2003: 13) argues that they are a unique form of design because the context is crucial to the research. While many other designs seek to eliminate the effect of context, it is central to case studies because the boundaries between the context and the case are often unclear. So, for example, if a researcher were studying a ward of a hospital, they would need to identify the effect of the hospital environment, and broader concerns such as national health policy and common patterns of illness, then consider how far these factors impacted on the staff and patients of the ward that had been selected for study.

Sampling

In some cases, a researcher will be able to collect data from everyone in the group, or population, that is of interest. For example, they may be able to ask to interview every employee at a place of work or seek to involve every adult in a village in focus group discussions. While collecting data from the entire population is ideal, there will be many cases, usually involving larger groups, where resources are insufficient for this to be achieved. In this situation a sample must be chosen, which means that the researcher must decide which members of the population to collect data from. Discussions of sampling often assume that a sample of people is being chosen, but the selection can involve other entities: for example, a researcher conducting content analysis (see below) on the newspapers published on a particular day may have to decide which newspapers to include in the sample and which to exclude. The important point here is that a selection is being made – sampling involves selecting.

For the quantitative researcher, random sampling is an important technique and a necessary pre-requisite for statistical tests that can establish how likely it is that a pattern seen in a sample will be reproduced in a population. However, qualitative researchers, who are less concerned with generalisation, tend to use very different techniques for choosing sample members. One method of qualitative sampling – theoretical sampling – was discussed above when considering grounded theory.

Even when not using a grounded theory approach, the selection of subjects in qualitative studies is often flexible, evolving once fieldwork begins. Fetterman (1989: 43) argues that ethnographers use a process that he describes as judgemental sampling, i.e. 'ethnographers rely on their judgement to select the most appropriate members of the subculture or unit, based on the research question'. A more commonly used term – but one that involves a similar principle – is purposive sampling. The researcher is quite deliberately subjective, choosing those respondents who will best fit the purpose of the research. The danger is that the subjectivity will become bias, so the researcher should reflect on their method of choosing respondents, and how this may influence the study, as a means of checking validity (discussed in Chapter 1).

While it is often difficult to define a qualitative sampling strategy in advance, commonly used ones identified by Patton (2002, cited in Flick, 2009: 122 and with my examples added) include:

Selecting extreme or deviant cases – an approach used when it is thought that sampling the extremities may give the best understanding of the field as a whole. So a researcher wishing to examine the strategies that lead to effective learning may collect data from some of the students who achieved the highest marks in a group and some who achieved the lowest marks.

Selecting typical cases – here the idea is to understand the field from the centre. So, in seeking to establish how an organisation has changed to adapt to different economic circumstances, a researcher may collect data from workers with average salaries who fit the most common profile of staff in terms of age and experience.

Seeking maximum variation in the sample – this approach seeks to demonstrate the range of differences within the population. So, for example, a study of the attempts of former prisoners to re-settle into the community might seek the maximum variation between sample members in terms of length of sentence, strength of family ties, level of skills relevant to the labour market, etcetera.

When using any of these sampling methods, it is important to use appropriate criteria: there would, for example, be little point in seeking maximum variation among the former prisoners in terms of their height.

There are two methods of sampling that are often used out of necessity but which should be avoided if possible. The first is convenience sampling, which refers to the selection of those cases where access is easiest. Many street surveys use convenience sampling and students will sometimes collect data from their friends and contacts. One difficulty with this approach is that, as the name suggests, respondents are being chosen for reasons of convenience rather than because they are most likely to contribute data that could help to answer the research question(s) or achieve the research objectives.

Snowball sampling tends to be used when there is a 'hidden' population such as people with HIV or people who have been abused as children. Here the researcher is unlikely to have a list of the people who belong to the population, so they may have to begin by collecting data from one suitable respondent and then asking if they know of other people in similar circumstances. As the populations concerned are usually vulnerable as well as hidden, snowball sampling is often used in research where there are difficult ethical questions to address (see below).

Negotiating access

In many cases there will need to be some negotiation over access before a sampling strategy can be put into practice. Often this negotiation must be at two levels: gaining access to the institution and gaining access to individuals, e.g. gaining permission from the head teacher or principal to undertake research within their school and then gaining the agreement of teachers for their pupils to take part in a focus group. Negotiating access is often more time consuming than the researcher expects: the person approached may take time to respond, be off work due to illness or need to refer the request for access to a committee. So it is important that the researcher makes the initial approach some time before they hope to collect the data.

In some cases, particularly when undertaking ethnographic work, the researcher may be able to negotiate access through an 'insider' within a community. Fetterman (1989: 44) notes the benefits of being introduced by a respected member of a group: 'A strong recommendation and introduction strengthen the fieldworker's capacity to work in a community and thus improve the quality of the data.'

In other cases, the method of introduction, although necessary, may have a negative impact on the willingness of potential respondents to take part in the research. For example, research in prisons will inevitably require permission from senior staff members, but their support may provoke suspicion among prisoners. In this situation, the researcher will need to work particularly hard to convince potential respondents of their impartiality, the confidentiality of data and the potential value of the research.

Maximising response

Maximising response is particularly important in quantitative studies, where a high response rate gives greater confidence that the findings can be generalised from a random sample to a population. For qualitative researchers, it can be more acceptable to replace a non-respondent by adding someone else to the sample. However, it is clearly advantageous if the people who were originally chosen for the sample are the ones whom data is collected from, so the researcher should consider which measures can be taken to ensure that as many as possible respond positively when asked to take part. Oppenheim (1992: 103–106) provides a list of steps that can be taken to maximise the response to questionnaire or interview surveys; the most relevant to the qualitative researcher are:

1 Covering topics that are likely to be of interest to respondents.
2 Giving as much notice as possible that the research is to take place.
3 Explaining how respondents have been selected, to demonstrate the importance of them providing data rather than assuming that someone else can take their place.
4 Giving clear guarantees of confidentiality and/or anonymity (see the ethics section below).
5 Providing small incentives for participation. There are some ethical questions as to whether offering incentives is coercive or creates undue pressure, but Grant and Sugarman (2004) argue that this is unlikely to be the case, particularly when the incentives are small.
6 In addition to often being necessary to secure access, obtaining the support of someone in a powerful position such as the chief executive of an organisation can encourage response.

Forms of data collection

A major decision affecting any research project is the choice of method or methods by which data is collected. Some forms of data collection, most notably postal and online questionnaires, are used mainly for quantitative studies. The methods that are most commonly used in qualitative research are outlined below, together with the reasons for using them and the issues that they raise.

Secondary analysis of existing data

Strictly speaking this is not a method of data collection but of using data that has already been collected and analysed by someone else. There is a longer tradition of secondary analysis in quantitative research, where datasets can be stored in an SPSS or Excel file with no information that could enable an individual respondent to be identified.

Heaton (2004: 29–31) notes a number of reasons why secondary analysis of qualitative data is more problematic. More physical space may be required to save materials such as transcripts, photographs, audio and video tapes than is the case for a single electronic data file. Qualitative data is more difficult to anonymise than the responses to a structured questionnaire; there is a danger that, in removing identifying information from an interview transcript (for example), a researcher may either distort what was said or leave little that is of value to analyse. While the type of national surveys made available for secondary analysis tend to cover a wide range of issues, qualitative studies may have more specific and limited research questions or objectives, which mean that it is not appropriate to use the data for a different purpose. Finally, there are questions as to how far qualitative data can be understood without being fully aware of the context in which it was collected.

However, some research funding councils are now insisting that qualitative data is anonymised and stored for secondary analysis, suggesting that they see potential for this activity. It is an option for the qualitative researcher to consider, particularly if they are familiar with the context in which the research has taken place, the original researcher is available to discuss the study and the respondents have agreed that their data can be used by other researchers.

Documentary analysis

Wharton (2006: 79) defines documentary analysis as:

> The detailed examination of documents produced across a wide range of social practices, taking a variety of forms from the written word to the visual image.

Academic sources such as books and journal articles tend not to be the subject of documentary analysis: it is an approach that is usually applied to materials such as public records, newspapers, letters and diaries. Macdonald (2008) suggests that, although there may be a tendency to think of documents as being 'objective', they are socially produced and so can be analysed by questioning their authenticity, credibility and representativeness. Careful consideration should be given to the position and meaning of the writer. What are they trying to achieve by producing the document and how might this affect what is written?

Bryman (2008: 528) notes that the methods for analysing documents include content analysis, discourse analysis and critical discourse analysis. Content analysis is defined by Scott (2006: 40) as a specifically quantitative method, which involves counting the frequency with which certain words or phrases appear. However, it is a term that can also be used more broadly, referring to the counting of references to themes or concepts in many forms of qualitative data, as was noted in Chapter 1. Discourse analysis and critical discourse analysis are qualitative methods that can be used with both written and spoken words: they will be considered further in Chapter 7.

A key advantage of using documents is that they are often easy to access (in the case of newspapers, for example) and the researcher is saved much of the time that is usually associated with data collection. However, the data collection is not interactive and limited to the topics that the documents cover; the researcher has no opportunity to ask for further information or for clarifications.

Observation

The use of observation has historically been closely tied to a qualitative methodological approach to social research, and particularly ethnography, because it is seen to embody the principle of naturalism: people are observed in everyday settings without the artificial structure of asking them to take part in an interview or to complete a questionnaire (Coffee, 2006: 214–216). Bryman (2008: 257) makes two important distinctions. The first is between structured and unstructured observation:

Structured or systematic observation – the researcher employs explicit rules as to what to record and observes for a specific length of time, so what is looked for is pre-determined. This method can be associated with a quantitative approach but tends to be used less frequently than unstructured observation in the social sciences.

Unstructured observation: the researcher records as much as possible of what they see in order to develop a narrative account of the behaviour observed. As the research progresses, the researcher will tend to decide which are the key areas to concentrate on, so the focus will become narrower.

The second distinction is between participant and non-participant observation (Bryman, 2008: 257):

Participant observation – the researcher immerses themselves in the social setting that they are studying and takes part in relevant activities.

Non-participant observation – the researcher observes a social situation but takes no part in it. Non-participant observation can either be simple, where the researcher has no control over the situation they are observing, or contrived, where the researcher alters or even creates the situation. Simple observation would, for example, involve sitting in a shopping area and observing the behaviour of people as they go in and out of shops. In contrast, one example of a contrived piece of non-participant observation was the creation of a simulated prison by Haney et al. (1981) in order to observe how research subjects would react to being given the role of prisoner or guard.

Most observation will be classified as either structured or unstructured and as either participant or non-participant. For example, televised sport usually incorporates structured, non-participant observation, with teams of observers producing statistics such as the amount of time that one team has spent in possession of the ball. In contrast, ethnographers have tended to use unstructured, participant observation, taking part as fully as possible in the environment that they are studying and trying to record as much as they can, at least in the early stages of the study.

Observation can quickly provide a large amount of data, although this often makes analysis a more complicated task. If respondents are not aware that they are being observed, this raises difficult ethical questions around informed consent. However, if they are aware that observation is taking place, they may change their behaviour, making the research less 'naturalistic'. The researcher usually has little control when using observation (except in the case of contrived non-participant observation) and so may need to use additional data collection methods such as interviews to ensure that specific issues are addressed.

Interviews

Interviews have historically been assumed to be the 'gold standard' for qualitative research (Barbour, 2008: 113) and there is sometimes an assumption that a decision to use this data collection method requires no justification. However, it is important to consider the reasons for choosing interviews, such as their flexibility and adaptability (Robson, 2011: 280). The qualitative interview provides an opportunity for the researcher to listen to the views or experiences of one respondent for an extended period of time and to ask probing questions to explore ideas further. Hennink et al. (2011: 109–110) note a range of areas where interviews are particularly helpful:

- in determining how people make decisions;
- in examining people's beliefs and perceptions;
- in identifying motivations for behaviour;
- in determining the meanings that people attach to their experiences;
- in examining people's feelings and emotions;
- in extracting people's personal stories or biographies;
- when covering sensitive issues; and
- in examining the context surrounding people's lives.

Hennink et al. (2011: 110) comment that: 'In-depth interviews are thus primarily used when seeking to capture people's individual voices and stories.' Miller and Glassner (2011: 133) argue that interviews do not provide an objective view of the social world that the respondent inhabits but demonstrate the meanings that they attribute to this world and their experience of it.

Interviews require a researcher to spend a substantial amount of time with each respondent, so are resource intensive. In addition, they lack some specific advantages of other techniques, being seen as less 'naturalistic' than observation and not providing the same opportunities to explore collective understandings that are offered by focus groups.

Focus groups

Wilkinson (2011: 168) defines focus group research as:

> ... a way of collecting qualitative data, which usually involves engaging a small number of people in an informal group discussion (or discussions), 'focused' around a particular topic or set of issues.

Barbour (2007: 19–22) suggests that focus groups can bring into a research project either those who are reluctant to participate or hard to reach groups. Liamputtong (2011: 19–22) argues that they are a valuable data collection tool for feminist research because they have the potential to redress power imbalances and enable the collective voices of women to be heard. Similarly, using focus groups may be particularly relevant in cross-cultural research because of their ability to elicit the collective voices of relatively powerless groups of people (Liamputtong, 2011: 127–130).

The distinguishing feature of a focus group is the interaction between the group members, which contrasts with an interview, where the interaction is solely between the respondent and the interviewer. Interaction between respondents has disadvantages because the researcher has a limited amount of control: it may be difficult to prevent the discussion from drifting into areas that are not relevant. However, as Barbour (2007: 35–37) notes, focus groups take some of the burden of interpretation from the researcher because participants themselves can provide insights and commentaries in the course of the discussion. Oates (2000: 187) argues that focus groups force individuals to explain to others why they hold particular views and this can give a greater insight into the reasoning behind opinions that are held. Disagreement may also demonstrate the strength with which individuals hold their convictions.

Bloor et al. (2001: 5–6) note that focus groups also have a role in relation to shared understandings, both revealing shared values and identifying difficulties associated with such norms. This point is illustrated by Onifade's (2002) finding that police officers from minority ethnic groups were more likely to acknowledge racism when data was collected through focus groups than through individual interviews. However, it is often difficult to be certain that a consensus or shared understanding exists, as will be demonstrated in Chapter 8.

There are some situations in which focus groups are clearly not a suitable method of data collection. They are unlikely to be effective when collecting data on sensitive topics or for institutional contexts where people may not be willing to express their views in front of each other. They are also unlikely to produce useful data where personal narratives are required or where participants strongly disagree with each other (Liamputtong, 2011: 8).

Both interviews and focus groups are discussed further in Chapter 3.

Ethical issues

The importance of conducting research ethically is perhaps best illustrated by considering Sir Cyril Burt, a British psychologist whose publications argued that identical twins brought up in different environments tended to have very similar intelligence. This apparent triumph of genetics over upbringing influenced the system of streaming used in British schools. However, after Burt's death it emerged that he had invented results, faked data and included co-authors to his papers who did not exist (Homan, 1991: 7).

While such blatant dishonesty is rare, a researcher has a moral responsibility, both to respondents and to those who may want to conduct social research in the future, to ensure that their study is conducted ethically. Organisations such as the British Sociological Association and the American Psychological Association have developed their own codes of professional practice to ensure that ethical standards are maintained. A student or member of staff of a university will usually have a local ethics committee that they need to present their research proposal to before being allowed to proceed.

Miles and Huberman (1994: 288–297) discuss a range of ethical issues that should be considered by qualitative researchers. The most important of these are presented briefly below, with some of my own examples:

Worthiness of the project

In order to justify the time and energy expended on a project, both by the researcher and the respondents, there must be the potential for some beneficial outcome. The clearest indication that some research projects fail to satisfy this ethical criterion are the existence of the spoof Ig Noble prizes awarded by Harvard University each year for research that 'cannot or should not be reproduced.' One example was a study that suggested that humans can swim equally quickly in sticky syrup as they do in water (*Guardian*, 7 October 2005).

Benefits and costs

The benefits of conducting research are usually obvious for the researcher: they may be paid for their work, obtain a qualification or be able to publish the results, so increasing their self-esteem and enhancing their career prospects. There are not the same benefits for the respondent, although they may appreciate being listened to or having the opportunity to reflect on their own views or actions. However, the respondent may also face potential costs: speaking about some subjects may damage their self-esteem, they may risk being ostracised within their community for talking to an outsider or they may have fears that confidentiality could be breached. In view of this inequitable relationship, the researcher must seek to minimise the potential costs of taking part in the research.

Competence boundaries

For research to be worthy, and for the potential benefits to outweigh the costs, it is essential for the researcher to have the necessary skills to conduct their study. So the new researcher should not attempt the most difficult forms of data collection such as contrived non-participant observation, or undertake research into sensitive issues such as people's experience of bereavement, until they have developed their skills with simpler projects in areas that they feel comfortable with. Supervisors and colleagues can often provide helpful guidance as to how ambitious a researcher should be in the type of study that they undertake.

Informed consent

It is important to remember that respondents are being placed in an unfamiliar position when taking part in research, so the consequences should be explained to them as clearly as possible: for example, how long an interview is likely to last and which topics will be covered. A balance must be sought between seeking to maximise the number of people who agree to take part and ensuring that no one feels pressurised into participating. As was noted above, observing people without their knowledge appears to breach the principle of informed consent, although in this case the researcher usually asks for respondents' consent at the end of data collection rather than at the beginning. However, for the new researcher, it is advisable to use research designs where informed consent can be sought at the start of the study.

Honesty and truth

Linked to the issue of informed consent, some of the most complex ethical questions arise in situations where a researcher uses some level of deception. Classic studies of this nature include Humphreys' (1970) research in which he posed as a lookout for men who undertook sexual acts in public toilets. Humphreys (1970: 171) offered a spirited defence of his own actions but it is highly unlikely that any ethical committee would even consider approving such a piece of research today, despite Humphreys undoubtedly gaining information about the type of people who were involved in such acts that would not have been available using more conventional methods.

Such controversial examples are rare and likely to fall well beyond the experience of the new researcher. Miles and Huberman (1994: 292) suggest that a more subtle form of deception is the 'fake persona', where the researcher adopts a role in order to gain or maintain access. A researcher should not, for example, express an opinion that they do not hold simply to gain the trust of respondents. This must be balanced against the need to establish rapport and to listen to opinions which the researcher does not agree with, both of which are discussed further in Chapter 3.

Privacy, anonymity and confidentiality

In the current age of reality television, privacy is a concept that often seems to be of little importance. However, it is an important element of social research: participants have not usually volunteered to have their most intimate secrets requested by the researcher. It is very important that the researcher limits their data collection to information that is essential to the topic under study.

The concepts of confidentiality and anonymity are often confused. At one level anonymity can only be promised where no one (not even the researcher) is aware of which respondent has provided which piece of information, usually when data is collected through postal or online questionnaires. However, anonymity should usually be maintained in the manner in which findings are reported, to ensure that no one reading the research output can identify which respondent has expressed which opinion. For example, if a researcher were conducting research among a group of trainee primary school teachers, only one of whom was male, the principle of anonymity would be breached if their findings were reported in the following manner: 'One of the respondents felt that the training had not equipped *him* to deal with difficult classroom situations'.

Confidentiality means an agreement as to how the data will be used and who will have access to it. Typically a researcher conducting interviews will be able to guarantee that the only people who will be aware of individual responses will be the research team and anyone involved in transcribing audio files. The researcher should also be able to give guarantees about data storage, for example that the recording will be kept in a locked filing cabinet when it is not being used for transcription.

Confidentiality is impossible to promise when conducting focus group research because the researcher can only ask that focus group members keep the views of other respondents confidential (Liamputtong, 2011: 25). All focus group members should be aware of the limits to confidentiality before the discussion begins.

Use of results and conclusions

The researcher should give thought to the ownership of their research output and the manner in which their findings might be used. I have supervised a number of part-time dissertation students whose employers have supported them in collecting data from their workplace. However, some of these employers have then expected to have control over the use of the findings, e.g. by limiting the number of people who can read the dissertation. If the researcher is not able to have complete control over the dissemination of their output, they should at least have an agreement in advance as to the use that they can make of their findings.

There may also be difficulties with the interpretation of the researcher's findings. For example, the government's reaction to a research project that found that there were insufficient job opportunities in one geographical region might be to encourage industry and commerce to re-locate to that region, but could equally be to encourage people to move to where the jobs were, leaving the region to decline further. While the new researcher is unlikely to undertake a project with such major implications, the type of action or argument that their research might be used to support is an important ethical consideration.

Intervention and advocacy

Miles and Huberman (1994: 293–294, citing Van Maanen, 1983) reflect on this issue in the case of a researcher who witnessed police brutality but chose not to intervene because this would have ended their research. Such examples are rare, but a researcher may well be faced with a situation where they see the opportunity to do some good, e.g. they interview someone who could claim a benefit that would boost their income or could contact a group that would give them support. In this case, the researcher has to decide how far they should maintain the role of detached observer and reporter of information and how far they have a moral obligation to intervene. Many would resolve this dilemma by completing the data collection and then offering the respondent information as to where they could access help.

Summary

This chapter has highlighted some of the key decisions that must be made by any researcher before beginning to collect data. A qualitative approach is often chosen on pragmatic grounds, but it is important that the researcher is aware of some of the underlying differences with quantitative and critical methodologies to ensure that inappropriate steps are not taken. For example, qualitative researchers may become too concerned with generalising findings, instead of drawing on the strengths of a qualitative approach such as its ability to reveal different perspectives and to allow respondents to define what is most important to them.

Similarly, thinking where their research lies on the inductive–deductive continuum should help the researcher to ensure that they design their research appropriately. If the approach taken is primarily deductive, with the literature being thoroughly searched in order to determine how the study can fit with what is already known about a subject, it is appropriate to consider whether a specific theory should be tested or a specific research question addressed. Alternatively, if the research is primarily inductive (which may or may not mean taking a grounded theory approach), with the data analysed first before a substantial examination of the existing literature, then it is usually more appropriate to think in terms of broader research objectives. The research design should reflect the research question(s) or objectives, although qualitative designs tend to be more flexible than quantitative ones, with more scope to change direction part way through the study, even when using a primarily deductive approach.

Turning to methods, although the ideal is to collect data from every member of the population being studied, this is often not feasible, in which case the qualitative researcher should have a clear purpose in choosing from a range of sampling techniques. They should also consider carefully the advantages and disadvantages of different data collection methods and have a clear reason for the choice(s) that they make.

Finally, the researcher should take account of a range of ethical issues when planning their research. While some of the striking examples discussed in this chapter, such as those involving police brutality and public toilets, are very unlikely to be reproduced by the new researcher, some of the principles that they illustrate have relevance for many studies.

All the decisions that are made by the researcher in planning their research, and the unexpected developments that mean that plans have to be adjusted in the course of their study, should be reflected in the methodology section of the research output, which will be discussed in Chapter 9. Before writing the output, of course, the researcher must collect and analyse their data: data collection is the focus of Chapter 3.

Further reading

There are a wide range of issues discussed briefly in this chapter; much more could have been written if space allowed. For a more detailed overview I recommend:

Flick, U. (2009) *An Introduction to Qualitative Research*, 4th edn. London: Sage (1st edn, 1998).

The different principles underlying quantitative and qualitative methodologies can be difficult to grasp but the most accessible explanation, in my opinion, is provided by:

Bryman, A. (1988) *Quantity and Quality in Social Research*. London: Routledge.

There are many discussions in the literature of the principles underlying grounded theory, but few examples of how these principles have been put into action. To read about grounded theory being used in practice, I recommend:

Goulding, C. (2002) *Grounded Theory: A Practical Guide for Management, Business and Market Researchers*. London: Sage.

A helpful example of an ethnographic study that combined data collected through observation and interviews is:

Roy, A. (2011) 'Tobacco consumption and the poor: an ethnographic analysis of hand-rolled cigarette (bidi) use in Bangladesh', *Ethnography*, 13(2): 162–188.

For an example of a qualitative study that used secondary analysis see:

Chew-Graham, C., Kovandzic, M., Gask, L., Burroughs, H., Clarke, P., Sanderson, H. and Dowrick, C. (2012) 'Why may older people with depression not present to primary care? Messages from secondary analysis of qualitative data', *Health and Social Care in the Community*, 20(1): 52–60.

3

Collecting and managing interview and focus group data

Introduction

This chapter will discuss the practice of collecting data through interviews and focus groups, which are the two most popular forms of qualitative data collection. It will consider the planning that should take place beforehand, including conducting pilot work and the creation of a guide for the interviews or the focus group meeting(s). Advantages and disadvantages of collecting data face to face, via telephone or online will be identified.

The skills of the researcher are central to the collection of data through interviews or focus groups; these skills will be described and examples will be provided where they were used to a greater or lesser extent. Important questions will be considered around the recording of the data collection and the differences that are evident when recordings are changed from audio to written format. The chapter will focus first on interviews, then on focus groups and finally on a number of areas that affect both forms of data collection.

Distinctive features of qualitative interviews

Structured interviews are used in quantitative studies, where data are often collected through standardised interview schedules, with the same questions being asked to each respondent in the same order and the answers recorded mainly by indicating which of a number of pre-set alternatives has been chosen. Interviews in qualitative research – whether semi-structured or unstructured – may appear similar, with the interviewer asking the respondent a number of questions, but there are important differences, as noted by Bryman (2008: 437):

- The quantitative, structured interview is designed to answer specific questions, while the qualitative interview begins with broader objectives; it is more interested in drawing out the respondents' perspectives and addressing the issues that most concern them.

- Qualitative interviewers often encourage respondents to 'ramble' – to talk without interruption for an extended period – which can demonstrate what is important to them, while a quantitative interviewer would regard this as a distraction.

- In qualitative interviews, the interviewer can ask new, unplanned questions as a result of something that the respondent has said; they can also vary the order or wording of questions. In contrast, structured interviews are inflexible.

Types of qualitative interview

The reasons why a qualitative researcher might choose interviews as their method of data collection were considered in Chapter 2. Having made this decision, they then face a further choice between a number of different types of interview. Although there are many options, the discussion here will be limited to three that are frequently used: semi-structured interviews, unstructured interviews and biographical interviews.

Semi-structured interviews

Semi-structured interviews are likely to be appropriate in many research situations and are recommended for the new researcher because, as their name suggests, they provide some structure and guidance to the interviewer, without taking the standardised approach of the quantitative interview. The researcher has a guide to follow and analysis is likely to be easier because there will be a number of topics on which every respondent will have made some comment.

The interview guide can consist of a list of topics or of specific questions. Where questions are identified, they will be open ended in nature and in either case the researcher will need to use planned and/or unplanned probes. The list of topics/questions will be used only as a guide for the interview; the topics may be raised in a different order and the researcher needs good listening skills in order to be able to establish whether all the required topics have been covered (Roulston, 2010: 14–15). A specific semi-structured interview guide will be discussed later in this chapter, but for now it should be helpful to consider an example of a question that was used in semi-structured interviews with homeless people who were living in temporary accommodation projects:

Can you tell me how you came to need support from this project?

Probe for:

a Offending

b Drugs/Alcohol

c Family issues

d Episodes of homelessness

e Physical/mental health

It is important to note here that, although the initial question asked was an open one, there were specific issues that the researcher wanted respondents to discuss. So if a respondent's answer to the open question only covered the areas of family issues and episodes of homelessness, the researcher would ask specific follow-up questions (or probes – discussed later in this chapter) about any offending history, any problems with drugs or alcohol and any experience that the respondent may have had of physical or mental health problems. However, follow-up questions could also be asked in the areas that the respondent had already mentioned – i.e. family issues and episodes of homelessness – if the researcher thought it would be useful to explore these issues further. In addition, if a respondent mentioned an issue that was not on the list to probe for, such as being forced to leave accommodation, the researcher could also ask further questions about this.

Unstructured interviews

While many qualitative researchers tend to prefer a semi-structured approach, Gillham (2005: 45) suggests that there are three situations in which an unstructured interview may be most appropriate:

- in the early stages of the research, when the researcher is looking to identify key themes which can then be asked about specifically in subsequent, more structured data collection;

- when a more structured approach might be inhibiting or constraining for the respondent;

- when discussing an aspect of the respondent's life where asking questions might interrupt the thread of the narrative.

The unstructured interview appears on the surface to operate in a similar manner to a conversation. The interviewer may have a single question that they begin with, then ask follow-up questions based on the response to the first one, or they may have notes of a number of points that they wish to raise in the course of the interview (Bryman, 2008: 438). However, this list of points is shorter than would be the case for a semi-structured interview.

Unstructured interviews tend to produce the 'richest' data. However, they are also very time-consuming to analyse, as it may be difficult to find commonalities between different interviews. In addition, the potential for interviewer bias is particularly high, because the interviewer may decide to ask follow-up questions about the topics that they are most interested in and ignore others.

If the interviews with homeless people (discussed above) had been unstructured, the question given as an example above might have been presented on the interview guide without any suggested topics to address in follow-up questions, i.e.

Can you tell me how you came to need support from this project?

Of course, it is possible that the homeless person would have mentioned some or all of the topics identified above, such as offending and use of drugs and/or alcohol, in their answer. However, in an unstructured interview there is no need to probe for issues that are not mentioned by the respondent – and so presumably are less important to them – leaving more time to ask further questions about issues that they choose to discuss.

Life history interviews

As their name suggests, these interviews focus on the life of one person, or one part or period of their life, and are often combined with the collection of various kinds of personal document such as diaries, photographs and letters (Bryman, 2008: 440). However much or little of a respondent's life the interview covers, the focus is on process. Life experiences are examined in a more holistic way than with other types of interview: breadth of topics covered is likely to be sacrificed for depth of information. Life history interviews can be semi-structured or unstructured but they lend themselves particularly well to an unstructured approach, with the researcher allowing the respondent to give their narrative as they see best (Fielding, 2006: 159–161; Hesse-Biber and Leavy, 2011: 133–134).

Life history interviews are a particularly popular method of data collection in the humanities (see Plummer, 2001). They have been little used historically in the social sciences, partly because life stories cannot be generalised, but their popularity has grown in recent years as a number of advantages of this form of data collection have been identified (Bryman, 2008: 440). The area of homelessness is one where life history interviews have proved particularly useful in seeking to map the sequence of events or 'pathway' by which a respondent reached their present situation (for example, May, 2000; Mayock and Sheridan, 2011).

Data collected through life histories is often suitable for narrative analysis, which is discussed in Chapter 7.

Modes of data collection

In addition to the type of qualitative interview that is to be used, another choice for the researcher is between different modes of data collection, i.e. the face-to-face interview, the telephone interview and various forms of electronic interview. There is an assumption in much of the literature on qualitative interviews that these will be conducted face to face if possible: arguments in favour of other forms tend to be made entirely on the grounds of expediency, i.e. costs are lower or access easier (Gillham, 2005: 5). One of the reasons for the preference for face-to-face interviews is that a full range of communication is possible, with both interviewer and respondent able to respond to the non-verbal signs given by the other. For example, the interviewer may note that a respondent looks uncomfortable when asked a question and offer to move on to the next topic. However, it is in face-to-face interviews that the interviewer faces the greatest risk of creating bias, as will be discussed in the next section.

Another reason for telephone interviews frequently being considered an inferior alternative to face-to-face interviews is that respondents may slip into their habitual method of telephone conversation: either the brief and to the point answers typical of the workplace or a conversational style used in discussions with friends. These difficulties can be reduced by informing respondents about the likely duration of the interview, briefing them thoroughly about the purpose, pre-arranging a time of day for the call when a respondent is unlikely to be disturbed and encouraging them to find a private setting in which to take the call (King and Horrocks, 2010: 80–82). However, there remains a risk that the conversation may become too task focused and stronger probing (see later section) may be necessary if responses become too 'factual'. Specialist devices are available for recording telephone conversations (King and Horrocks, 2010: 82–83).

There are a variety of options available for undertaking online interviews, including email, chat rooms and instant messaging services. These forms of communication have the advantage of being familiar and available to many people and enable researchers to reach participants worldwide. Concerns over the degree of rapport that can be achieved in online interviewing have decreased with time as the amount of communication that takes place in this format has increased (King and Horrocks, 2010: 86–93). This must be balanced against the disadvantage of the lack of visual clues to guide the interview and the limitations that online interviewing presents in terms of choice of respondents: it is not an option that is available for collecting data from most prisoners, for example, or from people living in the poorest parts of developing countries.

Email interviews can take place through exchanges on a number of occasions, sometimes over substantial periods of time, but they present unique challenges such as ensuring that as many interviews as possible are completed. It is good practice for a researcher to give respondents an indication of the timeframe in which they are expected to respond. They must also consider carefully how many times they should remind respondents who have not replied to an email. One of the advantages of email interviews is that there is no need for a transcript, but editing together a number of email exchanges can be a substantial administrative task (King and Horrocks, 2010: 86–93). Other forms of online interview, such as instant messaging services, are thought to produce more conversational styles of interaction, reflecting the type of communication that many individuals use these services for. However, 'real time' forms of interviewing may present difficulties in terms of typing quickly and accurately. Care must also be taken to save the dialogue before closing down the messaging service (King and Horrocks, 2010: 94–97).

Qualities of the qualitative interviewer

Oppenheim (1992: 67) notes that it is a highly skilled task to persuade people to talk freely about their thoughts and feelings for a period of up to an hour. The nature of the relationship between the researcher and the respondent is clearly crucial to the success of an interview. Steinke (2004: 185) suggests that a key check for the validity of an interview is to examine whether a working relationship has been developed between the researcher and the respondent: if it has not, the interview is likely to yield little useful data.

The researcher should consider carefully how their observable (or hearable) characteristics may bias the interview, particularly when interviewing face to face. For example, Lewis (2006: 184) found that offenders from black and minority ethnic (BME) groups were more likely to say in an interview that they would like to be supervised by a probation officer from the same ethnic group if the person conducting the interview was themselves from a BME background. The face-to-face interviewer should, as far as possible, ensure that their appearance is in keeping with the situation: smart dress is appropriate when interviewing professionals but is likely to inhibit respondents of lower social status such as those with addiction problems.

Hesse-Biber and Leavy (2011: 94–95) argue that qualitative interviews involve the researcher and the respondent participating in meaning making and that the extent of division and hierarchy should be low. Similarly, Hennink et al. (2011: 124–128) note the importance of the early stages of the interview for establishing and maintaining rapport: they suggest that it is very important to take some time to engage in everyday conversation after meeting a respondent and to continue to encourage them to relax as the interview progresses. Building rapport is more difficult, but particularly important, in telephone or online interviews, where (as noted previously) the researcher and respondent cannot provide each other with visual clues.

However, the need to establish rapport must be balanced against the danger of creating bias. Hennink et al. (2011:109) suggest that a good interview should feel like a conversation to the respondent, but does not represent a two-way dialogue: the role of the interviewer should be to elicit information and views. Legard et al. (2003: 159–161) note the dilemma as to whether the interviewer should provide personal information about themselves in the course of the interview. Some feminists have criticised the notion that the researcher is a 'depersonalised extractor of data' (Legard et al., 2003: 160) but providing too much personal information may lead to the respondent wanting to keep the interview to an area where they know they have something in common with the researcher or not discussing a topic because they assume that the researcher is fully aware of it. Offering to answer questions at the end of the interview may be the most effective method for the researcher to maintain both rapport and an appropriate distance.

It may be particularly difficult to maintain a neutral approach when faced with a subject that the interviewer feels strongly about or when the respondent expresses views that the researcher finds offensive. Legard et al. (2003: 160) suggest that it is the role of the researcher to understand what underpins offensive views rather than to challenge them. This approach was taken, for example, by Ray et al. (2004) when studying the thinking of racist offenders. However, Pryke (2004) took a different view when he felt that he had colluded during an interview by failing to challenge views that justified genocide. As a result, he found methods to subtly present an opposing point of view in later interviews where similar opinions were expressed. Such emotive examples are unlikely to be directly relevant to the new researcher, who will usually be steered towards less controversial issues and may be unable to examine particularly sensitive topics on ethical grounds (see Chapter 2). However, it is important for the interviewer to think in advance about their response if presented with a point of view with which they profoundly disagree.

To take a much simpler issue, the interviewer needs to establish credibility by asking relevant questions. This can be achieved by having read thoroughly about the interview topic and by being very aware of their interview guide (Legard et al., 2003: 143).

Another issue that affects the nature of the relationship between the researcher and the respondent is positionality, i.e. the power relationship between the two parties. For example, a lecturer interviewing one of their own students would need to constantly be aware of the power that they had over the respondent, providing particularly thorough assurances that questions could be refused and that the data would only be used for research purposes. However, in the case of a student going to interview someone in a senior position in an organisation, the power relationship would be completely different and the student might feel inhibited in trying to build rapport, although this would still be important. The researcher should think carefully about how they position themselves in terms of their role and the influence that this may have on the interview (Hennink et al., 2011: 122–123).

Further skills required by the qualitative interviewer are listed by Bryman (2008: 445, adapting Kvale, 1996):

- structuring and finishing the interview, making clear when the interview is complete and asking if the respondent has questions;
- balance – not talking too much and dominating the interview, but equally not saying so little that the respondent feels that their answers are 'wrong';
- clarity – asking simple and easy to answer questions;
- gentleness – letting the respondent finish and giving them time to think;
- critical – while being gentle also being prepared to point out apparent inconsistencies in the respondent's answers;
- remembering and referring back to what has previously been said;
- interpreting and clarifying what is said, but without imposing their own meaning on the responses.

Planning the interview and the interview guide

Despite the flexibility that is the hallmark of qualitative data collection, there is still a need to prepare an interview guide, even for unstructured interviews. As its name suggests, this simply guides the interview, rather than prescribing the format, and is essentially a memory aid (Hennink et al., 2011: 112). However, putting together an interview guide is a task that the new researcher often finds difficult.

King and Horrocks (2010: 38–39) suggest that the guide may include full questions or, alternatively, words or phrases as reminders of topics to cover. The advantage of full questions is that the researcher can think in advance about the wording and so avoid questions that are leading or confusing. The disadvantage is that the guide may be used inflexibly, almost like a structured interview schedule, in which all questions are asked in the same order without any unplanned follow-up questions. However, despite this danger, having full questions written is likely to provide reassurance for the new researcher.

King and Horrocks (2010: 36–17, citing Patton, 1990) describe different types of question that can be asked during an interview. Background/demographic questions ask for factual information that may influence the analysis such as the respondent's age, ethnicity or occupation. These questions are usually asked near the start of the interview. A number of other types of questions will usually be asked as the interview progresses:

- Experience/behaviour questions that focus on actions that could have been observed by the researcher had they been present.
- Opinion/value questions that seek to establish what the respondent thinks about the topic and how their thoughts relate to their values.
- Feelings questions that focus on participants' emotional experiences. They should be worded carefully to avoid confusion with opinions/values questions, so questions are better to begin with 'What feelings are provoked by …' rather than 'How did you feel about …'.
- Knowledge questions that are concerned with what a participant considers to be a 'fact' rather than anything that is necessarily true objectively.

In addition to these types of questions, semi-structured interviews depend heavily on the use of probes. Hennink et al. (2011: 119–120) discuss topical probes, which are written in advance and involve the interviewer listing specific issues to raise if they are not covered by a respondent in answer to a question. The semi-structured interview question presented earlier in this chapter included topical probes for factors such as offending and drug/alcohol use. Other types of probe, which cannot be planned and need to be devised in the course of the interview, are considered in the next section.

Where a researcher is conducting a piece of deductive research (see Chapter 2), the questions or topics on the interview guide are heavily influenced by the research question(s), which arise from the literature on their chosen subject. Inductive approaches are less prescriptive, although the questions/ topics addressed should be consistent with the research objectives.

Part of an interview guide is presented below. The guide was used to conduct the interviews with lecturers at a case study university, which were introduced in Chapter 1 and provided the data which is analysed in Chapters 4–7. As a reminder, the objectives of this research were:

1 to identify the motivation of lecturers for their choice of career;

2 to identify feelings about, and practical difficulties associated with, different elements of the job;

3 to discuss different types of students and the experience of teaching them;

4 to identify feelings about reflective practice and methods by which it was put into practice; and

5 to discuss changes with time in relation to the above factors.

Questions were devised to give the best possible chance that these research objectives could be met. The first two sections of the topic guide are shown below, together with classifications for the questions and probes that were used.

Guide for interviews with lecturers at the case study university

Introduction

Remind respondent of purpose of interview; no obligation to answer all questions; limits of confidentiality. Ask to sign consent form and for permission to record.

Background

How long have you been in this job? (*background/demographic question*)

Have you had any other roles within this university? (*background/demographic question*)

Have you taught at other universities? (*background/demographic question*)

Motivation

Why did you want to work in higher education? (*opinion/value question*) – satisfaction, financial reasons, flexible working (*topical probes*)

What were your initial hopes and fears for the job? (*feelings question*)

Have your expectations changed? (*feelings question*)

Has the university changed since it was a polytechnic (if applicable)? (*knowledge question*)

Do you believe that you are recognised and appreciated for your role? (*opinion/value question*)

What are your feelings about your workload? (*feelings question*)

The question about a polytechnic refers to a change of status of the institution (from polytechnic to university) that took place in 1992; it was only applicable if the respondent had worked there before 1992.

You will now be presented with two exercises where you are asked to perform tasks in relation to later sections of the interview guide.

Exercise 1

The questions shown below were from part of the interview guide that dealt with experiences of teaching different types of student. Some elements of these questions proved to be problematic: please read them and identify what the difficulties might have been. (Please note that mature students are usually defined in the UK as those who begin their course at the age of 21 or more, while traditional students are those who begin at 18, 19 or 20).

What is your view of the attendance and motivation of students?
What are your experiences of teaching mature students?
What are the differences between teaching traditional and mature students? – expectations, motivation, preferred methods of teaching, satisfaction of teaching

Please complete the exercise before looking at my criticisms of these questions, which appear below.

Reflecting on this section of the interview guide, I can see two major areas of weakness:

1 The first question is a very broad one to ask without any topical probes. While attendance is a relatively straightforward idea, motivation is multi-faceted and the provision of some probes could have helped to guide the interviewer. These probes could have included motivation for different tasks – to complete assessed work, to undertake independent study, to take part in discussions, to engage with the subject area, and so on.

2 The question 'What are your experiences of teaching mature students?' could have been treated as an experience/behaviour question or an opinion/value question. This is because a respondent might have answered in a factual manner, e.g. 'I have been teaching mature students for five years and, at present, teach a mixture of mature and traditional students on a professional practice course.' However, it could also have been answered by a respondent discussing the expectations, motivations and preferred teaching methods of mature students, and the satisfaction gained from teaching them, in comparison to traditional students. Such a response would make the next question unnecessary, but might mean that information was not collected about the extent of the respondent's experience. So it would have been preferable to have re-worded the first question to indicate clearly that it was an experience/behaviour question, i.e. 'To what extent have you been involved in teaching mature students?'

Please note that, although these are the key weaknesses that occur to me, there may be other problematic elements that you have identified and I have not.

Exercise 2

One of the objectives of the research was to 'identify feelings about reflective practice and methods by which it was put into practice'. You are invited to devise a small number of questions and topical probes that could be used to explore the issue of reflective practice, i.e., respondents reflecting.

Please complete this exercise before looking at the questions that I devised below.

A reminder that, for all the exercises in this book, it should not be assumed that my responses are the 'correct' ones and that a differing response on your part is of no value. This is particularly true in the case of this exercise, where a range of useful questions could be devised. However, it should still be useful to compare the questions and probes that you have devised with mine, which are shown below:

Reflective practice

What is your understanding of reflective practice? (*knowledge question*)

How important is reflective practice to you? (*opinion/value question*) – mechanisms used for reflection (*topical probe*)

What is your motivation for reflective practice? (*opinion/value question*) – internal or external (*topical probes*)

Reflective practice is an issue that is discussed extensively in Chapter 4, so you will be able to judge how effective these questions and probes were in meeting the research objective.

Unplanned probes

In addition to the topical probes discussed previously, a qualitative researcher will need to use probes that cannot be planned in advance. A key judgement during an interview is to know when and how to use unplanned questions, comments or sounds in order to elicit further information. A number of types of probes are shown in Table 3.1.

A more daunting form of clarification probe is one that challenges apparent inconsistencies in a respondent's account, using a format such as 'Earlier you expressed the opinion that ... However, you've just said that ...'. Respondents can also be challenged gently by presenting an alternative opinion or course of action using phrases such as 'Did you ever consider ...' (Legard et al., 2003: 152). The use of this type of probe is linked to the question discussed previously as to how far it is appropriate to disagree with a respondent or to hint at disagreement. It is an area where a less experienced researcher may prefer to err on the side of caution.

Table 3.1   Types of probe

Type of probe	Purpose	Typical words used
Motivational probe	To show that the interviewer is listening and encourage a respondent to say more	'Ah-ha' 'Mmm' or 'Yeah'
Amplification probe	To encourage a respondent to provide more detail	'Can you tell me a little more?' or 'Can you give me an example?'
Exploratory probe	To explore a respondent's feelings about a situation they have discussed	'How did you feel when ...' or 'Why did you think it was important to ...'
Explanatory probes	To encourage the respondent to explain opinions, feelings or behaviour	'What exactly made you feel ...' or 'Could you tell me why you believe ...'
Clarification probe	To provide greater clarity in areas such as the order of the events that a respondent is discussing or the definition of a term that they are using	'Could you just confirm ...' or 'Would you mind just explaining to me ...'

Sources: Hennink et al. (2011: 129–130); Legard et al. (2003: 150–152)

Legard et al. (2003: 152–153) note that a single probe is often insufficient and that a researcher may need to ask a number of follow-up questions. This may sometimes feel artificial but is often necessary to achieve the level of understanding that is needed in qualitative research. Good probing can be the key to carrying out an effective interview.

Planning a focus group

Mode of data collection

When planning a focus group, there is no equivalent choice to the one between semi-structured, unstructured and biographical interviews, although the researcher will need to decide how far to direct the discussion, as will be shown below. Instead, the first major decision is likely to be which mode of data collection should be used, i.e. whether the focus group should be conducted face to face, via telephone or online. As with interviews, there is an assumption in much of the literature that face-to-face data collection is the norm and that other modes should be evaluated by considering their advantages and disadvantages in comparison to this norm.

Telephone conferencing has advantages in terms of reducing the cost of bringing people together: it can reach remote populations or respondents who are geographically dispersed. In addition, focus groups conducted by telephone have been found to be less easy for an individual to dominate, probably because they cannot use body language to demand preferential treatment or assert their superior status (Barbour, 2007: 150). Of course, the lack of body language can also be a major disadvantage, as individuals cannot take clues from each other, most notably that one person is about to speak. As interaction is one of the defining features of focus groups, limiting this to what can be heard is clearly a major restriction. Of course, telephone conferencing also requires the appropriate equipment, which may not be available to an undergraduate student, for example.

There has been more academic interest in conducting focus groups through online mediums such as discussion boards. The advantages and disadvantages of the lack of visual communication also apply here. Bloor et al. (2001: 83) identify further advantages that researcher effect is reduced (as people cannot make assumptions based on the researcher's appearance or voice), people tend to be familiar with computer mediated forms of communication and data arrives readily transcribed. Although focus groups are not usually suitable for discussing sensitive issues, respondents may be more willing to discuss such issues in an online environment.

However, there are also a number of disadvantages of conducting focus groups online. Pressures to type may lead to an individual abbreviating their comments, meaning that a full picture of their views is not established (Barbour, 2007: 150–151). Bloor et al. (2001: 83) note that, in an online environment, it is difficult to detect deceit or probe issues, rapport can be difficult to establish and there is no opportunity to identify non-verbal clues. The researcher cannot be certain who is participating in the study, even down to their most basic demographic characteristics such as age and gender (Tonkiss, 2012). Partly because of difficulties such as these, Barbour (2007: 151–152) suggests that online focus groups will not replace the face-to-face mode of data collection, but provide a useful extra tool for the qualitative researcher.

Choosing respondents for the focus group

Whatever the mode of data collection, and bearing in mind the difficulties of verifying the identity of people contributing to online focus groups, the researcher will need to decide who to ask to take part in the discussion. Sampling was discussed in general terms in Chapter 2, but there are specific questions to resolve when choosing respondents for focus groups, namely the number of people who are involved and their relationships to each other. There is no ideal number of participants for a focus group: the number whose voices can be accommodated will depend on the skill of the moderator and also on the desired complexity of the discussion. Marketing research material tends to recommend a group of 10–12 people (Barbour, 2007: 60), while the figure is more often 6–8 for the social sciences. Practical factors need to be considered: too few focus group members can make it difficult to generate discussion and risks the meeting needing to be cancelled if people do not turn up; too many can leave participants frustrated that they do not have the opportunity to express their views (Bloor et al., 2001: 26–28). A larger group may also create greater difficulties in finding a suitable location.

Another distinctive feature of choosing members for focus groups is that it is often advantageous to create a 'community of interest', where all members will be motivated to discuss the chosen topic. This means that focus group members should have something in common: there should be homogeneity of interest although not necessarily of views (Barbour, 2007: 59). Where pre-existing groups are used, the data can say much about the relationships between the people involved, in addition to the subject matter that they are discussing (Barbour, 2007: 67), as will be demonstrated in Chapter 8. Where a group is too large to all be involved in one discussion, several focus groups can meet. Alternatively, a researcher may select some individuals rather than others to take part using one of the qualitative sampling techniques discussed in Chapter 2 such as maximum variation sampling (Onwuegbuzie et al., 2009: 4). Creating two or more focus groups, while involving more work, also adds validity to the findings (Barbour, 2007: 59): patterns observed in the discussions of several groups are less likely to be due to unrepresentative views of the individuals concerned or to misinterpretation of contributions by the researcher.

One important point to consider when choosing focus group members is whether there is any element of hierarchy between the individuals. In the case of the focus group discussion that was introduced in Chapter 1 – where lecturers from one academic department discussed their experiences of teaching seminars – an open invitation to the discussion was offered, because I felt that the staff could be considered to be a community of interest. One member of the department who attended the focus group discussion (Nick) was the line manager of the others, although he regularly taught students through both lectures and seminars. I thought that it was appropriate that Nick took part because he had much to say on teaching related subjects and had a management style that encouraged individuals to exchange views. There was no evidence of other group members being inhibited by Nick's presence, although on one occasion he asserted his authority when a discussion threatened to focus on an approach that was not permitted by university policy. Nick diverted discussion away from this approach and back to an issue that had been raised earlier:

> **Neil**: I have colleagues in other places as well where people ask students who's read and who hasn't and then they actually ask those who haven't read to leave the seminar. They actually ask them to go and come back next week when they've read it.

> **Nick**: That's not something that we can do; we'd better not discuss that. I think that one issue that needs to be put aside to come back to is the feeling that if not all students come to the seminar, that's a plus. Then we get only students who come to discuss things so I think that's worth coming back to. The other thing I do think is interesting is Ian leading us down that road of thinking about year one, year two and year three and whether we have different expectations of students at different levels …

Nick's attempt to steer the discussion was successful: several contributions about expectations at different levels of study followed and the question of whether the university should allow the exclusion of students who had not read in preparation for the seminar was not returned to. While Nick made a very positive contribution to the discussion, this example illustrates a dilemma that may face the qualitative researcher when deciding whether to include people of different rank or status in the focus group meeting.

The focus group guide

As with interviews, it is helpful for the researcher to prepare in advance either topics to cover, or specific questions to answer, in order to guide the focus group discussion. Although focus groups typically last longer than individual interviews, the guide is likely to be shorter, because interaction between respondents should ensure that issues are discussed for a greater length of time. Although the researcher should be prepared with probes, these are often not needed if group members interact effectively and explore each other's views. Less has been written about the types of question that can be asked in focus groups than is the case for individual interviews. Krueger (1998a: 24–28) provides a list of types of questions which, although helpful, simply marks different stages of the discussion:

- Opening question – one that can be answered very quickly by everyone, often just a simple introduction.

- Introductory questions – broad questions that encourage respondents to discuss the areas of interest and to interact with each other.

- Key questions – these are most important and are central to answering the research question(s) or achieving the research objectives. Most of the discussion should be devoted to these questions.

- Ending questions – questions that finish the meeting by allowing respondents to state their final position, to respond to a summary of the discussion provided by the researcher or to discuss any matter that they consider important and which has not previously been mentioned.

However, this typology does not indicate how questions should be asked or what should be asked about. Considering the list of possible types of questions that were identified earlier for interviews, feelings questions are unlikely to be appropriate because sensitive topics are not usually suitable for focus group discussions. In addition, knowledge questions are unlikely to produce the interactions that are necessary for focus groups, unless respondents have different views of what is factually true. Background/demographic questions might be appropriate at the introductory stage, but most of the questions asked are likely to be about experience/behaviour or opinions/values.

Below is the guide that was used for the focus group with academic staff which examined good practice in the delivery of seminars. There was no need to include an introductory question as the respondents were well known to each other. As noted in Chapter 1, this focus group was part of a broader educational project, where one objective was to: 'Research, identify and disseminate good practice in the organisation and delivery of seminars'. The guide largely reflected this objective:

Guide to seminar focus group

Please could you give one example of a seminar that you deliver and some of the issues that it raises? (*This was the introductory question.*)

What are the aims of your seminars? – defined outcomes, learning, skills, participation

What is the relationship between lectures and seminars?

Should specific qualities in students be developed through seminars? – academic skills, social skills, other skills

What prevents you from delivering effective seminars? – practical factors, ability of lecturer, nature of student body

What are the advantages of reflecting with others on seminar practice? – reassurance, sharing ideas, improved practice

How can staff be encouraged to reflect with others on seminar practice?

What practical steps can be taken to ensure that seminars are effective?

Is there anything that we have not covered that you think is relevant to a discussion of good practice in seminars? (*This was the ending question.*)

The extent to which I, as the moderator of the group, used this guide effectively is discussed in the next section.

Moderating a focus group

The person who leads a focus group is usually referred to as the facilitator or moderator. Moderating focus groups is a highly skilled task and, as with interviews, the quality of the data collected is highly dependent on the researcher. This section considers specific abilities that are required. It is assumed here that the focus group is being conducted face to face, although many of the skills will be needed in any mode of data collection.

Preparation

Finding a convenient time for all the focus group members to meet, and choosing and booking a suitable location, require good organisational skills on the part of the researcher. Making thorough preparations also involves undertaking tasks such as visiting the venue in advance and finding the best position for the recording equipment in the middle of the table (Barbour, 2007: 75–76). Although most focus groups consist of a moderator simply asking questions, they may also decide to show members materials such as newspaper articles or film clips to stimulate discussion (Onwuegbuzie et al., 2009: 4). Ensuring that all such materials are available at the required time is another important element of the preparation.

Encouraging interaction

Once the focus group begins, a key task of the moderator is to encourage interaction between the group members. As Wilkinson (2011: 169) notes, focus groups are not the same as group interviews and it is neither necessary nor desirable for questions to be answered by each respondent in turn; instead it is hoped that group members will respond spontaneously to the comments of others. The introductory question is crucial; it should encourage as many people as possible to participate and give the maximum opportunity for discussion of the issues that emerge (Finch and Lewis, 2003: 178–179).

As was noted above, if a focus group is working well, the moderator will need to do little probing, because respondents will explore and sometimes challenge the views of other group members. However, when there is a limited amount of interaction, the moderator needs to take a more active role. Krueger (1998a: 46) notes that unplanned probes may be crucial; the moderator must know when to ask follow-up questions based on the importance of the issue, the amount of time available and the level of detail that is hoped for in the data.

To take an example of a probing question, a colleague of mine was moderating a focus group with trainee teachers, where one of the objectives was to establish the extent to which they were critically curious. When one respondent discussed curiosity only in the context of their current academic course, my colleague asked a probing question that not only encouraged the original respondent to think further, but also led to a reaction from another group member:

> **Louis**: I think we all have a curiosity for everything we do because we're still in that learning phase and we are learning all the time in whatever we do; certainly the curiosity thing is a big thing for us; you know there's lots of 'why does that happen, do we need to do that sort of thing?'.

> **Moderator**: And do you think that once you leave university that curiosity will leave or do you think that will always continue?

> **Louis**: I think that the good people will always keep that because I think that's what will make you effective. I think that's what will keep making sure that you're trying to better your practice all the time. I think if you stop being like that then you're going to have problems and probably be in the wrong profession.

Andrea: Especially with a teacher because, if you expect your children to learn, you need to keep learning new things as well. As society changes and science is forever changing as well, so you need to keep up to date and you're constantly learning as a teacher.

Maintaining an appropriate level of control

Finch and Lewis (2003: 180–184) identify an important skill of the moderator as being to ensure coverage of topics to answer the research question(s) or satisfy the research objectives while also providing the flexibility to facilitate discussion of the issues raised by group members. Similarly, Liamputtong (2011: 157) suggests that the moderator needs, on occasions, to provide some direction and to keep the group focused.

When moderating the focus group on seminars, I failed on occasions to provide sufficient direction, as demonstrated by the discussion not covering some of the areas on the focus group guide, such as the two questions about reflection. One specific failure is illustrated below. I wanted to examine further the issue that Nick had steered the group towards – namely whether academic staff should expect different amounts of preparation for seminars from students in different years of study. I thought it would be useful to probe whether two views expressed were in conflict with each other, but the issue became lost in a more practical question about monitoring attendance:

Moderator: I am thinking about what Eric said about having different expectations at different levels which perhaps slightly contrasts with what Leanne said about having that culture from day one that you read before a seminar. Are those two incompatible do you think? Do you think we should be saying in the first year ...

Ian: I was just wondering is seminar attendance compulsory? Is the lecture compulsory at all?

Eric: It's not, it's not. Not recorded.

Melissa: We can request for anything to be monitored ...

I was then unable to stop the discussion focusing on attendance; it never returned to the issue raised by my probing question. On reflection, it would have been appropriate to have interjected after the question of Ian or the answer of Eric with a comment along the lines of: 'We can return to the question of monitoring attendance in a moment, but for now could we just give some thought to the opinions expressed by Eric and Leanne ...' This would have represented an appropriate balance between steering the discussion and ensuring that issues that respondents wanted to discuss were covered (provided, of course, that the discussion had returned later to the monitoring of attendance).

Ensuring that all contribute

One of the consequences of focus groups being different from group interviews is that the moderator does not have control over the order in which people speak or the number of times each member contributes. Finch and Lewis (2003: 180–184) note that one role of the moderator is to regulate the dynamics of the group by ensuring that contributions are received from each group member, limiting the contributions of dominant respondents, drawing out reticent respondents and preventing people from talking simultaneously. Moderators must be aware of a group member who has not yet contributed and sensitively invite them to do so, possibly through a direct question or by picking up on body language such as smiling or nodding: for example, 'I see that you are nodding there, can you tell me your views?' (Barbour, 2007: 80–82). It is important that the moderator indicates from the beginning that the views of all group members are wanted and that disagreements should be voiced (Bloor et al., 2001: 49). Conversely, the moderator must be able to shift attention away from a dominant speaker without them or others feeling that their views are being dismissed (Liamputtong, 2011: 81). In the case of the seminars focus group, one group member sought to close down discussion in response to a question and I had to be quite forceful in seeking the views of others:

> **Moderator**: So, going back to Kevin's question, how do we measure whether a seminar's worked?
>
> **Evan**: You can't.
>
> **Moderator**: Well, others might think that you can.

Here this very blunt approach was effective, encouraging participation in the discussion from others without stopping Evan from taking part. In other cases, the moderator may need to be gentler in ensuring that all are encouraged to participate without one speaker feeling that their contributions are not welcomed.

Piloting for interviews and focus groups

In any form of research, a pilot study is crucial because it can identify potential difficulties and so reduce the danger that flawed data is collected. When designing questionnaires or interview schedules for quantitative studies, there are sophisticated multi-stage piloting procedures that should be employed to reduce the danger that large numbers of questionnaires or schedules will be returned with incomplete or misleading information (see De Vaus, 2002: 114–118). In the case of qualitative interviews, the need is not quite so obvious, as minor changes may be made to the interview guide as the interviews progress. Similarly, if more than one focus group is conducted, the guide may be adjusted in the light of the first experience of data collection. However, it is clearly advantageous to ensure that as few changes as possible need to be made once the research has begun.

Hennink et al. (2011: 120) recommend that a small number of pilot (or practice) interviews are conducted with people who are as similar as possible to the group who will be the respondents to the research. They suggest that such pilot interviews can help to establish:

- if questions are understood;
- if the words and ideas used are appropriate to the context of the respondent;
- if any questions need to be rephrased;
- if the order of questions is logical;
- if the research question(s) can be answered, or research objectives can be met, with the information gathered from the interviews; and
- if the interview guide is of an appropriate length.

In addition to the researcher's own perceptions, it is helpful to seek the views of the interviewees on these matters. At the end of the pilot phase, the researcher should have a revised interview schedule that they feel confident to use.

It is more difficult to pilot focus group research. However, where it is possible to assemble people similar to the respondents who will take part in the focus group(s), this opportunity should be taken and feedback sought from them about the questions and the dynamics of the discussion.

Recording and transcription of interview and focus group data

There are substantial advantages to recording data collected from interviews and focus groups rather than having to take notes. Indeed, the speed of discussion of a focus group, and the limits to the control that can be exercised by the moderator, mean that it would be all but impossible for the moderator to keep comprehensive notes on the discussion and difficult even for a second researcher to do so. The disadvantages of making notes are also substantial when conducting interviews: the interviewee may become distracted by the note taking and the researcher is unlikely to be able to make a sufficiently detailed record to use direct quotations (Oppenheim, 1992: 69–70). Recording the exact words of a respondent is essential if the researcher wishes to use techniques such as discourse analysis or conversation analysis (see Chapter 7).

Interviews are almost always recorded in audio form (King and Horrocks, 2011: 46–47). Video recording of focus groups can overcome difficulties of identifying who is speaking and recording non-verbal behaviour, but may present problems in positioning the recorder to ensure that everyone is covered. It may also increase the self-consciousness of respondents (Barbour, 2007: 76–77). When using audio recording for focus groups, having a note-taker in addition to a moderator is a major advantage. They can keep track of the order of speakers (which may be difficult to tell from an audio recording), record the key issues to emerge from the discussion and note group activities and movements that cannot be captured by an audio recording device. In addition, in the later stages of the discussion, they can inform the moderator if there are any topics that have not yet been covered (Liamputtong, 2011: 63).

However, there are situations where a respondent refuses the use of a recording device. In the case of a focus group, the researcher may have to very politely suggest that the objecting member does not take part in the discussion because, as noted above, it is very difficult to use written notes as the only method of recording focus group data. In the case of an interview, note taking is more feasible, although very challenging: the researcher must strike a balance between keeping the interview flowing and ensuring that the key points are recorded. A respondent should not be asked to repeat a point unless the researcher judges it to be essential. It is helpful to write well spaced notes so that detail can be added as soon as possible after the interview, while it is still fresh in the mind of the researcher (King and Horrocks, 2011: 47).

Where a recording of an interview or focus group has been made, the researcher or somebody else will need to transcribe it, i.e. convert it from audio to written form. Transcribing inevitably involves an element of interpretation; spoken language needs punctuation to be added to it as it is written down and the position of full stops, dashes, and so on, reflects the transcriber's interpretation of what was said. Hesse-Biber and Leavy (2011: 158) note that there are further important decisions to be made when transcribing: for example, whether to eliminate noises such as 'um' and whether to correct grammar. They argue that it is important for the researcher to reflect on these decisions because they have an impact on the manner in which 'knowledge' is presented through the transcript; a consistent approach is needed to recording 'pauses, laughter, the raising or lowering of voice, tonal change, the elongation of words, and so forth' (Hesse-Biber and Leavy (2011: 143).

The role of different forms of transcription is illustrated below using an extract from an interview with a man living in a temporary accommodation project. The organisation that transcribed the interview recorded only the words and edited some of the grammar: their version is the first one that appears. The second was produced by me on listening back to the audio recording, noting the words and also some of the non-verbal elements. The parts that have been added to the second account are shown in italics.

Extract from interview: words only and grammar edited

Basically, all my problems started after a bad break-up with my ex-partner. We were together five years and actually on our anniversary we split up. And instead of trying to sort that out, I turned to drink. At this time I'm a recovering alcoholic, trying to sort things out that way.

For the first few months I just drank and drank, I lost my house, managed to find another place to stay which was all right. And then I moved to Glasgow, I moved in with my mum, who I hadn't actually seen for years, just got back in contact with her. Basically, I was offered a job and a place to live up in Glasgow and everything was going all right, nice job, I kept on drinking. I was turning up for work hung over all the time and then I moved out of my mum's place and then into a flat above a bar, which obviously didn't help with the drinking, because then I was obviously drinking every night and it just ... It messed with my head.

Extracts from interview: fuller transcription

Um, Basically, all my problems started after a bad break-up with my ex-partner. *Um* We were together five years and *on* – actually on our anniversary we split up. And *I actually turned* – instead of trying to sort that out, I turned to drink. *Um*, At this time I'm a recovering alcoholic, *um* trying to sort things out that way. And, *err*, for the first few months I just drank and drank, I lost my house, *um*, managed to find another place to stay which was all right. And then I moved to Glasgow? [*raises voice*], I moved in with my mum, who I hadn't actually seen for years, just got back in contact with her. *Um* Basically, I was offered a job and a place to live up in Glasgow and [*yeah and*] everything was going all right, nice job, *but I* – I kept on drinking. *Um*, I was turning up for work, *sort of*, hung over all the time and then I moved out of my mum's place and then into a flat above a bar, which obviously didn't help [*half laugh*] with the drinking, because then I was obviously drinking every night and it just, *it just* ... It messed with my head.

(Some details of the account have been changed to protect the identity of the respondent).

Reflections on the two versions of the extract

So how much more does this second version of the extract tell us? Many people make sounds such as 'um' and 'err' when they hesitate in their speech so it is difficult to determine how to interpret them. Perhaps more is to be gained by considering the reasons for the respondent sometimes stopping and reconsidering mid-sentence, which is usually indicated by a dash. A good example is: 'And I actually turned – instead of trying to sort that out, I turned to drink.' Here it appears that he began to say how he reacted to the relationship breaking down, but then stopped in order to indicate that he was aware that this was not the best response and that he should instead have 'sorted it out'. The second version notes that the man raised his voice when saying Glasgow, as though this were a question. He may have been checking that the researcher was aware where Glasgow was, but another explanation is that he was suggesting that moving away was an unusual step to take. The half laugh when he discussed moving in above the bar could be interpreted in a number of ways – most obviously that he felt that this was a foolish step to take for somebody who had a problem with alcohol.

Interpretations such as these are particularly subjective and are discussed further when considering discourse analysis in Chapter 7. However, the point in showing these two versions of the same account, and discussing briefly the extra data that is available from the second one, is to demonstrate that any transcription is likely to involve an element of interpretation and to remove some of the detail of the verbal record. A researcher who is conducting their own transcription should decide in advance what level of detail they will transcribe. A researcher who is able to ask someone else to transcribe their data should be aware of the level of detail that will be included and the implications of this for the analysis that is to follow.

Summary

Qualitative researchers must choose between collecting data through interviews, focus groups or other methods. If they choose interviews, there are further choices to be made between different types: semi-structured, unstructured and biographical interviews are among the most frequently used. Another important choice for the qualitative researcher is between modes of data collection, i.e. whether data should be collected face to face, by telephone or online. For the new researcher, face-to-face data collection is likely to be the most appropriate method to begin to use, although they should be aware of the particularly strong impact that their appearance and characteristics can have when collecting data in this manner.

Designing a guide for an interview or a focus group is an important element of the preparation. The researcher should give careful thought to how the questions to be asked, or topics to be raised, will contribute to answering the research question(s) or achieving the research objectives. It is very important to pilot the data collection and adjust the guide accordingly, although piloting is often difficult in the case of focus group research. Focus groups often raise extra questions in terms of the selection of respondents: the number in the group needs to be appropriate and, where possible, a 'community of interest' should be created, although with careful thought given to matters of power and hierarchy.

The manner in which an interview or focus group begins is likely to have a crucial impact on the quality of the data collected. The interviewer needs to establish rapport without becoming involved in a two-way conversation, while the focus group moderator needs to ensure that the opening questions facilitate discussion. Probing is a particularly important skill for qualitative interviewers; some possible probes can be identified in advance but it is often necessary for the researcher to make a very quick decision as to when one or more supplementary questions should be asked. When a focus group is operating effectively, the moderator may not need to encourage discussion, but instead to steer it on occasions and to ensure that all have the opportunity to contribute. However, a focus group moderator should also be ready to ask probing questions if a topic they wish to explore fails to generate sufficient discussion.

Recording, usually audio recording, of interviews and focus group discussions is advantageous, although this should, of course, only be undertaken with the consent of the respondent(s). The researcher should think carefully about the impact that converting data from audio recordings to written records has on the content: information is inevitably lost in terms of tone of voice, pauses, and so on.

Once the data has been collected the challenging task of data analysis begins. The next few chapters are devoted to different methods and techniques that can make sense of data.

Further reading

For discussion of a range of topics in the area of interview and focus group data collection, I recommend:

Roulston, K. (2010) *Reflective Interviewing: A Guide to Theory and Practice*. London: Sage.

Another comprehensive guide, which has been cited extensively in this chapter, is:

King, N. and Horrocks, C. (2010) *Interviews in Qualitative Research*. London: Sage.

There are a range of sources that discuss conducting interviews and focus groups in specific situations. Even if your own context does not match any of these, reading some and considering the different issues that arise should help you to adapt your approach to different situations:

Williams, H. (2011) 'Strategies for conducting elite interviews', *Qualitative Research*, 11(4): 431–441.

Philipin, S. M., Jordan, S. E. and Warring, J. (2005) 'Giving people a voice: reflections on conducting interviews with participants experiencing communication impairment', *Journal of Advanced Nursing*, 50(3): 299–306.

Allen, L. (2006) 'Trying not to think "straight": conducting focus groups with lesbian and gay youth', *International Journal of Qualitative Studies in Education*, 19(2): 163–176.

Strickland, C. J. (1999) 'Conducting focus groups cross-culturally: experiences with Pacific Northwest Indian people', *Public Health Nursing*, 16(3): 190–197.

4

First stages of analysing interview data – making summaries and making comparisons

Introduction

This chapter focuses on the first stages of the analysis of interview data, where the researcher has the transcripts and faces the challenge of trying to make sense of them. As was explained in Chapter 1, the approach taken can best be described as thematic analysis, although it incorporates elements of other approaches. When using thematic analysis, the researcher is seeking to achieve three aims: examining commonality, examining differences and examining relationships (Gibson and Brown, 2009: 128–129).

However, for the new researcher such aims may feel beyond them; the task of making sense of the complex data that qualitative researchers collect can seem an overwhelming one (Patton, 2002: 440). This chapter discusses two processes which can assist in the identification of themes running through different transcripts. The first, making summaries, is an initial step which facilitates further analysis. Reducing an interview to the key points can enable the researcher to see through the mass of detail and repetition to the points that are most relevant to the research question(s) or objectives. It facilitates the identification of similarities and differences. In this chapter you will be shown how sections of one interview can be reduced to a small number of bullet points, then invited to carry out a similar process for a second interview.

The second process that the researcher may find helpful in the early stages of analysis is the use of the constant comparative method. It will be shown that the first step in this process can be as simple as to make lists of similarities and differences between two cases, which can prepare the researcher for more difficult tasks as further cases are added.

Summarising and the constant comparative method can be used either separately or together when analysing a dataset. They can also be used alongside coding; much of the literature relating to the constant comparative method assumes that codes are used. Coding is discussed in Chapters 5 and 6 but it is suggested that the new researcher uses the constant comparative method separately in the first instance because, as is noted by Yin (2011: 188): 'coding routines can produce their own distractions – for example having to attend to the mechanics of the coding process rather than struggling to think about the data.'

This chapter will demonstrate that many of the decisions made during qualitative analysis are subjective and require a judgement on the part of the researcher as to the most suitable of two or more courses of action. It will include an example of a methodological memo to record a key decision, which is a method of ensuring the validity of research findings, as discussed in Chapter 1.

Summarising interviews

As was noted in Chapter 3, it is very important to read and re-read transcripts thoroughly before beginning analysis; this is a simple technique to enhance validity, making it more likely that the findings of the study will accurately reflect the original data. Although reading and re-reading is time consuming, it should ensure that the researcher does not neglect any ideas or sections of the transcripts when conducting their analysis (Schmidt, 2004: 255). Once the reading is complete, the process of summarising can begin. This process will be demonstrated using an interview with a lecturer referred to as Fern.

Case summary sheets have been used as a data reduction device since the early twentieth century (Fielding and Lee, 1998: 24). Miles and Huberman, (1994: 51) argue that the strength of summarising is that it enables the researcher to focus on the main questions raised by the respondent because 'it is easy to get lost in a welter of detail'. Paraphrasing the content into a shorter form can eliminate unnecessary features such as repetition (Flick, 2009: 325).

As Miles and Huberman (1994: 51–52) argue, the full transcript should be reduced to a summary that fits onto one sheet of paper and so is easy for the researcher to compare with other summaries. A glance at the full transcript of the interview with Fern, which appears in Appendix 1, will demonstrate that this means that the material must be substantially reduced.

It is often helpful to summarise one section of a transcript at a time. The process of summarising usually involves the following steps:

1 Identify the research objective(s) that the section of the transcript is most relevant to.
2 Decide which pieces of information or opinion are most relevant to this objective/these objectives and which are detail that do not need to be included in the summary.
3 Decide where (if at all) there is repetition that needs to be eliminated.
4 On the basis of these decisions, write brief notes.

The first step assumes that an inductive approach is being taken and that the study is seeking to meet research objectives. If a deductive approach were being used instead, the researcher would need to consider how the section of the transcript could contribute to answering the research question(s).

Summarising interviews: examples

I will now demonstrate how the first section of the interview with Fern was summarised according to this procedure. This section, which dealt with how and why the respondent became a lecturer, appears below:

Interviewer: First we're going to look at motivation. How long have you been in this particular job?

Fern: A large number of years now.

Interviewer: Right, okay. Have you had any other previous roles within this university?

Fern: I have progressed from a basic lecturer to a senior position.

Interviewer: Have you taught at any other universities?

Fern: Yes I've taught at one other.

Interviewer: Okay, why did you decide to enter into higher education?

Fern: Never wanted to do anything else.

Interviewer: But what were your reasons for doing that? Was it for your own satisfaction, financial reasons, flexible working?

Fern: Because I wanted to research and teach. I wanted to do the job and I didn't think about the money. It wasn't very well paid to start with. It never crossed my mind to do any other job to be perfectly honest.

Interviewer: In the beginning, what were your initial hopes and fears for the job?

Fern: I just wanted to be a good academic and I wanted never to have to leave. I didn't think about getting promoted; I just wanted to be a researcher and a teacher. My worry was perhaps I would have to leave because, like I say, I could never imagine doing anything else.

Step 1: identify the research objective(s) that the section of the transcript is most relevant to

As discussed in Chapter 1, the objectives of the research were:

1   to identify the motivation of lecturers for their choice of career;
2   to identify feelings about, and practical difficulties associated with, different elements of the job;
3   to discuss different types of students and the experience of teaching them;
4   to identify feelings about reflective practice and methods by which it was put into practice; and
5   to discuss changes with time in relation to the above factors.

It was clear that the first of these objectives was most relevant to this section of the transcript.

Step 2: decide which pieces of information or opinion are most relevant to this objective/these objectives and which are details that do not need to be included in the summary

The first three questions of the interview were included in order to provide some context and to establish rapport between the interviewer and the respondent; the responses did not need to appear in the summary because they were not central to the relevant research objective. Similarly, the discussion of the elements that did not motivate Fern – i.e. money and promotion – were eliminated because they were elements of detail; the point that I judged to be central to the research objective was what did attract Fern to the job, i.e. the desire to research and teach.

Step 3: decide where (if at all) there is repetition that needs to be eliminated

The fourth, fifth and sixth questions addressed motivation. There was repetition that could be eliminated because Fern made three very similar points in response to these questions: 'Never wanted to do anything else', 'It never crossed my mind to do any other job' and 'I could never imagine doing anything else.'

Step 4: on the basis of these decisions, write brief notes

Having made the decisions above, it was possible to write brief notes to appear in the summary of the interview, which looked like this:

- intrinsic motivation, wanted to research and teach;
- no interest in any other career.

Decisions as to which points to include in, and which to exclude from, a summary can clearly have an impact on the outcome of the research and a bearing on validity, i.e. the extent to which the conclusions drawn are an accurate reflection of the data that has been collected. To enhance validity, it was useful to write a methodological memo, which could be referred back to when writing the methodology section of the research output, as will be discussed in Chapter 9. The memo looked like this:

Methodological memo: factors excluded from the summary of the interview with Fern

The summary largely took out the detail of the interview, rather than ignoring issues completely. However, there were a small number of exceptions. Fern's previous experience, although specifically asked about, was not discussed: questions on this subject were asked mainly to orientate the interviewer and establish rapport with the respondent. The factors that Fern said did not influence her to become a lecturer were also not mentioned, in order to concentrate on those factors that provided her motivation.

The process of summarising will now be demonstrated again with another part of the interview with Fern – a section where reflective practice was discussed. This section appears below:

Interviewer: Okay we're going to move on to reflective practice now. What's your understanding of that?

Fern: It's about reflecting on how I do my teaching, how I practise my trade. Reflection is something that is required in every area of work these days.

Interviewer: And how important to you is reflecting on your own practice?

Fern: Oh I've always been interested in student feedback. I always want to know how it's gone and I don't like if I feel I haven't been on top form or I haven't explained things right: that really annoys me. So I do think, I do feel it over in my mind what I've done and how I've done; how I've answered questions and that kind of thing. I think I do it almost all the time, I don't think, 'another lecture over, on with the next'; I always want to feel it's gone well and if it hasn't gone well then why hasn't it gone well? And so if I'm understanding what reflective practice actually does, then it's my natural condition.

Interviewer: And what is your motivation to be reflective of your practice?

Fern: Pride.

Interviewer: Pride?

Fern: Yes I want to do a good job; I would not wish to produce poor research or produce poor teaching.

The same four steps were taken to summarise this section:

Step 1: identify the research objective(s) that the section of the transcript is most relevant to

Again, it was easy to see which of the research objectives was most relevant, i.e. to identify feelings about reflective practice and methods by which it was put into practice.

Step 2: decide which pieces of information or opinion are most relevant to this objective/these objectives and which are details that do not need to be included in the summary

Most of Fern's answers were relevant to this objective. However, her comment that 'Reflection is something that is required in every area of work these days' was not central either to feelings about reflective practice or methods of putting it into practice, so did not need to appear in the summary.

Step 3: decide where (if at all) there is repetition that needs to be eliminated

Much of what Fern said in this extract was elaboration of points that had already been made. So, for example, the first sentence of her second answer – 'Oh I've always been interested in student feedback' – established that she believed reflective practice to be important and that one mechanism that she used was student feedback. The remainder of the answer developed this initial statement. Similarly, after answering that her motivation for reflective practice was pride, Fern's next answer simply developed this point further. So, in each case, it was only the initial point or points that needed to appear in the summary.

Step 4: on the basis of these decisions, write brief notes

Based on the first three steps, the summary of this section was written as:

- reflective practice important;
- reflective practice mechanisms: personal reflection and student feedback;
- reflective practice motivation: pride.

Summarising interviews: exercise

Exercise 3 asks you to make some of your own summaries. You should use the same four stage process as above, i.e.

1 Identify the research objective(s) that the section of the transcript is most relevant to.

2 Decide which pieces of information or opinion are most relevant to this objective/ these objectives and which are detail that do not need to be included in the summary.

3 Decide where (if at all) there is repetition that needs to be eliminated.

4 On the basis of these decisions, write brief notes.

Exercise 3

You are now invited to read two sections of the transcript from an interview with another lecturer, referred to as Susan, and to write your own summary notes.

Section 1: reasons for entering the job

Interviewer: Have you worked in other universities?

Susan: Yes, I was at two other universities before I came here.

Interviewer: Okay, and why did you decide to enter your job? Particularly higher education?

Susan: By accident to tell you the truth! I was going to do it part time for six months while I finished my Master's and years later realised I was still at the same university and it had carried on so it wasn't an actual career choice, it was more by accident than choice I think really.

Interviewer: Okay, and would you say that you went into it for financial reasons?

(Continued)

(Continued)

Susan: Definitely not, no.

Interviewer: What about flexible working?

Susan: I did work on the belief that it was going to be flexible and good when I had a family but in reality I think it's exactly the opposite. For someone with a family it's probably the least flexible. You think it's going to be and there are all these misconceptions that you're going to be off for three weeks at Easter and all the way through the summer and that kind of thing. People aren't often aware about weekend teaching and you've got to be here at weekends. If you have a family, it's obviously much more difficult. So the stereotypical image is of a lecturer who does five or six hours a week and sits in the bar the rest of the time and it's all very flexible, but the reality is very different.

Interviewer: Okay, and did you have any hopes and expectation of the job?

Susan: I hoped that I was going to excite people as much as I was about what I'd studied and what I'd learnt and I feel very passionate about what I teach and what I do. My expectation was that other people would be excited, but the reality is just because you're excited doesn't mean other people will be but you can make it exciting and try to engage them. So I think that's probably why I stayed in education for so long, wanting to find someone like me who gets excited about the same types of things really.

Section 2: reflective practice

Interviewer: Moving on, what's your understanding of reflective practice?

Susan: It's about looking back at what you've done, how you do it, what experiences you've gained from that. You've got to constantly be a reflective practitioner and look at not just what we're teaching but how we teach it, how we impart that knowledge and the students' experience. You can reflect but it needs to be two ways with the people who you've been working with – how they've engaged that process and how they have seen it. I think it's critical; it's a two way engagement.

Interviewer: So you think it's important?

Susan: Oh yes, there are people who don't do that in this line of work; I'm thinking beyond the faculty to other academics who I've worked with who don't do it and churn out the same lecture year on year. They teach this because it's week eight, never mind if things have changed. It's dry and they don't excite or engage the students; they don't want to learn in that environment.

Interviewer: And what would you say was your motivation to be reflective of your practice?

Susan: For students to enjoy my teaching, and it comes back to wanting to be seen as a teacher.

Interviewer: So would you say that was internal?

Susan: In the sense of me?

Interviewer: Yes.

Susan: Yes, very much. There is pressure, in the fact we have to write personal teaching reviews and we do practise within the faculty to look at how you teach and the experience and the student expectations. But it's very much for me, that it's enjoyable for me and it's not enjoyable to teach if you look at a room full of students who look blank, don't ask questions and don't respond back. If you're sat in a seminar and thinking, 'ugh I've got two hours to wade through this', why would you ever want to keep doing that? It's about being enjoyable for me but also so that I can see students have been excited by what we've done and what we've covered.

Please complete the exercise before looking at how I would have tackled it below.

My summary of section 1

The objective of the research that was linked to this section was, of course, 'To identify the motivation of lecturers for their choice of career'. The parts of the extract that I felt were not relevant to this objective were that Susan had worked in two universities previously, that she felt that lecturers were wrongly stereotyped and that she disagreed strongly with the perception that academic work is flexible. Deciding what was essential and what was repetition or detail proved more difficult. When considering the question as to why Susan went into the job, the answer 'by accident' indicated that it was a pragmatic choice; the remainder of the answer simply developed this point. The next two answers gave two reasons for Susan making this pragmatic choice; in each case the key point was made at the start of the answer with the rest largely consisting of further detail. So my summary of this section was:

- pragmatic choice to enter higher education;
- attracted by the belief that academic job was flexible;
- excited by subject and wanted others to be excited.

My summary of section 2

The objective to consider in this section was 'To identify feelings about reflective practice and methods by which it was put into practice'. Most of what Susan said was very relevant to this objective, but her comment that some lecturers did not engage in reflective practice was clearly an aside that did not need to appear in the summary. Turning to the question of what was detail or repetition, the two methods of reflecting that Susan identified in her first answer (personal reflection and student feedback) were clearly of key importance. Her second answer established that reflective practice was important to her and suggested that her motivation was to see students enjoying learning – a point which was repeated in her third answer. Her final answer made this point again, but also introduced another element of motivation – Susan wanted to enjoy teaching. In addition, the mention of personal teaching reviews and making comparisons with practice in other parts of the faculty added further to the list of methods of reflective practice. So the points that I included in my summary were:

- reflective practice important;
- reflective practice mechanisms: personal reflection, student feedback, personal teaching reviews, making comparisons with other parts of the faculty;
- reflective practice motivation: for students and lecturer to enjoy teaching.

The value of summaries

As was noted above, summarising enables the researcher to reduce the large amount of information that is available through any interview transcript to a form where it is easier to identify the main points. It also facilitates the next method of analysis to be discussed here, i.e. making comparisons between cases. The full summaries of the interviews with Fern and Susan appear in Table 4.1. Such a table eases the process of identifying similarities and differences and also demonstrates one of the strengths of semi-structured interviews: because Fern and Susan were asked about the same issues, it was possible to make direct comparisons in many cases. For example, Fern preferred teaching lectures to seminars, while for Susan the reverse was true. However, there are still likely to be some areas talked about by only one respondent: for example, Fern made comparisons to when the university was a polytechnic (i.e. before 1992, see Chapter 7), while there was no such comparison made by Susan, who had been working in higher education for a shorter period of time.

Table 4.1   Summary of interviews with Fern and Susan

Fern	Susan
Intrinsic motivation, wanted to research and teach	Pragmatic choice to enter higher education, but excited by subject
No interest in any other career	Attracted by the belief that academic job was flexible
	Excited by subject and wants others to be excited
Difficulties of mass higher education and heavy workload compensated for by job satisfaction	Satisfaction in getting good feedback from students (but difficult to obtain feedback with large student numbers); less concerned about evaluation of peers
Work less pressurised when university was a polytechnic	
Research historically seen as optional; there remains more pressure from self than from university to do research	Teaching more important than research; research should feed into teaching
Large amounts of guidance tutoring but 'don't mind' doing it, most satisfying when get to know students	Finds guidance tutoring rewarding; needs to know how far to support students and when to refer to other staff/agencies
Used to enjoy teaching mature students but hindered by changes to financial support	Enjoys teaching mature students, particularly their preference for interactive teaching
Language a barrier to teaching international students but can be overcome with high student motivation	Cultural differences a greater barrier than language among international students; danger of using terminology that is too academic
Reflective practice important	Reflective practice important
Reflective practice mechanisms: personal reflection and student feedback	Reflective practice mechanisms: personal reflection, student feedback, personal teaching review, making comparisons with other parts of the faculty
Reflective practice motivation: pride	Reflective practice motivation: for students and lecturer to enjoy teaching
Prefers lectures to seminars; 'not so much in control' in seminars and difficult to persuade students to speak; sets lots of exercises. Workshops also hard.	Prefers seminars to lectures; varies seminar approach according to year of study; requires students to prepare for seminars
Views student attendance as voluntary; happy to teach students who are most motivated, i.e. those who attend	Student attendance influenced by whether material interesting and timing of teaching sessions; worried about monitoring attendance when there may be good reasons for absence

It is recommended that you read the full transcript of the interview with Fern in Appendix 1 and consider how much more difficult it is to make comparisons between cases if summaries are not made. This is not to suggest, of course, that the full transcript has no further use once the summary has been written. Indeed, further stages of analysis examine the full transcript in considerable detail, as will be demonstrated in later chapters. However, the point here is that basic similarities and differences are much easier to identify with summaries.

The constant comparative method

The constant comparative method is a helpful approach to identifying similarities and differences between cases in a dataset. It can be used alongside summaries or independently; as noted above, one of the values of summaries is that they make the task of comparing cases considerably easier.

The constant comparative method was originally advocated by Glaser and Strauss (1967) as part of their grounded theory approach but Barbour (2008: 217) argues that it is at the heart of all qualitative data analysis, which relies on constantly comparing and contrasting. It is described by Charmaz (2006: 54) in the following manner:

> At first you compare data with data to find similarities and differences. For example, compare interview statements and incidents within the same interview and compare statements and incidents in different interviews.

Later stages of the process involve creating categories in which to place data and then building theory (Flick, 2009: 407), but it is comparisons between interviews that this chapter will concentrate on.

The key reason for using the constant comparative method is identified by Dey (2004: 88): 'Comparison is the engine through which we can generate insights, by identifying patterns of similarity or difference within the data'. Barbour (2008: 217) also discusses the importance of identifying patterns when using the constant comparative method. So while this method is, of course, closely linked to comparative analysis, its aims overlap substantially with those of thematic analysis, particularly the examination of commonality and of differences.

A helpful approach to using the constant comparative method, and one which is demonstrated below, is to divide the process into three steps:

1 Make a list of similarities and differences between the first two cases to be considered.

2 Amend this list as further cases are added to the analysis.

3 Identify research findings once all the cases have been included in the analysis.

Step 1 – make a list of similarities and differences between the first two cases

This is a fairly simple first step and one that may help to build the confidence of the researcher who is worried about using the constant comparative method, or about qualitative analysis more generally. It will be illustrated using the example of the interviews with Fern and Susan. In the case of some issues, it will be immediately obvious whether respondents' views and/or experiences should be listed as similar or different. For example, the summaries discussed above showed clearly that Fern and Susan had different reasons for working in higher education: Fern had always wanted to be a lecturer while Susan came into the job for more pragmatic reasons.

Even in areas where there are broad similarities, there are likely to be differences of detail. For example, Fern and Susan both agreed that reflective practice was important and both used personal reflection and gaining feedback from students as methods of reflection. However, there were also some differences: Susan added personal teaching review and comparing practice with other parts of the faculty to her list of mechanisms. In addition, she said that her motivation was to enjoy teaching, while Fern's was pride.

So, when I made lists of similarities and differences in relation to these two issues, they looked like this:

Reasons for entering the job

Similarities

None.

Differences

Fern always wanted to do the job; Susan's reasons were pragmatic.

Reflective practice

Similarities

Agreed it was important.
Used personal reflection and student feedback as mechanisms.

Differences

Susan used personal teaching reviews and comparison with other parts of the faculty as mechanisms.
Susan was motivated by a desire to enjoy teaching, Fern by pride.

The next exercise examines the comments made by Fern and Susan about the experience of teaching mature students. The notes made on this subject in the summaries suggest a difference between the two respondents, but the exercise invites you to consider what was said in more detail:

Exercise 4

Read the comments of Fern and Susan in relation to teaching mature students, then list the similarities and differences:

Fern on mature students

Interviewer: Okay, what is your experience of teaching mature students?

Fern: Oh it used to be fabulous; in the good old days when there were grants we had loads and loads of mature students and sometimes up to a third of a course was made up of mature students. And there would be all sorts of people, we had vicars, we had retired miners – all sorts of people coming in. And lots of women who had returned to work after having children. And several of them struggled with it but some of them were really fabulous. In fact we had a couple of mature students just recently on the course; I wouldn't say more so than other students, but they were here because they wanted to be here. And they were desperate to learn and desperate to know; some of the brightest students we had were the mature students. And I thought it was marvellous taking somebody who had no chance of education and suddenly had the confidence to realise that they could come to learn and I think it's fabulous. I really, really enjoyed that; you don't have that now because of course they can't afford to take the loans out, mature students, they have to work. You know, no government grants, there's no support for them so they've all gone, nearly all gone … I think all students now need the information, they want to know what the assessment is; they want to know what they need to do because they want to know how to get the marks. They really are quite instrumental, whereas the mature students never were here just to get the qualification – that was the icing on the cake. They were here to learn and to enjoy the process. I'm not sure that students enjoy the process any more.

Susan on mature students

Interviewer: How do you find teaching mature students?

Susan: I really enjoy it because they bring different life experience to the classroom. It's not just a one way situation; it's two way; you can impart academic knowledge and they can bring practice knowledge and life experience with them.

Interviewer: Have you noticed any difference in the preferred teaching methods of traditional and mature students?

Susan: Yes, I find the mature students much prefer non-lecture based environments and prefer more discussion so it's two way. I think that

> traditional students do like that as well but because of the numbers there isn't always the capacity to be able to do it, so they get stuck in a rut of the lecture–seminar structure. It's not necessarily their desire but it's the structure of the university, the way we deliver and it's normally bigger numbers so it's less easy to offer other methods.
>
> Please complete this exercise before looking at how I would have tackled it below.

My first thoughts about the similarities and differences were that both Fern and Susan felt very positively about teaching mature students but for different reasons: Fern spoke about their motivation while Susan discussed the life experience that they could bring to interactive teaching situations. There also appeared to be differences as to whether this positive view of mature students only related to the past or was applicable to the present: Susan's use of the present tense – 'I really enjoy it' – indicated that she saw the advantages of teaching mature students as ongoing. In contrast, Fern spoke positively about the experience of teaching mature students in the past but then seemed ambiguous about the present-day experience: she spoke warmly about the motivation of two students who had recently been on her course but then suggested that mature students, like others, now tended to be quite instrumental in their method of learning.

So my list of similarities and differences in relation to mature students was:

Mature students

Similarities

Positive about teaching mature students.

Differences

Susan enjoyed teaching mature students in the present; Fern was unclear as to whether her enjoyment had mainly been in the past.
Fern valued mature students for their motivation, Susan for their life experience and the opportunities this provided for interactive teaching.

As noted previously, there are likely to be some areas where comparisons cannot be made, even when examining only two cases. In the above example, Susan did not discuss the impact of changes to financial support for students so this issue could not be the subject of comparisons.

Step 2 – amend the list of similarities and differences as further cases are added to the analysis

One of the great strengths of qualitative data, but one of the factors that makes it difficult to analyse, is the complexity that it can capture and record. The greater richness is a key difference between qualitative and quantitative data (Denzin and Lincoln, 2008: 16). As more cases are added to the analysis, it is likely that any simple list of similarities and differences will need to be substantially modified. This section will show how the introduction of an interview with a third lecturer from the case study university, Rachel, added to the complexity of the analysis of two of the issues discussed above, i.e. reflective practice and the experience of teaching mature students.

Following is a reminder that the similarities and differences between Fern and Susan in relation to reflective practice were:

Similarities

Agreed it was important.
Used personal reflection and student feedback as mechanisms.

Differences

Susan used personal teaching review and comparison with other parts of the faculty as methods.
Susan motivated by a desire to enjoy teaching, Fern by pride.

The section from Rachel's transcript on this subject is shown below:

Rachel on reflective practice

Interviewer: What is your understanding of reflective practice?

Rachel: Looking at what you do, looking back at what you do, and looking at how you can improve.

Interviewer: Do you find it important?

Rachel: Yes, because I think you can slip into a certain way of doing lectures, a certain way of doing seminars and a certain way of dealing with students and you forget that time's moved on and actually you should be. You should move with the times and I think changing jobs has given me a new lease of life. I've done things I haven't done ever before and just thinking about what you're doing and what you're teaching and what you want to get across is something we should do all the time.

Interviewer: Do you feel under pressure from anywhere to reflect?

Rachel: From myself.

Interviewer: Just yourself?

Rachel: Yes, it is surprising that there is no external pressure. I want to write good lectures and to always have great images and things like that. So a lot of pressure from myself but I don't think that's such a bad thing, because if I didn't give myself that pressure then I probably wouldn't bother any more.

Incorporating Rachel's data demonstrated three likely effects of adding further cases to the analysis of similarities and differences.

First, factors are likely to disappear from the list of similarities. Rachel agreed that reflective practice was important and that personal reflection was a method of achieving this. So here were two areas of continuing agreement. However, she did not discuss incorporating student feedback into reflection so this could not be considered a similarity between all the cases.

Second, the list of differences is likely to become more complex as the researcher seeks to keep track of who said what. It now needed to be recorded that Fern and Susan discussed using feedback from students in their reflective practice but Rachel did not. I also noted that Rachel gave different reasons to both Fern and Susan for undertaking reflective practice, i.e. to teach to a high standard and to stay updated.

Third, comparisons are likely to become possible in some new areas, which were discussed in some interviews but not others. So, for example, I noted that Rachel and Susan both discussed where the pressure to reflect came from, but Fern did not. The comparison showed that Rachel only identified internal pressure (indeed, she commented on the lack of external pressure), while Susan said that it was mainly internal but two of her identified mechanisms – personal teaching review and comparisons with other parts of the faculty – were required activities and so a reflection of external pressure. This difference needed to be recorded, but it was also necessary to record that the issue was not discussed by Fern.

As a footnote to this third point, it sometimes emerges that comparisons of issues that appear to be new could, in fact, have been made earlier. To take an example, Rachel suggested that reflective practice was something that should be done 'all the time'. On looking back to see whether this idea was referred to in previous interviews, I noted that Susan referred to the need to 'constantly' be a reflective practitioner. I then re-read the interview with Fern and saw that she described reflective practice as her 'natural condition'. I interpreted this phrase as meaning that she reflected very regularly, so a further similarity emerged, one that I missed when initially comparing the interviews of Fern and Susan, i.e. that all three respondents reflected continuously on their practice. Of course, the interpretation of 'natural condition' is a subjective one and this interpretation could be recorded using a methodological memo.

So having incorporated the material from Rachel's interview, the list of similarities and differences in relation to reflective practice looked like this:

Similarities

All agreed it was important.
All used personal reflection as a method.
All thought that reflection should be a continuous process.

Differences

Susan and Fern used student feedback; Rachel did not.
Susan was the only one to use personal teaching review and comparison with other parts of the faculty as methods.
Susan was motivated by a desire to enjoy teaching, Fern by pride, Rachel by a wish to teach to a high standard and to stay updated.
Rachel thought the pressure to reflect was entirely internal while Susan discussed both internal and external pressures and the issue was not addressed by Fern.

Now I suggest that you undertake a similar exercise to examine the impact of adding Rachel's data relating to mature students to the comparisons made previously between Fern and Susan. You will recall that the list of similarities and differences between the interviews with Fern and Susan looked like this:

Similarities

Positive about teaching mature students

Differences

Susan enjoyed teaching mature students in the present; Fern was unclear as to whether her enjoyment had mainly been in the past.
Fern valued mature students for their motivation, Susan for their life experience and the opportunities it gave for interactive teaching.

In addition to this list of points, it will be useful to read again the relevant extracts from the interview with Fern (pp. 59–60) and with Susan (pp. 68–69) before undertaking Exercise 5.

Exercise 5

You are invited to read through the section of the interview with Rachel that referred to mature students and consider how the list of similarities and differences should be adjusted:

Rachel: I taught a lot of mature students in my previous job, but in this post at the moment I'm teaching predominately undergraduates.

Interviewer: And have you noticed any differences between traditional and mature students?

Rachel: No, nothing huge.

Interviewer: What about in terms of preferred teaching methods?

Rachel: With mature students you can probably be a bit more flexible with your teaching methods and you can also expect them to read. They'll probably take it quite seriously so, for instance, when I was teaching some mature students in my last job, if you asked them to read something, they would come back having made notes. So I think they tend to take studying more seriously while traditional undergraduates are less likely to read. So you have to rely on different teaching methods so in that respect, yes there is a difference. Mature students are also more likely to bring their work to you for guidance. This may be just a lack of confidence because they haven't been in higher education before or for a long time or just because they feel more committed to the course they're doing.

Interviewer: And do you get more satisfaction from teaching mature students as opposed to traditional students or vice versa?

Rachel: I like to teach them all: it's different and there's great satisfaction if you have a good traditional student sitting there and they've read something because they're interested in it after you've given the lecturer about it. If they hadn't thought about something before, but now they are reading about it, then the satisfaction is immense. On the other hand, it's quite demoralising when you feel that you've give your heart and soul to a lecture and then the students come along to a seminar and are just not interested – it's quite demoralising. It's also frustrating because you can't actually make people do work for seminars.

Please complete this exercise before looking at how I would have tackled it below.

When adding the material from the interview with Rachel to the list of similarities and differences, I found that the analysis partially followed the pattern that was established in relation to reflective practice. However, there were no similarities that disappeared from the list – the one similarity between Fern and Susan remained because Rachel also made positive comments about teaching mature students.

As was the case with the material on reflective practice, the list of differences became more complex as another respondent was added to the analysis. When considering changes with time, I simply aligned Rachel with Susan in that she did not make any distinction between the present and the past. However, on the question of the advantages of teaching mature students, the picture was more complex: Rachel identified one advantage that was also noted by Fern – that mature students were sometimes more committed; one advantage that was also identified by Susan – that it was possible to be more flexible with teaching methods to mature students; and one advantage that was identified by neither of the other respondents – that mature students were more likely to read between teaching sessions.

Another common feature with the reflective practice analysis was that a comparison became possible in a new area. Rachel commented that, in addition to their motivation, another reason for mature students being more likely to bring their work for guidance was that they lacked confidence. This was not an issue that was discussed by Susan but Fern commented on the moment when a mature student 'suddenly had the confidence to realise that they could come to learn'. So a need for confidence on the part of mature students could be identified as a similarity between the comments of Fern and Rachel.

So, after adding the interview with Rachel, my amended list of similarities and differences looked like this:

Similarities

Positive about teaching mature students.

Differences

Susan and Rachel identified no difference with time in teaching mature students; Fern was unclear as to whether she had enjoyed teaching them more in the past.
Fern and Rachel valued mature students for their motivation; Susan and Rachel for the greater opportunities that there were for interactive teaching; Susan for their life experience; Rachel for the greater likelihood that they would read between teaching sessions.
Susan did not identify specific difficulties experienced by mature students; Fern and Rachel both discussed a lack of confidence.

Reaching findings using the constant comparative method

There were, of course, further interviews to consider in the case study but there is not space to take you through the process of adding each of them to the analysis. Instead this section will consider briefly the method by which themes and findings may be identified once the process of using the constant comparative method is complete. Some writing about the constant comparative method discusses continuing to add new cases to the dataset until the point of 'saturation' is reached, i.e. new cases are not adding anything to the analysis (e.g. Charmaz, 2006: 113–114; Boeije, 2010: 83–84). However, it is unlikely that many research projects can offer this level of flexibility. In practice, the point at which a researcher stops collecting data is usually determined by the amount of time or other resources that can be devoted to the research project.

So a researcher often has less data than they would ideally like from which to draw their findings. As noted previously, the process for identifying findings using the constant comparative method can reflect the aims of thematic analysis identified by Gibson and Brown (2009: 128–129), i.e. examining commonality, examining differences and examining relationships. Each of these aims will now be considered using the data analysed in this chapter.

Examining commonality

It was noted previously that, as more cases are added to the analysis, it is probable that the list of similarities will dwindle because the likelihood of identifying an experience or a view common to all is reduced. However, in the case of reflective practice, one similarity that persisted across all the respondents at the case study university was an agreement that reflective practice was important.

Gibson and Brown (2009: 128) suggest that, where a commonality has been identified, the next stage is to analyse further and to look for sub-divisions. In the case of reflective practice, there were sub-divisions to explore such as differences between respondents who involved students in the process of reflection and those who did not, between respondents who had different types of motivation for their reflective practice, and so on. These subdivisions are not investigated here because they are the subject of further analysis in Chapter 5.

There are two reasons why the unanimous agreement about the importance of reflective practice was unusual. The first is that, while there should be some subjects that are discussed by all respondents, this will not be the case for every issue. The second is that there are likely to be individuals who disagree even where there is a broad consensus. One method of dealing with such disagreement is analytic induction: an advanced form of analysis which involves examining cases that differ from the norm and seeking to explain this difference (Flick, 2006: 4–5). However, a more obvious question for the new researcher is how many cases should have a common feature for it to be counted as commonality. One simple method of resolving this dilemma is by counting: Miles and Huberman (1994: 253) suggest that this is an essential part of qualitative analysis and Barbour (2008: 217) argues that it is a key element of using the constant comparative method. So how much agreement is needed for a factor to be considered as a commonality? My very rough rule of thumb is that, if three quarters of respondents or more share an experience or a view, then it should be considered to be a commonality. However, this is an entirely subjective decision and one which should be recorded using a methodological memo.

Examining differences

It was noted above that the pattern of differences tends to become more complex as more cases are added to the analysis; almost by definition, seeking to reach findings and identify themes in relation to differences is likely to be less simple than doing so in relation to similarities. The findings that can emerge in relation to differences will also be considered further in later chapters. One example will be provided here, using four cases for illustrative purposes; the subject matter is the reasons for going into lecturing. Fern and Susan's reasons were discussed earlier; Rachel's reasons are now considered briefly, together with those of another lecturer referred to as Laura.

Rachel took a number of jobs before becoming a contract researcher and studying at Master's level. A degree that she was particularly interested in began to be taught at a local university and, seeing an opportunity for a permanent job, she successfully applied for a post as a lecturer.

In contrast, Laura's prime motive for taking the job was similar to that of Fern: she said that a career as an academic was 'something I've always been keen to pursue'. The attractions of the job had included autonomy and flexibility, but also love for her subject.

The first type of finding is to simply note a broad difference: in this case, that some lecturers (i.e. Fern and Laura) had long-standing aims to go into the job while for others (i.e. Susan and Rachel) the reasons were more pragmatic. Second, sub-divisions can be noted: while Susan and Rachel both had pragmatic reasons, the supposed flexibility was a key factor for Susan while the permanent nature of the post advertised was important for Rachel. Third, common factors can sometimes be found even where there are broad differences: Susan, Rachel and Laura all discussed their enthusiasm for the subject area.

Examining relationships

The most challenging (and sometimes impossible) type of finding to draw is one that examines and seeks to explain relationships between different issues within a dataset. Richards (2009: 141) argues that the most important findings of a study can consist of making systematic comparisons to determine why cases are different. As was noted in Chapter 2, identifying the causal relationships between concepts was an important principle underpinning the development of quantitative methodology (Bryman, 1988: 30). However, Bryman (1988: 101–102) notes that a search for factors that are statistically linked can draw attention away from the process which links them and argues that:

> The qualitative researcher is in a better position to view the linkages between events and activities and to explore people's interpretations of the factors which produce such connections.

One possible outcome of examining relationships can be the creation of a typology; Richards (2009: 182) argues that this process involves examining the characteristics of cases that co-occur in order to explain the manner in which they are connected. A slightly different perspective is offered by Rosenthal (2004: 61), who argues that types can be developed by examining contrasting cases. Looking for types can be a frustrating experience and one where the researcher must often admit defeat. This will be demonstrated by discussing an apparent pattern of differences which I had thought might be built into a typology, but where the pattern that emerged from the early data was not subsequently sustained.

The differences between Fern's long-standing commitment to go into a job as a lecturer and the more pragmatic motivation of Susan and Rachel have already been noted. I then considered whether motivation could be linked to the level of priority that respondents gave to two key parts of the job of a lecturer, i.e. research and teaching. Fern demonstrated how central research was to her work when she interrupted the interviewer:

> **Interviewer**: Okay, we're going to move on to a little bit about research. You already mentioned it, is it very important to you personally that you ...
>
> **Fern**: Absolutely! 100 per cent. Yes, most important.

Fern also demonstrated that research was her priority by saying that she went into the job to 'research and teach' and that she wanted to be a 'researcher and teacher'. She discussed the importance of doing research even when she was not required to.

In contrast, Susan made very clear that research was of secondary importance to her after teaching, saying: 'It [*research*] is important but it always comes second to your teaching and you've never got enough time to get your research done'. In addition, it was clear that research was an important activity for its own sake for Fern, while for Susan it appeared to be a means to an end – she said of research: 'because I see myself as a teacher I want whatever I'm doing to feed in to my teaching'.

Rachel similarly made clear that teaching was her main task and that research would only be undertaken if she had spare capacity:

> It's hard for me to see it as important because I just feel at the moment I'm just writing lectures and teaching: it's hard. I'd like to have the time and space for research ... it's probably not the most important thing to me about my job.

So the question I sought to examine through my analysis was: could differences in the level of priority that respondents gave to research be linked to their reasons for entering the job? More specifically, did respondents who had a long-standing ambition to become a lecturer regard research as their first priority, while those who entered the job for more pragmatic reasons were most concerned with teaching? Or, if I wished to express this idea as a typology, was there one type of lecturer who had a long-standing desire to do the job and gave priority to research, while a second type of lecturer entered the job for more pragmatic reasons and gave priority to teaching?

However, the answer to all three questions turned out to be 'no' when I examined Laura's transcript. It has already been noted that Laura had a long-standing wish to be a lecturer but she made very clear that teaching and research had equal levels of priority for her: she said that she was 'interested in being able to combine both the teaching aspect of a subject that I'm really interested in and also carrying out research into that subject'. There were also two other respondents from the case study university who could not be placed on either side of the research/teaching divide: Paula said she had wanted a job that combined research and teaching, while Thomas commented that he loved research and teaching, but fought against administration.

This example illustrates that seeking to establish patterns of relationships is one of the most difficult elements of qualitative analysis; you should not be too disappointed, when analysing your own transcripts, if patterns that look as though they are emerging from the early data are not found in later cases. As with the discussion of commonality above, there is a subjective decision to be made as to how many cases must fit a pattern or a typology for it to be considered as such. However, it is often the case that no clear pattern of relationships can be established.

Despite the failure to find a clear pattern in this case, it is useful to consider the types of relationships and linkages between issues that can sometimes be revealed by studies that use the constant comparative method. Some examples are provided below:

1 Rager (2004) found that one issue had an impact on several others. American women who undertook self-directed learning were able to point to four benefits: empower-ment (they felt more in control), connectedness (they were able to make contact with people in similar situations), selective learning (they could choose which subjects they learnt about) and the search for meaning (they were better able to articulate what meaning the experience should have for them).

2 In contrast, the research of Lawson (2003) among boys who had sexually abused children found that central to their thinking was the idea that, after treatment, they wished to become a 'success story'. This idea of success was shown to incorporate three issues: avoiding a relapse into offending, complying with what others expected them to do and making decisions based on the correct information.

3 Baildon and Sim (2009) examined the impact of two issues that were in tension with each other. They found that Singaporean school cultures that emphasised teaching to enable students to pass assessments were in conflict with the need for people who could think critically and develop innovations in an increasingly globalised world. The result was anxiety for teachers.

4 Radwin et al. (2005) developed a typology of the factors that cancer patients used when describing their nursing care. They found that most comments centred on the concepts of whether the staff were laudable, whether the approach used was caring, whether professional standards were maintained and the outcomes of their care. Illustrative issues that contributed to each of these concepts were identified: for

example, staff were considered commendable if they were hard working, approachable and inspired gratitude. While, of course, some respondents gave descriptions that covered more than one of the concepts, the typology proved a helpful manner of classifying the elements of care that were most important to patients.

The new researcher will typically (and correctly) be very happy to achieve two of the objectives of thematic analysis using the constant comparative method, i.e. to examine commonality and to examine differences, without progressing to the next stage of examining relationships. However, these examples are included to demonstrate the types of relationships that may be present within a qualitative data set.

Summary

This chapter has examined two processes that are likely to prove useful when beginning the daunting task of analysing qualitative data for the first time: making summaries and using the constant comparative method. These processes can be employed either separately or together and they can also be used alongside (or separately from) codes, which are discussed in Chapters 5 and 6.

Making summaries is essentially a means to an end; a method of reducing the large amounts of data present in an interview to an at-a-glance view of the points that are likely to be most useful in analysis. It is helpful to divide the interview transcript into smaller sections to analyse and then to reduce each section to a list of summary points by taking the following steps:

1 Identify the research objective(s) that the section of the transcript is most relevant to.

2 Decide which pieces of information or opinions are most relevant to this objective/ these objectives and which do not need to be included in the summary.

3 Decide where (if at all) there is repetition that needs to be eliminated.

4 On the basis of these decisions, write brief notes.

Summaries can begin the process of highlighting similarities and differences between interviews. This process can be developed further through the constant comparative method, which is usually discussed in the context of grounded theory but is also seen by some as an essential element of all qualitative data analysis.

An advantage of the constant comparative method for the new researcher is that it can begin by comparing two cases and making a simple list of similarities and differences. There are likely to be more differences than similarities because, even in an area where there is broad agreement or a shared experience, there are often differences in terms of detail. Adding more cases to the analysis increases the complexity and is also likely to reduce the number of similarities further; the likelihood of achieving a complete consensus is reduced as the number of respondents increases. In contrast, the list of differences is likely to grow longer and more complicated as further cases are added and records must be kept of the differing views of greater numbers of respondents.

The likely reduction in the number of similarities as more cases are added will usually face the researcher with a difficult decision when seeking to achieve the first aim that has been identified for thematic analysis, i.e. examining commonality. How many respondents need to share an experience, or agree on an opinion, for it to be considered a commonality? There is no definitive answer to this: I have suggested three-quarters of respondents as a very rough figure, but this is a subjective judgement. Even in areas where a broad commonality has been identified, there are likely to be sub-divisions, which should be the subject of further analysis.

Analysis of differences is likely to be a substantial task due to the long and complex list that develops in relation to most issues. Broad differences and areas of sub-difference should be noted, together with factors that are common even in an area where there is broad disagreement.

The final aim of thematic analysis, examining relationships between factors, is the most difficult. Unless a researcher has the resources to pursue their data collection and analysis to the point of saturation – where new cases are adding nothing to the analysis – it remains an incomplete task. Although many studies have used the constant comparative method to identify patterns of difference, including typologies, looking for these is likely to be a frustrating task, as patterns that appear to be emerging from early cases may not be present in later ones. Again, the researcher will need to reach a subjective decision as to how frequently a pattern should occur for them to conclude that it provides an explanation for relationships.

Indeed, the early stages of analysis are filled with subjective decisions by the researcher such as which factors to include in a summary and how to interpret slightly ambiguous comments made by respondents. It is important that decision making is as consistent a possible. Keeping a record of decisions through methodological memos is good research practice which should ensure consistency and be helpful at a later stage in assessing the validity of the findings.

Further reading

For an easy to read and accessible discussion of the constant comparative method, I recommend Barbour, R. (2008) *Introducing Qualitative Research*. London: Sage.

A more thorough discussion of the complexities of the topic is provided by Boeije, H. (2010) *Analysis in Qualitative Research*. London: Sage. However, please note that this account makes references to codes, which will be discussed in Chapters 5 and 6.

For a series of ideas for steps that can be taken in the early stages of analysis, see Miles, M. B. and Huberman, A. M. (1994) *Qualitative Data Analysis*, 2nd edn. London: Sage (1st edn, 1984). It is important to treat the steps that they discuss as suggestions to try in order to identify what works best with your data.

5

Using codes to analyse an illustrative issue

Introduction

This chapter introduces codes as an important tool for conducting a comprehensive thematic analysis of an issue. The use of codes is not incompatible with the constant comparative method (discussed in Chapter 4) – indeed the two are frequently discussed as part of the same process (see, for example, Boeije, 2010: 83–86).

Gibson and Brown (2009: 130) helpfully note that 'a code draws attention to a **commonality** within a dataset'. Moreover, when a code applies to one case but not to another, this can alert the researcher to a difference between cases. In addition, identifying patterns as to where codes do and do not appear can assist the researcher in exploring relationships. So coding helps to achieve all three of the aims of thematic analysis identified in previous chapters, i.e. examining commonality, examining differences and examining relationships. The role of codes in examining relationships will be demonstrated in Chapter 6; this chapter will show how they can contribute to identifying similarities and differences between cases. The data used for examples is sections of the interviews with seven lecturers at a case study university that were introduced in Chapter 1. The issue selected for analysis is reflective practice.

Perhaps the most obvious question to ask about codes is what they look like. Codes are usually notes made in the margin of interview transcripts and can take a number of forms. Miles and Huberman (1994: 59) use a complex system of abbreviations, while Matthews and Ross (2010: 332–326) demonstrate systems that use both abbreviations and numbers. Other writers (e.g. Charmaz, 2006: 52; Barbour, 2008: 199–200; Saldana, 2009: 3) have tended to use full words and short phrases as their codes. This chapter will use words and phrases; the only abbreviation used will be the shortening of reflective practice to RP.

Numerous coding strategies are discussed in the literature on qualitative methods (see, for example, Saldana, 2009). Various distinctions are made between different types of codes and coding: for example, Neuman (2006: 461–464) distinguishes between open, axial and selective coding and Richards (2009: 99–104) discusses descriptive coding, topic coding and analytical coding.

However, perhaps the most helpful distinction is the one that Gibson and Brown (2010: 132–133) make between apriori codes and empirical codes. Apriori codes are created to reflect categories that are already of interest before the research has begun; empirical codes are derived while reading through the data, as points of importance and commonality are identified. Empirical codes are more likely to be used in inductive pieces of research, where the data is examined and analysed before consideration of the existing theory and literature, as discussed in Chapter 2. In contrast, apriori codes, since they tend to derive at least partly from the researcher's previous reading, are more appropriately used as part of a deductive approach. However, it is important to emphasise that these two forms of coding are not entirely separate: even when using empirical codes, it is likely that the researcher's prior knowledge of the subject will influence decision making to some extent. Similarly, when using apriori codes, it is almost certain that some issues and themes will emerge that were not anticipated from the researcher's prior reading in the subject area; this type of coding will be discussed further in Chapter 7.

Rapley (2011: 280) suggests that beginning to code data can be a frightening process. However, this chapter will seek to quell the new researcher's quite natural fear by breaking down the process of using empirical codes into four steps and considering each step in turn. These steps are:

1 identifying initial categories based on the reading of the transcripts;

2 writing codes alongside the transcripts;

3 reviewing the list of codes, revising the list of categories and deciding which codes should appear in which category;

4 looking for themes and findings in each category.

The four steps will now be discussed in turn.

Step 1: identifying initial categories based on reading the transcripts

As with other elements of qualitative data analysis, coding should begin with a very thorough reading of the full transcripts to be analysed (Neuman, 2006: 461). It is important for the researcher to engage with every line of the transcripts and, at this stage, it may be useful to underline key phrases or make a note of what is of interest in order to assist in the process of thinking holistically about the data (Rapley, 2011: 280).

Initial thorough engagement with the data is very worthwhile for a number of reasons, one of which is that it will usually enable the researcher to identify categories that codes can be placed into and so save time in the analysis that follows. Charmaz (2006: 45) suggests that coding is a process of selecting, separating and sorting data; identifying categories is a major part of the separating and sorting. However, it is difficult to suggest specific tactics or techniques for creating categories (Berg, 2009: 350). The researcher can only use their judgement to identify broad subject areas under which the data could be grouped.

The initial list of categories will almost inevitably be modified in the course of the analysis, as will be demonstrated when discussing Step 3 below. However, the coding process is likely to take less time and to seem less daunting if the researcher is able to draw up a preliminary category list at the start of the coding process.

To take the example of the lecturers at the case study university, you may recall that, in Chapter 4, we looked at sections of the transcript relating to reflective practice for Fern (pp. 59–60), Susan (pp. 62–63) and Rachel (pp. 70–71). Similarities and differences were identified in the areas of motivations and mechanisms for reflective practice. On reading through the sections of the interview about reflective practice for all seven of the lecturers, I became aware of two other categories that codes could be placed into, meaning that the full list of initial categories looked like this:

1   mechanisms for undertaking reflective practice;

2   motivation for reflective practice;

3   aims of reflective practice; and

4   limitations to reflective practice.

Step 2: writing codes alongside the transcripts

After deciding on the initial list of categories, and the form that their codes should take (e.g. abbreviations, words and phrases), the researcher should begin to write the codes alongside the interview transcripts. The application of codes involves three elements:

Summarising – coding reduces the space taken up by different ideas in order to facilitate analysis; a process sometimes referred to as data reduction (Hennink et al., 2011: 227). This data reduction helps the researcher to see beyond the detail of the individual case and to identify themes (Richards, 2009: 93).

Selecting – Rapley (2011: 280) suggests that a function of coding it to label the things that are important, as there are too many to remember. Barbour (2008: 203) emphasises the importance of selection by highlighting the dangers of using too many codes so that the list becomes unmanageable. However, this must be balanced against the risk of failing to code a part of the transcript that could assist in the identification of an important theme. It is better to err on the side of caution and to limit the amount of selection, introducing codes that may need to be discarded later, rather than risk failing to code an idea that could become an important feature of the analysis.

However, even when taking this cautious approach, the researcher must still make choices as to what should be coded and what should not. Matthews and Ross (2010: 334) suggest that such decisions should be taken with reference to research objectives. However, a difficulty with relying too heavily on objectives is that there may be an important theme that emerges from the data and that was not anticipated when they were devised. As a key element of the inductive approach is that the development of theory is driven by the research findings, rather than existing theory directing the nature of data collection and analysis (Bryman, 2008: 9–10), the researcher must be alert to an unexpected theme arising from the data.

A more helpful guiding principle in the decision as what to code is the search for commonality. A thorough reading of the transcripts – particularly if it incorporates making summaries, as discussed in Chapter 4 – is likely to sensitise the researcher to the information, ideas and feelings that are discussed frequently within their dataset. This can then guide them to the most important areas to code.

Interpreting – Some codes involve a substantial element of interpretation; examples will be provided later in the chapter. Interpreting phenomena in their context is a key feature of qualitative research (Moses and Knutsen, 2007: 154–155). To correctly interpret the words of respondents, the qualitative researcher must be empathetic, i.e. able to consider how the world looks to other people (Hennink et al., 2011: 9). In the case of comments where the meaning may not be obvious, the researcher needs to consider the context of what has been said and apply a code that reflects the most likely meaning of the speaker.

However, in many cases, a code does little more than re-state very slightly the spoken words: for example, as will be shown later, where respondents said that reflective practice was important to them, this was simply coded as 'RP important'. So the extent of interpretation required to apply a code can vary considerably.

I will now use a section of an interview with a lecturer from the case study university, who is referred to as Thomas, to show how codes can be applied. There follows the relevant section of the interview transcript and the codes that I wrote, followed by an explanation of the coding process. Please remember that the four categories that had been identified initially were:

- mechanisms for undertaking reflective practice;
- motivation for reflective practice;
- aims of reflective practice; and
- limitations to reflective practice.

Where codes could fit into one of these categories, they were written accordingly.

Notes on reflective practice from interview with Thomas

Interviewer: What's your understanding of reflective practice?

Thomas: What's my understanding of reflective practice? Well you do something and you think, 'ooh did I do that well, or could I have done it better?', and you try and make it better the next time. And I think I do that given time but if you're only teaching the same things, or doing the same things, with little pressure you can reflect and learn and develop. But if I go back to when I first came to this university, in terms of the ability to do the job, there's no comparison; I'm a million miles away from when I first came. And I think that's down to reflection. When I came here, new members of staff had to do a course in teaching in higher education. But working with colleagues and thinking about the job and wanting to do better, I think has been more valuable than that particular course. There was a lot of information given, a lot of sensible things said but I think you learn from your peers and you learn from yourself but the situation here is now there's no time to sit and reflect. When I first came here there was time to do that informally; we would do it together, we would sit and talk about how to make seminars better and I used to do quite a lot of team teaching early on here and I would watch how the others did it and would try to adapt. We can all improve over time but I don't think there's the time now to really think about what you're doing. It's like what do I need to do for this week, what do I need to do tomorrow? And it's difficult, it is difficult.

Mechanism – personal reflection

Limitation to RP – time

Limitation to RP – teaching new subjects (implied)

Mechanism – working with colleagues

Personal reflection and working with colleagues more effective than teaching course

Limitation to RP – time
Used to be greater opportunities for RP
Mechanism – watching the teaching of colleagues

Interviewer: Do you think it is important?

Thomas: Absolutely, we should all do it in our own lives, every aspect of our lives. You're talking about ambition; I would like to be able to teach like a colleague who's the best teacher in this faculty. And we all strive to that but there's not the time; we used

RP important

to talk about these issues when we had time but there's not now; you try to do it yourself. I had a lecture yesterday that I spent most of Sunday writing and it was ****. But the way things are at the moment I won't even be able to really go back and think what made it bad or how I could make it better until I have to do it again next year. There's not time now to sit and think about it which means, by the time I re-write it, I will have forgotten what half the problems were.

No opportunity to reflect on bad lecture until next year

Delay means reflection will be less effective

Interviewer: What motivates you to do reflective practice? Is it internal or external?

Thomas: It's internal, absolutely internal. This might sound silly but when I started work someone taught me if you're going to do something then you should do it the best you can. And I've tried to live by that, even in a work situation.

Motivation internal

Motivation – to do the best possible job

Interviewer: Would you say there is any pressure from the university to be reflective?

Thomas: No. That's what I find strange. We have timetables so we've got to be in rooms at particular times but what we do in those rooms nobody checks up on. Nobody listens to my lectures; nobody asks to see my PowerPoint slides. We're given the autonomy to do this. The oversight is on how many lectures we have to do, what do we publish, where do we publish: those things are quantifiable but the quality of our delivery is never tested. The only oversight is we have this system of peer review where one of our colleagues will sit in on a lecture or a seminar. It's supposed to be done every year but I've never done it for two years; it just never happens – we're too busy; we just don't do it.

Surprised by lack of external pressure for RP
No oversight of quality of teaching

Mechanism – peer review

Peer review limited by time

In this example, I used all three of the elements of applying codes which were discussed above:

Reducing/summarising: the interview with Thomas demonstrated that points can often be made more succinctly in written form than when they are made verbally; reducing/summarising information through codes can often be quite a simple task. The first code used above, 'Mechanism – personal reflection', reduced substantially quite a long statement made by Thomas while retaining the key element.

Selecting: the creation of categories in advance assists with the process of selection; I knew to code any comment about mechanisms, motivations, aims or limitations as these had already been identified as areas discussed by a number of respondents. The search for commonality also drove other decisions as to when to code and when not to. As an example, consider Thomas' comment about where the pressure to reflect comes from: 'It's internal, absolutely internal. This might sound silly but when I started work someone taught me if you're going to do something then you should do it the best you can. And I've tried to live by that, even in a work situation.' Codes were placed alongside this statement about Thomas' motivation, because it was one of the pre-set categories, and his belief that the pressure to reflect was internal, because this was an issue on which a number of other respondents commented. However, the material about the advice he received when he started work was not coded because I knew from reading other transcripts that they included no similar discussion of early influences or influencers while working in other occupations.

Interpreting: Thomas' comment that 'And I think I do that given time but if you're only teaching the same things, or doing the same things, with little pressure you can reflect and learn and develop' was interpreted to mean that time and teaching different subjects were limitations on his ability to reflect on his practice. This interpretation arose from my attempts to understand Thomas' perspective and the context in which this comment was made. My understanding that Thomas felt that time limited his opportunities to reflect was drawn from a number of comments that he made elsewhere, e.g. 'There's not time now to sit and think about it'. However, there were no similar comments to support my interpretation that having to teach new subjects limited opportunities to reflect, so I relied on the context – Thomas appeared to be discussing the ideal conditions for reflection, then saying that these conditions did not exist. This is the type of occasion where a methodological memo is useful, noting the element of interpretation in the coding, to facilitate later reflection on the judgements that were made during the analysis and how these judgements might have affected the research findings. I wrote the memo like this:

Methodological memo: interpretation of Thomas' comments in relation to limitations imposed on reflective practice

Some interpretation was needed for Thomas' comment, 'And I think I do that given time but if you're only teaching the same things, or doing the same things, with little pressure you can reflect and learn and develop'. It was clear from the context of what was said that 'do that' meant 'reflect on practice'. It also seemed clear from comments that were made elsewhere in the interview that Thomas thought that lack of time was a factor that limited his use of reflective practice. A further interpretation that was made, although one with less supporting evidence, was that Thomas believed that being asked to teach different subjects limited his ability to reflect. The reason for this interpretation was that Thomas seemed to be discussing the conditions under which reflection could most easily take place – having time, teaching the same subjects, not being under pressure – but then implying that, where any of these conditions did not apply, reflection was more difficult. However, as the issue of the subjects taught was not referred to elsewhere in the interview, this was a particularly subjective interpretation.

You are now invited to write codes in the exercise that follows.

Exercise 6

Please read below the section of the transcript relating to reflective practice, from an interview with a lecturer who is referred to as Lewis, and write a list of codes. As part of the process you should reduce/summarise, select and, if necessary, interpret the material. The process of selection is made more difficult because you have not seen all of the transcripts and therefore do not have full information with which to judge what is likely to be a commonality. However, you have seen enough (from the extract of the interview with Thomas and the material about reflective practice in Chapter 4) to be able to make some judgements of this nature. Where appropriate your code should fit into one of the pre-determined categories, i.e. 'Mechanism –', 'Motivation –', 'Aim –' or 'Limitation –'. You should also reproduce exactly the codes from the interview with Thomas where possible as this will clearly make the identification of commonalities easier. However, you will also need to create some new codes that do not fit into pre-set categories.

Interviewer: What is your understanding of reflective practice?

Lewis: That it is what it says it is, I hope. We have to take time to look back at what we do, evaluate what we do, and change what we do on the basis of reflections. We tend to do that; I would see that as something we would do individually and something we should do collectively.

Interviewer: Do you find it important, to be reflective of your own practice?

(Continued)

(Continued)

Lewis: Yes, it is. But that doesn't mean I do it as well as I should and it doesn't mean I've got the time always because you rush from one lecture to another sometimes and there'll be times I'll come in, just put down my lecture notes, PowerPoint presentation on the table, grab another set and go out and do it and I'm not reflecting. But I think the lecturers generally – me anyway certainly – are probably their own worst critics. I think I can come out of a lecture and go, 'that was rubbish!' And the students might think that was fine but I can think to myself, 'that needs changing, I need to do that better next time'. So I think that with reflective practice you may not use that language all the time – 'oh I'm doing a bit of reflective practice' – but you're walking out going 'no, don't do that again, change that! That seminar really didn't work'. So in an informal way I think lecturers should be doing that all the time.

Interviewer: So what would you say your motivation to be reflective of your practice was? Would you say internal?

Lewis: It's driven internally by wanting to be good at what I do. And thinking that I should be good at what I do. But lecturing is communicating effectively with students. So what should also drive me is if I've failed to communicate something. That's usually very clear from students' puzzled looks or students coming up to me afterwards and saying, 'I don't understand that.' And that's not a student's responsibility; it's my responsibility. If I'm not communicating effectively that's not their problem, it's my problem, so I need to change. So it's really important.

Please complete the exercise before looking at how I would have tackled it below.

Section of interview with Lewis with my codes

Interviewer: What is your understanding of reflective practice?

Lewis: That it is what it says it is, I hope. We have to take time to look back at what we do, evaluate what we do, and change what we do on the basis of reflections. We tend to do that; I would

Mechanism – personal reflection

see that as something we would do individually and something we should do collectively.

Interviewer: Do you find it important, to be reflective of your own practice?

Lewis: Yes, it is. But that doesn't mean I do it as well as I should and it doesn't mean I've got the time always because you rush from one lecture to another sometimes and there'll be times I'll come in, just put down my lecture notes, PowerPoint presentation on the table, grab another set and go out and do it and I'm not reflecting. But I think the lecturers generally – me anyway certainly – are probably their own worst critics. I think I can come out of a lecture and go, 'that was rubbish!' And the students might think that was fine but I can think to myself, 'that needs changing, I need to do that better next time'. So I think that with reflective practice you may not use that language all the time, 'oh I'm doing a bit of reflective practice' but you're walking out going 'no, don't do that again, change that! That seminar really didn't work'. So in an informal way I think lecturers should be doing that all the time.

Interviewer: So what would you say your motivation to be reflective of your practice was? Would you say internal?

Lewis: It's driven internally by wanting to be good at what I do. And thinking that I should be good at what I do. But lecturing is communicating effectively with students. So what should also drive me is if I've failed to communicate something. That's usually very clear from students' puzzled looks or students coming up to me afterwards and saying, 'I don't understand that.' And that's not a student's responsibility; it's my responsibility. If I'm not communicating effectively that's not their problem, it's my problem, so I need to change. So it's really important.

Margin codes:

Should be collective reflection

RP important

Limitation to RP – time

RP should be constant

RP should be informal

Motivation internal
Motivation – to be good at job
Motivation – wants to communicate effectively
Accepts responsibility for students' reaction

Please note that, if my codes are different from yours, this does not necessarily mean that mine are 'right' and yours are 'wrong'. However, it should be useful for me to explain how I chose the codes, which principally involved two of the elements listed previously:

Reducing/summarising: again, this was the simplest step, largely reflecting a human tendency to express ourselves at greater length verbally than we do in written form. So, for example, the code 'Motivation – wants to communicate effectively' was adequate to record something that Lewis said at greater length in his final answer.

However, there were also a small number of occasions when the code or codes re-phrased what was said but hardly reduced it. For example, two codes – 'RP should be constant' and 'RP should be informal' were used for the comment that 'So in an informal way I think lecturers should be doing that all the time'. This demonstrates that, while codes usually involve reducing the data, this is not always the case.

Selecting: some of the areas to code were obvious, because they fell into the pre-set categories of mechanisms, motivation, aims and limitations. In other cases, I used my knowledge of the other transcripts to decide which material should be coded. The code 'Accepts responsibility for students' reaction' may seem to have limited relevance for a discussion of reflective practice, but I knew from reading other transcripts that there was a similarity to comments made by another respondent: this code helped to develop the theme of responsibility, which will be discussed in Chapter 6. In contrast, I knew that lecturers being self-critical was not something that was discussed by others, so did not include a code for Lewis' comment on this issue. However, as you did not have this knowledge, you may well have included a code about self-criticism which would have been appropriate, given the advice that I offered earlier to err on the side of caution in deciding whether to use a potential code.

Although all coding involves **interpreting** to some extent, there was not anything said by Lewis where an alternative interpretation to the one provided in the codes seemed likely, so this element had a limited role.

Step 3: reviewing the list of codes, revising the list of categories and deciding which codes should appear in which category

This third stage of the coding process is central to the search for commonality.

Rapley (2011: 280) suggests that a reason for coding is that it enables the grouping together of data that addresses similar themes. However, this grouping is rarely achieved at the first attempt, which is why the researcher is almost certain to need to adjust categories, and the codes that appear in them, as the analysis progresses.

The outcome of applying codes to transcripts is often that there are large numbers that appear to apply to only one case. At this point the researcher needs to look for connections between codes which were not initially obvious. Boeije (2010: 108) notes the need to adjust categories and to put data back together again as new connections are made. Other writers (for example,

Hesse-Biber and Leavy, 2006: 352; Charmaz, 2006: 57–62; Flick, 2009: 307–312) provide examples of how they have adjusted their initial coding schemes in order to identify themes.

A number of practical measures can be taken with an initial list of codes and categories in order to make better sense of the data. These include:

- Identifying codes which should belong in the initial categories but were not placed there when the coding first took place.
- Creating sub-categories within the initial categories.
- Identifying new categories which can bring together a number of codes.
- Identifying codes that apply to sufficient numbers of respondents to be part of the findings even though they stand outside any category.
- Identifying codes that stand outside any category and should be discarded because they do not apply to sufficient numbers of respondents.

Each of these steps is demonstrated below for the data relating to reflective practice, where the initial list of codes was long and unwieldy. The list is shown below with the name(s) of the respondent(s) to whom each code applied. Despite its length, it is included in full, in the hope that you will not be disheartened if your initial list looks equally unmanageable.

Complete list of codes used in relation to reflective practice

RP important: Fern, Susan, Rachel, Lewis, Laura, Paula, Thomas

Mechanism – student feedback: Fern, Susan

Mechanism – personal reflection: Fern, Susan, Rachel, Lewis, Laura, Paula, Thomas

RP should be constant: Fern, Susan, Rachel, Lewis, Paula

Motivation – pride: Fern

RP for both teaching and research: Fern

Lecturers who do not reflect become outdated and stale: Susan

Motivation – for students and lecturer to enjoy teaching: Susan

Internal and external motivation for RP: Susan

Mechanism – personal teaching reviews: Susan

Mechanism – comparing with practice elsewhere in the faculty: Susan

Danger of dreading teaching: Susan

Aim of RP – to excite and engage students: Susan

Accepts responsibility for students' reaction: Lewis, Laura

Motivation – to teach well: Rachel

Motivation – to stay updated: Rachel, Paula

Failure to reflect leads to outdated practice: Rachel

Change of job helpful: Rachel, Paula

Motivation internal: Rachel, Lewis, Thomas

Need for internal pressure: Rachel

Surprised by lack of external pressure for RP: Rachel, Thomas

Should be collective reflection: Lewis

Limitation to RP – time: Lewis, Laura, Thomas

Motivation – to be good at job: Lewis

Motivation – wants to communicate effectively: Lewis

RP should be informal: Lewis

Mechanism – reflecting with a colleague: Laura

Aim of RP – improved practice: Laura, Paula

Helpful to write down evaluation of a teaching session: Laura

Value of more experienced colleagues: Laura

External pressure only from teaching course: Laura

External motivation only from teaching course: Laura

Motivation mainly internal: Laura

Motivation – to improve teaching practice: Laura

Publishing teaching material can assist in reflection: Paula

Likes to experiment with teaching methods: Paula

Mechanism – sharing experiences with colleagues: Paula

Mechanism – reflecting on the practice of colleagues in other universities: Paula

Important to encourage students to reflect: Paula

Motivation mainly external (mechanism not specified): Paula

Limitation to RP – teaching new subjects (implied): Thomas

RP has led to improved practice: Thomas

Mechanism – working with colleagues: Thomas

Personal reflection and working with colleagues more effective than teaching
  course: Thomas

Used to be greater opportunities for RP: Thomas

Mechanism – watching the teaching of colleagues: Thomas

No opportunity to reflect on bad lecture until next year: Thomas

Delay means reflection will be less effective: Thomas

Motivation – to do the best possible job: Thomas

Motivation internal: Thomas

No oversight of quality of teaching: Thomas

Mechanism – peer review: Thomas

Peer review limited by time: Thomas

When I first looked at this list, I was disappointed because so many codes applied to only one respondent – a common experience for the qualitative researcher. However, by using the five measures listed above, I was able to change the list in a manner that made it possible to identify findings.

Identifying codes that should have been placed in pre-set categories

The categories identified when first reading through the transcripts were the obvious starting point in seeking to identify themes. Including the name of the category in the code makes it very easy to bring the relevant codes together. In the case of mechanisms for reflective practice, the codes that were easy to place in this category were:

    Mechanism – student feedback: Fern, Susan
    Mechanism – personal reflection: Fern, Susan, Rachel, Lewis, Laura, Paula, Thomas
    Mechanism – personal teaching reviews: Susan
    Mechanism – comparing with practice elsewhere in the faculty: Susan
    Mechanism – sharing experiences with colleagues: Paula
    Mechanism – reflecting on the practice of colleagues in other universities: Paula
    Mechanism – working with colleagues: Thomas
    Mechanism – watching the teaching of colleagues: Thomas
    Mechanism – peer review: Thomas

However, the researcher may well find, on re-considering their codes, that some of them should appear in one of their initial categories even though they did not see this when the codes were first written. On reading back through the list of codes on reflective practice, I was able to identify two that I had initially failed to see were about mechanisms:

    Helpful to write down evaluation of a teaching session: Laura
    Publishing teaching material can assist in reflection: Paula

These were re-written as:

    Mechanism – written evaluation of a teaching session: Laura
    Mechanism – publishing teaching materials: Paula

There may also be codes which are related to others in the category, although in a less direct manner. I realised that Lewis' suggestion that reflection should be informal could be seen to cover a number of mechanisms for reflection – e.g. watching the teaching of colleagues – as could his suggestion that reflection should be collective. Similarly, Laura's comment that experienced colleagues could be particularly helpful in the process of reflection added detail to Thomas' discussion of the value of working with colleagues. So the following three codes were added to the mechanisms category:

    Should be collective reflection: Lewis
    RP should be informal: Lewis
    Value of more experienced colleagues: Laura

Creating sub-categories

A further stage of analysis may be helpful after the codes that should be placed in a category have been identified. Gibson and Brown (2009: 128) suggest that the process of identifying commonalities '... typically involves finding ways to pool together all the examples from across a data set that can be categorised as "an example of x". These commonalities are then subjected to further analysis and sub-division.'

One method of sub-dividing commonalities is the creation of sub-categories. It may be possible to identify common characteristics of some codes beyond membership of the main category, meaning that a sub-category can be created. The grouping together of codes into sub-categories can contribute substantially to the identification of themes.

To take an example, on re-reading the codes relating to mechanisms for reflective practice, I noted that several of them had the common element of working with colleagues in various forms. So I created a 'Mechanisms involving working with colleagues' sub-category into which the following codes were placed:

Mechanism – working with colleagues: Thomas

Mechanism – sharing experiences with colleagues: Paula

Mechanism – watching the teaching of colleagues: Thomas (*this was one specific method of reflecting on the practice of other lecturers*)

Mechanism – comparing with practice elsewhere in the faculty: Susan (*it was not clear whether this took the form of discussions with colleagues or reading documents but, in either case, was an examination of the practice of other lecturers*)

Mechanism – reflecting on the practice of colleagues in other universities: Paula (*this was more likely to be in the form of documents, but again would have involved learning from the practice of others*)

Value of more experienced colleagues: Laura (*as suggested above, this provides some more detail as to which colleagues might be most helpful to involve in reflection*)

The findings that could follow from placing these codes into a sub-category will be considered later in the chapter.

Creating new categories

This is often more difficult than creating sub-categories and may require some more conceptual thinking. While it may be obvious from the researcher's list of codes that some should go together, in other cases they may need to think a little further about a common factor that could justify the creation of a new category. There is no easy way to suggest how less obvious commonalities might be identified, other than to spend a substantial amount of time reading and re-reading through the list of codes and thinking carefully. It may be reassuring to know that this is a skill, like many others in qualitative data analysis, which develops with practice.

On reading through the list of codes relating to reflective practice, I was able to identify one fairly obvious new category and one that required a little more thought. The obvious one was called 'Teaching course run by the university' and incorporated the following three codes:

External pressure only from teaching course: Laura

External motivation only from teaching course: Laura

Personal reflection and working with colleagues more effective than teaching course: Thomas

The less obvious example emerged when I noticed two codes that were similar, i.e.:

Lecturers who do not reflect become outdated and stale: Susan

Failure to reflect leads to outdated practice: Rachel

The similarities between these codes led me to think that a new category called 'Consequences of failing to reflect' could be created. Reading back through my list of codes, I found another that could clearly be placed in this category:

Danger of dreading teaching: Susan

I also found one that, although not concerned with the dangers of completely failing to reflect, suggested that a time gap could reduce the effectiveness of reflection:

Delay means reflection will be less effective: Thomas

After consideration, I decided that this code could be added to my emerging new category if it was named 'Consequences of failing to make timely reflections'. So, by thinking again about possible commonalities, I had created a category incorporating four codes, which would prove helpful when identifying themes.

Identifying codes that apply to sufficient numbers of respondents to be part of the findings although they stand outside any category

Despite their best efforts to fit as many codes as possible into categories, qualitative researchers tend to find that they have some codes that simply do not have much in common with any others. They then have to make an important decision. Should the codes be retained, because they can contribute to the findings on their own, or should they be discarded?

There is no easy answer to this question but the simplest method of deciding is to look at the number of respondents that the code applies to.

To develop a point made in Chapter 4, while one of the characteristics of qualitative researchers is that they emphasise words rather than figures and are less concerned than quantitative researchers over measurement (Bryman, 2008: 21–22), this does not necessarily mean that all forms of quantification should be abandoned. Miles and Huberman (1994: 246) note that describing a method of analysis as 'thematic' means that patterns are being sought in the data – a pattern must occur more than once. While acknowledging that qualitative research goes beyond simple enumeration to provide detail about the qualities of the data, Miles and Huberman (1994: 253) argue that:

> ... a lot of counting goes on in the background when judgments of qualities are being made. When we identify a theme or pattern, we're isolating something that (a) happens a number of times and (b) consistently happens in a specific way. The 'number of times' and 'consistency' judgments are based on counting.

So how many respondents does a code outside any category need to apply to for it to be used when identifying the findings of the research? I can only suggest an approximate and subjective standard that, if a code that is outside any category applies to one-quarter or more of the respondents, it should contribute to the research findings. However, other researchers – if they were prepared to give a figure at all – might suggest a standard that was quite different from this. This is an area where a methodological memo would be useful, to recall at a later stage how the decision about which 'stand alone' codes to consider had been made.

To use the example of the reflective practice data again, in the course of the analysis I had created six categories:

- mechanisms for undertaking reflective practice;
- motivations for reflective practice;
- aims of reflective practice;
- limitations to reflective practice;
- teaching course run by the university; and
- consequences of failing to make timely reflections.

However, there were a number of codes that remained outside any of these categories. Using the 'threshold' of one-quarter of respondents, I included those codes which applied to more than one respondent when identifying findings, i.e.

> RP important: Fern, Susan, Rachel, Lewis, Laura, Paula, Thomas
> RP should be constant: Fern, Susan, Rachel, Lewis, Paula
> Accepts responsibility for students' reaction: Lewis, Laura
> Change of job helpful: Rachel, Paula

Identifying codes that stand outside any category and do not apply to sufficient numbers of respondents to be considered to constitute a theme

Of course, this action is very closely related to the previous one. If there is a 'threshold' for the number of respondents that a code outside any category should be applied to for it to be considered part of the findings, it follows that a code that falls below this threshold should be discarded. Using the threshold of one-quarter of respondents in this case meant that any code which stood outside a category and which applied to only one respondent should be eliminated from the analysis. Given the thematic nature of the analysis, this seemed particularly appropriate – a theme, by definition, must appear more than once. The codes that were eliminated were:

RP for both teaching and research: Fern

Likes to experiment with teaching methods: Paula

Important to encourage students to reflect: Paula

Used to be greater opportunities for RP: Thomas

No opportunity to reflect on bad lecture until next year: Thomas

Step 4: looking for themes and findings in each category

This section is not concerned with how to write about research findings because 'writing up' is covered in Chapters 9 and 10. Instead it covers the process by which the researcher looks at their list of categories and codes and decides on the key messages from the data. Three pieces of advice are offered when identifying findings:

1. Remember the purpose of thematic analysis

Identifying findings, like every part of thematic analysis, should be guided by the aims identified by Gibson and Brown (2009: 128–129), i.e. examining commonality, examining differences and examining relationships. However, not every dataset, or issue within a dataset, allows for the examination of relationships, so it may be that only the first two of these aims can be achieved. Examining relationships is associated more with conceptual findings and building theory, which will be discussed in Chapter 6. For the new researcher, identifying similarities and differences within the data is a very worthwhile first goal of analysis.

2. Be content with simple findings

If the process of creating and modifying categories and codes has been effective, then identifying findings becomes quite straightforward. Indeed, it is a common experience for the qualitative researcher to feel disappointed that their findings are simple and do not seem to be saying anything particularly profound. If this is the case with your own data, you should not be discouraged. It is the role of the researcher to report their findings accurately, even if they simply confirm 'common sense' knowledge or previous research. The findings still make a contribution, albeit a small one, to knowledge about the social world. Few pieces of research provide substantial new insights into social phenomena.

To reinforce this point, studies that have been published in internationally recognised journals often include simple statements of some of their findings, before going on to discuss more conceptual elements. For example, Sheikhattari et al.'s (2012) study of the role of community leaders and institutions in improving health in two remote Iranian villages includes the following statement: '...some of these NGOs [non-government organisations] funded and constructed water wells in the villages and improved the irrigation system for local residents' (Sheikhattari et al., 2012: 441). Similarly, Mathews et al.'s (2011) study of South African men who had killed their partners states simply that: 'The men described their childhood as "rough" or "hard". Talking about these experiences brought back strong memories and emotions, bringing some to tears' (Mathews et al., 2011: 964). So you should not feel that your findings are not useful because they make a statement about the data in quite simple terms. The skills that you develop through the analysis will be invaluable when examining more complex data, which may have a more complicated story to tell.

3. Find ways of expressing trends that avoid the use of numbers

While it was argued above that counting plays a greater part in qualitative data analysis than is sometimes acknowledged, it is rare for qualitative findings to be expressed in terms of specific numbers. Instead, other words are found to provide indications of trends within the data. For example, Mackie (2001) conducted a qualitative study of reasons for students leaving courses and gave broad indications of the frequency with which different themes occurred without actually using numbers:

> Few students feel fully integrated within the formal organisation by the beginning of term two ... Accommodation is a major source of dissatisfaction ... Financial issues feature ....

(Mackie, 2001: 269–270)

The use of the words 'major source' for accommodation suggests that accommodation difficulties were discussed more often than financial issues, which only 'feature'. So the qualitative researcher must find their own language with which to identify trends – findings are often expressed in terms such as 'some', 'the majority' and 'a number'. Of course, this will involve some subjective judgements on the part of the researcher: while the number of respondents referred to as 'all' is obvious, the researcher may need to decide at what figure 'few' respondents becomes 'some' respondents or 'a number' of respondents becomes 'many'.

Identifying findings from the data on reflective practice

The above three pieces of advice were taken into account when identifying some of the findings in relation to reflective practice. There were some obvious commonalities between respondents, which could be simply stated. For example:

- All respondents agreed that reflective practice was important.

When looking through the list of codes relating to mechanisms, there was another obvious similarity:

- All respondents used personal reflection as a form of reflective practice.

However, the findings in relation to some of the other codes – including those in the sub-category of 'Mechanisms involving working with colleagues' – needed a little more detail when they were noted:

- Several respondents discussed methods of involving colleagues in seeking to identify best practice. The methods discussed were both formal (e.g. peer review) and informal (e.g. watching the teaching of colleagues).
- A small number of respondents discussed incorporating student feedback into their reflective practice.
- There were a number of other mechanisms identified by individuals: personal teaching review, making a written evaluation of a teaching session and publishing teaching materials.

Please note my choice of words to indicate quantities here: four of seven respondents (Thomas, Susan, Laura and Paula) were attached to codes in the 'working with colleagues' sub-category; this number seemed to justify the use of the word 'several'. In contrast, only two respondents (Fern and Susan) discussed incorporating student feedback, so 'a small number' seemed an appropriate phrase here. While the wide range of methods of incorporating the views of colleagues meant that only two examples could be given (these were chosen to demonstrate the contrast between formal and informal reflection), all of the 'other' mechanisms could be listed under the final bullet point as there were only three.

There follows an exercise relating to another of the categories used to analyse the data. The exercise requires you to undertake one of the measures suggested as part of Step 3 – i.e. creating sub-categories – in addition to the Step 4 task of identifying findings.

Exercise 5

Creating sub-categories and identifying findings

Listed below are the codes that should be placed in the category of motivation for reflective practice. Your task is to sort them into sub-categories and then identify findings in relation to the theme of motivation.

Motivation – pride: Fern
Motivation – for students and lecturers to enjoy teaching: Susan
Motivation – to teach well: Rachel
Motivation – to stay updated: Rachel, Paula
Motivation internal: Rachel, Lewis, Thomas
Motivation – to be good at job: Lewis
Motivation – wants to communicate effectively: Lewis
Motivation – to do the best possible job: Thomas
Motivation mainly internal: Laura
Motivation mainly external (mechanism not specified): Paula
Internal and external motivation for RP: Susan
Need for internal pressure: Rachel
Surprised by lack of external pressure for RP: Rachel, Thomas
External pressure only from teaching course: Laura
External motivation only from teaching course: Laura
Motivation – to improve teaching practice: Laura
No oversight of quality of teaching: Thomas

Please note that codes can be placed in more than one category or sub-category: the codes about Laura's view of the teaching course are relevant here, in addition to appearing in the 'Teaching course run by the university' category. Similarly, there is no difficulty with putting a code in more than one sub-category if you think this to be appropriate.

Please complete the exercise before looking at how I would have tackled it below.

Again, it should be emphasised that there is no 'right' or 'wrong' way to undertake this task but it should be useful to compare your process and outcomes with mine. The sub-categories that I created, and the codes that appear under each of them, are shown below:

Balance between internal and external motivation

Motivation internal: Rachel, Lewis, Thomas
Motivation mainly internal: Laura
Motivation mainly external (mechanism not specified): Paula

Internal and external motivation for RP: Susan
Need for internal pressure: Rachel
Surprised by lack of external pressure for RP: Rachel, Thomas
External pressure only from teaching course: Laura
External motivation only from teaching course: Laura
No oversight of quality of teaching: Thomas

Motivation associated with personal satisfaction

Motivation – pride: Fern
Motivation – for students and lecturers to enjoy teaching: Susan
Motivation – to teach well: Rachel
Motivation – to stay updated: Rachel, Paula
Motivation – to improve teaching practice: Laura
Motivation – to be good at job: Lewis
Motivation – to do the best possible job: Thomas

Motivation associated with students

Motivation – for students and lecturers to enjoy teaching: Susan
Motivation – wants to communicate effectively: Lewis

As with so many stages of qualitative analysis, placing codes into sub-categories involves making subjective decisions: you may well ask why I placed the motivation of the respondents who wanted to teach well or do a good job in the 'Motivation associated with personal satisfaction' sub-category, while Lewis' desire to communicate effectively was placed in the 'Motivation associated with students' sub-category. This decision was made with reference back to the transcripts. Thomas, for example, presented the desire to improve his teaching as a desire to be as good as he could:

> This might sound silly but when I started work someone taught me if you're going to do something then you should do it the best you can. And I've tried to live by that, even in a work situation.

In contrast, Lewis made specific reference to the manner in which his teaching was received and understood by students:

> So what should also drive me is if I've failed to communicate something. That's usually very clear from students' puzzled looks or students coming up to me afterwards and saying, 'I don't understand that.' And that's not a student's responsibility; it's my responsibility.

This again demonstrates that qualitative analysis involves an element of interpretation; it is also a point where a methodological memo would be helpful.

My findings in relation to motivation were as follows:

- Most respondents identified stronger internal than external pressure to undertake reflective practice.
- Some expressed surprise at the lack of external pressure to be reflective.
- All identified motivation that was associated with personal satisfaction and the quality of the job that they did.
- Some also discussed motivation associated with the experience of students.

Again, I have not been afraid to state the findings very simply and have used words expressing quantities – 'all', 'most' and 'some' – which seek to differentiate the more frequent from the less frequent types of comments. However, presenting findings is a more varied task than simply giving indications of how many respondents codes applied to, as will be demonstrated in Chapter 9.

Summary

Coding is an important tool for qualitative researchers which can assist in the identification of commonalities and differences in datasets. When using an inductive approach it is likely that empirical codes will be used, i.e. those that emerge from the data rather than from existing theory or prior reading.

There is a huge diversity in coding systems and no 'right' or 'wrong' way to go about coding data. However, this chapter has suggested a four-step process that should prove useful to the new researcher. The first step, identifying initial categories, follows careful reading of the transcripts and represents an early attempt to sort through the mass of data that qualitative research typically provides. It is almost inevitable that this list of categories will be adjusted and added to in the course of the analysis, but this initial step can save substantial amounts of time, as codes can be written in a manner that demonstrates category membership.

The second step in the coding process is to write the codes alongside the transcripts; a step that involves summarising, selecting and interpreting. The most straightforward of these elements is summarising because much of what humans say can be reduced to smaller numbers of words without major changes to the meaning. Selection involves some difficult judgements as to what should be coded and what should not. This is straightforward when a comment fits into a pre-set category but more difficult in other cases; a researcher should use their knowledge of the transcripts to determine whether an idea is referred to elsewhere and therefore worth coding. It is recommended to err on the side of caution and to write too many codes rather than too few: it is better to remove a code at a later stage than to miss an area of commonality. The most difficult element of applying codes, although one that reflects the essence of qualitative research, is interpretation. While in most cases the words of respondents leave little room for differing interpretations, in others the researcher needs to consider carefully the context of what is said, and use their skills in understanding the perspectives of others, to identify the most likely meaning of the words used.

Reviewing the list of codes and categories is the third stage of the process and is often a substantial task. Any number of measures could be taken in order to refine the list into a format that better facilitates identifying findings, but some that may prove particularly useful are identifying codes that should be placed into pre-set categories but have not been, creating sub-categories and creating new categories. One of two actions can be taken with regard to codes that continue to stand outside any category: they can either be treated as part of the findings on their own or excluded from consideration. The decision as to which of these two options to take could be made on several grounds, but the most likely and obvious one is the number of respondents whom the code applies to. The figure to use as a 'threshold' is one of a number of subjective decisions that are likely to be made during the coding process: writing methodological memos to record such decisions is important if the validity of the findings is to be assessed at a later stage.

The final stage of the process, identifying findings, also involves some consideration of quantities: the researcher will, on occasions, need to choose between words such as 'some', 'many' or 'few' to give an indication of the number of respondents whom codes applied to. Findings should reflect the aims of thematic analysis: in all cases it should be possible to examine commonality and differences. Not all data lends itself to the third aim of thematic analysis, i.e. examining relationships between factors. The data on reflective practice, which much of the discussion in the chapter is based on, is one such example. In contrast, Chapter 6 will provide an example of data that facilitates the examination of relationships and the building of theory. However, it is hoped that, after reading this chapter, you will feel confident to use codes as a helpful tool for exploring your data and reaching simple findings.

Further reading

For a broad discussion of the process of identifying themes, which includes a critique of the process, I recommend Gibson, W. J. and Brown, A. (2009) *Working with Qualitative Data*. London: Sage.

One book that discusses making notes in the margin as a form of coding, which it refers to as annotating, is Dey, I. (1993) *Qualitative Data Analysis*. Abingdon: Routledge. The notes made are considerably longer than the ones that are used in this chapter but they are helpful as an illustration.

Another example and some helpful commentary is provided in Charmaz, K. (2006) *Constructing Grounded Theory*. London: Sage. Although coding is discussed as part of a grounded theory approach, many of the examples and points are relevant to any form of qualitative data analysis.

6

Identifying conceptual themes and building theory

Introduction

Chapter 5 discussed the analysis of illustrative issues, using the example of reflective practice. In this chapter, many similar tools are used – such as codes, categories and sub-categories – but a more advanced stage of analysis is discussed, which involves the identification and development of conceptual themes. Not every dataset will include such themes. However, where respondents have been able to discuss their experiences, opinions or feelings in some detail, it is often possible to identify principles, assumptions and ways of thinking that underlie what was said.

This chapter includes less detailed instructions than Chapter 5 and relies more heavily on an example because it is difficult to make generalisations about the process of identifying and analysing conceptual themes. Hennink et al. (2011: 205) suggest that qualitative data analysis is both an art and a science: some of the step-by-step processes discussed in previous chapters may (I hope!) seem logical and scientific. In contrast, identifying conceptual themes represents the more creative or artistic element of dealing with qualitative data. Although it is more difficult to provide detailed guidance for a more creative process, it is hoped that the ideas and suggestions made in this chapter will still prove helpful for applying to your own data. The theme that is used as an example, drawing on the data provided by the seven lecturers at the case study university, is responsibility for teaching and learning.

The chapter will identify characteristics of conceptual themes, introduce data memos and tables as helpful tools and discuss a four-step process for identifying and analysing such themes. The example which covers the major part of this chapter follows this four-step process, using data memos and a table, and includes a number of exercises to complete. Building theory will be shown to be one of the outcomes of the process.

Characteristics of conceptual themes

Although conceptual themes vary substantially, there are likely to have five characteristics. First, they are likely to be drawn from different sections of the interview transcripts and to use codes taken from the analysis of different illustrative issues. In the example below, it will be shown that codes that were initially created in relation to a number of issues, such as student attendance and preparation for teaching sessions, were used to analyse the concept of responsibility.

Second, the conceptual theme may not be referred to directly. Few respondents used the word 'responsibility', although it appeared to be a concept that underlay much of what was said. So there is likely to be a greater element of interpretation when considering a conceptual theme than when analysing an illustrative issue.

Third, the conceptual theme may not be spotted on the first reading of the transcripts. The identification and analysis of such themes illustrates particularly well the need for the qualitative researcher to return to, and re-analyse, their data. As Barbour (2008: 216) notes:

> Sometimes issues don't 'jump out' at you until someone says something particularly vehemently or articulately. However, this does not mean that it isn't present in earlier transcripts. Once sensitized, you may be surprised to find how many other instances you can find.

Fourth, the use of conceptual themes is likely to achieve the most difficult aim of thematic analysis identified by Gibson and Brown (2009: 128–129), i.e. examining relationships between different elements of the data. While the analysis of illustrative issues tends to be very helpful for examining commonalities and differences between respondents, it is the identification and analysis of conceptual themes that is most likely to contribute to understanding patterns of relationships. A conceptual theme is, of course, a finding in its own right, because it is a commonality. However, it is also an explanatory tool that can help the researcher to understand relationships between other themes and issues. It will be shown that the conceptual theme of responsibility not only underlay comments made by many of the lecturers but also provided an explanation for some of the differences between them.

Fifth, and linked to the previous point, identifying conceptual themes enables the researcher to move beyond identifying findings to building theory. Grbich (2007: 186) describes theory as 'abstract knowledge which has been developed as an account regarding a group of facts or phenomena'. She suggests that there are three levels of theory:

1 microtheory, which uses concepts to identify common aspects of phenomena.

2 middle-range theory, which combines concepts with variables and propositions to form explanations with a focus on a particular academic discipline.

3 grand theory, which combines concepts, propositions and statements and can be applied to a range of academic disciplines. (Grbich 2007: 188–189)

Dealing with these in reverse order, an example of a grand theory is Marxist ideas about the manner in which the ruling classes are able to use their economic power to their own advantage. This theory can be applied to a range of social science disciplines including Sociology (Giddens, 2001: 196), Criminology (Tierney, 2010: 22–23) and Politics (Kavanagh et al., 2006: 22–23). A linked middle-range theory, applied specifically to Sociology, covers a set of arguments that education, rather than reflecting meritocratic principles, systematically favours people from more affluent backgrounds (Bilton et al., 2002: 274–276). A microtheory might then focus on the more limited choices that tend to be available to disadvantaged groups when choosing universities (Reay et al., 2001).

From this example, it should be clear that the large majority of qualitative research studies are concerned with building microtheory. This is certainly likely to be the case for a student research project. It may be helpful to illustrate this point by giving examples of academic studies that have identified conceptual themes and used them to build microtheory:

- Kember et al. (2011: 215) used the concept of individual goal setting to explain the comments made by some community college students in Hong Kong about becoming distracted from studying. The microtheory they developed suggested that undergraduate students were better able to act in a manner consistent with their long-term goals than community college students.

- Wimshurst (2011: 308) used a concept that she referred to as 'deflecting' to explain how some Australian students of criminal justice education limited their engagement with theoretical ideas. One student discussed concentrating instead on the practical elements of criminal justice; another explained how she chose just one theoretical perspective to discuss; and a third concentrated only on passing assessments when studying the theoretical parts of the course. The concept of 'deflecting' contributed to the microtheory that Wimshurst built about students' understanding of the nature of their subject area.

Two helpful tools for identifying conceptual themes

Data memos

Chapters 4 and 5 demonstrated the use of methodological memos to record decisions that are made in the analysis of data. Data memos serve a different purpose: the researcher makes a note of a matter that they may wish to consider further in their analysis. Data memos are often discussed in the context of grounded theory (for example, Flick, 2009: 434) but can be used in a wider variety of qualitative contexts (Yin, 2011: 186).

Richards (2009: 80) suggests a method by which the qualitative researcher can use data memos to assist in their analysis:

> Develop a memo-writing routine that encourages quick and easy documentation of ideas and the way they grow. Treat memos as informal records of thinking aloud, never as finished research productions.

Miles and Huberman (1994: 72) argue that memos can be a tool for stepping back from the data and moving beyond codes to try to think more reflectively and conceptually. Similarly, Bryman and Burgess (1994: 5) suggest that memos elaborate data and can represent the first step in developing theory. Hesse-Biber and Leavy (2006: 352–354) demonstrate how a memo assisted in the analysis of data, and the building of theory, in a study of young African-American women. The memo identified a concept that appeared to underlie responses to several questions about weight and appearance. Hesse-Biber and Leavy refer to this concept as 'internal self-assessment', meaning that the young women were more interested in their own assessment of themselves than the opinions of others. This concept of 'internal self-assessment' proved helpful in explaining how the young women dealt with racism and pressures to be thin.

Tables

For more complex forms of analysis, the use of tables may help the researcher to see patterns in the data. Tables can take any number of forms. Table 6.1 is, in fact, the first few lines of a table which I used to compile the responses of a sample of people living in temporary accommodation about the accommodation that they were living in. It simply highlights the key point(s) made in relation to each issue in the form of a quotation.

Table 6.1   Table to show opinions of temporary accommodation

Respondent	Support from staff	Best thing	Worst thing
R1	'they've been very supportive'	'not being on the street'	'not being allowed people to come and visit you'
R2	'lots'; 'very good'	'it's a roof over your head at the end of the day isn't it, but it is a really, really, very, very, nice roof as you can see'	'you've got to put up with the other residents'
R3	'no, I just scramble up here and lock my door'	'safe – it's a roof'	'we don't get a breakfast in here – too many cereals'
R4	'helped with my drug issues and things like that'	'the support and stuff that you get'	'all the drunks coming in'
R5	'they have been helpful'	'I get on with the other people'	'nothing really'
R6	'help to get appointments'	'support with accommodation and stuff'	'sharing the bathrooms'

Table 6.2 is from the same study and represents a different type of table, which I used to try to establish some of the key life events that might explain respondents becoming homeless. Again, it is an extract from a larger table. Explanations of the abbreviations are shown below:

Table 6.2   Checklist of circumstances experienced by homeless people

	B	RB	LJ	E	HLPH	MHP	DP	AP	P	R
R1		X					x	x	x	
R2				x		x		x	x	X
R3	X	X			X			x		
R4						x	x			
R5				x		X	x			X
R6		X		x		X	x		x	

B: bereavement

R: raped

MHP: mental health problem

E: evicted/forced to leave accommodation

DP: drug problem

AP: alcohol problem

RB: relationship breakdown

LJ: lost job

P: prison

HLPH: had to leave parents' home

Although Table 6.2 is only an extract, it demonstrates how I was able to identify some of the commonalities within the data: for example, that the large majority of the respondents had had a difficulty with either alcohol or drugs. It also highlighted possible relationships between factors – for example drug problems often seemed to co-exist with mental health problems – which led me to examine closely the comments made about these two issues to try to understand the relationship better.

As you become more confident in your data analysis skills, you may wish to use more complex tables; Miles and Huberman (1994) provide a wide range of examples and demonstrate the role that they can play in qualitative analysis.

Analysing a conceptual theme step by step

It was noted above that the process of identifying conceptual themes is one where it is difficult to suggest an approach that can be generalised. However, the example that follows will take four steps and, although some modification may be necessary, these steps could form the basis for the analysis of many datasets. The four steps are:

1 identifying the conceptual theme and creating a category;

2 bringing together codes from different illustrative issues into the category;

3 creating sub-categories to reflect different elements of the conceptual theme;

4 using the conceptual theme to explain relationships between different parts of the data and to build theory.

Step 1: identifying the conceptual theme and creating a category

The conceptual theme of responsibility was mentioned when analysing the data relating to reflective practice in Chapter 5. A code that was applied to Lewis and to Laura was 'accepts responsibility for students' reaction'. However, the illustrative issue where I first identified the concept of responsibility was the attendance and motivation of students. An extract from the interview with Fern and the codes that I applied to it are shown below:

Interviewer: Okay, a question about the attendance and motivation of students.

Fern: I think that's difficult; I think now we're treating the preliminary degree as a career grade it's becoming a bit like school. In a sense you've got some kids who love to be there and other kids who can't be bothered because they're just going through the motions. And there used to be about 5–10% of people went to university so I imagine you were effectively teaching that minority who really want to be there. But now you have some who are not too bothered; they're here to get a qualification and get on with their lives, and they're quite instrumental with that. But people don't attend because they're working; they don't come in because as soon as they know what the assessment is they go to do it and don't want to learn. They're not particularly interested in learning they just want to get the assessment and that's it. So I think to a certain extent that I understand that's instrumental to students doing reasonably well. They don't have a breadth of education but they can technically get though the assignment. So I just let them get on with it and concentrate on those who really want to do it, you know. So really it's like the old university group inside the mass really, so you know I just focus – that's not true, I don't just focus on those who are interested. But if a minority, like lectures aren't compulsory, we don't take down registers so there might be people not there. But we do take registers in seminars so we have more people there. If I find some people haven't turned up to class I don't worry about it because I teach those that are there and those who are there by definition are the most interested. So attendance is a problem, that cynicism of 'oh let's get through this' 'oh we've got to do this degree let's get through it'. There's still loads of interested students but, if they're not there, then they're either working or not interested.

Codes

Some students very motivated

Some students not interested

Changes since smaller numbers attended university

Reason for non-attendance – lack of interest

Reason for non-attendance – employment

Reason for non-attendance – some students only interested in passing assessment

Response to non-attendance – monitoring attendance at seminars

Response to non-attendance – teaches those who are there

It was at this point that I noticed that many of these codes reflected an underlying question of who was responsible for non-attendance, so I wrote a data memo to record my thoughts:

Data memo – responsibility

It appears that Fern placed the majority of the responsibility for non-attendance at teaching sessions on the students. While being clear that some students were interested in their subject and in studying, she also indicated that there were some who 'can't be bothered' and were 'not particularly interested in learning'. These students, in her opinion, were driven by a desire to achieve a qualification rather than a desire to learn and felt that they could pass the assignment without attending teaching sessions. So negative attitudes were the reasons that some students did not attend regularly, although Fern also indicated that employment might be a factor. Fern made clear that she did not regard it as her responsibility to make changes to respond to students not attending when she said that: 'If I find some people haven't turned up to class I don't worry about it because I teach those that are there and those who are there by definition are the most interested.'

Looking at the list of codes that I had written for Fern in relation to the issue of attendance, I thought that all of them could be duplicated and placed in a category called 'responsibility', with one exception, i.e. Changes since smaller numbers attended university

In order to confirm my impression that responsibility was a conceptual issue that underlay much of the discussion on attendance, I read and coded the answer that Susan gave to a question on this subject:

> **Susan**: I think attendance is pretty good, and I think that students vote with their feet; if it's boring they don't turn up. So I think they're not just motivated by assessments but also what they're going to cover and if they think it's an interesting subject that they're going to cover and it's going to be taught in an interesting way then they'll turn up. So it says a lot about that but also about timing of classes; we've got one lecture from five o'clock to six o'clock but a lot of students work and have children so that's quite difficult. So I think we've got to be careful about looking at how we monitor attendance and whether it's appropriate at times to monitor the students because the motivation might be there to attend but it might be that there are barriers to them attending at certain times.

Students not just motivated by passing assessments

Reasons for non-attendance – boring subject matter

Reason for non-attendance – subject not taught in an interesting manner

Reason for non-attendance – teaching sessions at an inconvenient time

Reason for non-attendance – employment

Response to non-attendance – monitoring attendance at seminars, but may not be appropriate

I thought that all these codes were relevant to the concept of responsibility. Adhering to Richards' (2009: 80) suggestion of recording ongoing development of ideas through memos, I wrote a second data memo:

Data memo – responsibility (2)

Susan appeared to take a very different position from Fern in relation to responsibility for attendance. She specifically rejected the idea that students had the inappropriate attitude of only wanting to pass assessments and should therefore be held responsible when they did not attend. Instead she identified a series of reasons for non-attendance for which students were not responsible: boring subject matter, the subject not being taught in an interesting manner and teaching sessions being at an inconvenient time, particularly for students with children. The one common reason identified by both Susan and Fern for non-attendance was employment. Both also mentioned the monitoring of attendance but, while Fern described it in neutral terms, Susan's comment on this subject implied concern that students might be penalised when non-attendance was for reasons that were not their responsibility. So the concept of responsibility appeared to explain many of the differences in the reasons for non-attendance, and the responses to it, discussed by Fern and Susan.

Step 2: bringing together codes from different illustrative issues in this category

Conceptual themes tend to underlie discussions of a number of illustrative issues. Having identified the theme of responsibility, I next read through the interview transcripts again in full and found this theme to be evident in discussion of a number of other issues. One such issue was respondents' feelings about different teaching sessions and, in particular, students' preparation for seminars. Exercise 7 invites you to look for the theme of responsibility in a section of the transcript of the interview with Rachel, part of which was used in Chapter 4.

Exercise 7

Read through the following section of the interview with Rachel. Look at my list of codes, which could appear in an illustrative category called Teaching Sessions and Preparation for Them. Then decide which of these codes could also appear in a category called Responsibility.

(Continued)

(Continued)

Interviewer: And have you noticed any differences between traditional and mature students?

Rachel: No, nothing huge.

Interviewer: What about in terms of preferred teaching methods?

Rachel: With mature students you can probably be a bit more flexible with your teaching methods and you can also expect them to read. They'll probably take it quite seriously so, for instance, when I was teaching some mature students in my last job, if you asked them to read something, they would come back having made notes. So I think they tend to take studying more seriously while traditional undergraduates are less likely to read. So you have to rely on different teaching methods so in that respect, yes there is a difference. Mature students are also more likely to bring their work to you for guidance. This may be just a lack of confidence because they haven't been in higher education before or for a long time or just because they feel more committed to the course they're doing.

Interviewer: And do you feel, do you get any satisfaction from teaching mature students as oppose to traditional students or vice versa?

Rachel: I like to teach them all: it's different and there's great satisfaction if you have a good traditional student sitting there and they've read something because they're interested in it after you've given the lecture about it. If they hadn't thought about something before, but now they are reading about it, then the satisfaction is immense. On the other hand, it's quite demoralising when you feel that you've give your heart and soul to a lecture and then the students come along to a seminar and are just not interested – it's quite demoralising. It's also frustrating because you can't actually make people do work for seminars.

Interviewer: Do you like to give lectures?

Rachel: Yes, I don't mind now. I can't believe I'm saying that but I don't mind!

Interviewer: And how about seminars?

Rachel: I don't mind seminars either. I think the old fashioned way of expecting students to work for seminars has gone and that's the hardest thing; you can't go to a seminar and expect all the students to have prepared. So seminars can actually be really hard work, perhaps harder than lectures.

Codes in category of 'teaching sessions and preparation for them'

- Mature students more likely to read
- Mature students tend to take learning more seriously
- Need different teaching methods for mature and traditional students
- Mature students less likely to be confident
- Mature students more likely to seek guidance
- Some traditional students read
- Demoralising when students don't prepare for seminars
- Cannot force students to work for seminars
- Likes lectures and seminars
- Can no longer expect students to have prepared for seminars
- Lack of preparation makes seminars more difficult

Please complete the exercise before looking at how I would have tackled it below.

In deciding which codes should also appear in the category of 'Responsibility', I decided that any which focused on the amount of effort that students applied to their course reflected, at least partly, the level of responsibility that they took for their learning. So I placed the following codes in the 'Responsibility' category:

- Mature students more likely to read

- Mature students tend to take learning more seriously

- Some traditional students read

- Can no longer expect students to have prepared for seminars

There were also a number of codes that implied that, when students did not prepare for seminars, there was a responsibility on the part of the lecturer to adjust their teaching method. So the following codes were also included:

- Need different teaching methods for mature and traditional students

- Lack of preparation makes seminars more difficult

It seemed clear that two of the codes about mature students were about their needs rather than any element of responsibility, i.e. 'Mature students less likely to be confident' and 'Mature students more likely to seek guidance'. These codes were not copied to the 'Responsibility' category. The code 'Demoralising when students don't prepare for seminars' appeared to be primarily concerned with the lecturer's feelings rather than with responsibility, as did 'Likes lectures and seminars'. Possibly the most difficult decision was to exclude from the 'Responsibility' category the 'Cannot force students to work for seminars' code. This seemed to me to be primarily about the limitations of the lecturer's role, although it could also be seen as a denial of responsibility if students did not prepare. The context of the use of the code – Rachel discussing her feelings about teaching – seemed to support my interpretation. A methodological memo could have been written here to record this decision.

So six of the eleven codes that appeared in the category of 'Teaching sessions and preparation for them' could also be placed in the category of 'Responsibility'. There were also codes used to analyse a range of other issues that could be placed in the Responsibility category, for example some that considered where responsibility lay if students did not participate in seminar discussions. By the time the process was complete, a large number of codes had been placed into the 'Responsibility' category so it was necessary to consider whether it could be divided into sub-categories.

Step 3: creating sub-categories to reflect different elements of the conceptual theme

Creating categories and sub-categories was shown to be part of the process of analysing an illustrative issue in Chapter 5. It may be a more difficult task in the case of a conceptual theme because the data will be more complex and will usually deal with a number of illustrative issues. You may feel that you already understand the process of creating sub-categories and that there is no need to read this section. However, it is worth looking at a further example, where the sub-categories are not so obvious, before seeing to analyse a conceptual theme in your own data.

In relation to the conceptual theme of 'Responsibility', it has already been shown that there were differences between Fern and Susan as to who they held responsible for non-attendance at teaching sessions. Susan also appeared to have a slightly different view from Rachel as to who was responsible if students did not prepare for seminars, saying:

> I don't think it's about going away and looking at your teaching guide and turning up, but it's about having direction week on week to keep people motivated and coming prepared to have discussion and to be actively informed.

My interpretation of the phrase 'having direction' was that this direction should be provided by the lecturer. This suggested that, in the area of preparation as well as attendance, there were different views as to whether the students or staff (and the university, in the case of attendance) should be held responsible. So the first two sub-categories were:

1 *Attendance and learning: students held responsible*

2 *Attendance and learning: staff/university held responsible*

Although these two sub-categories captured the essence of the debate over responsibility, there were also some specific issues where respondents appeared to have different perspectives. One such area was employment, where Thomas explicitly expressed the view that students should not be held responsible for non-attendance if they had employment commitments:

> There is a problem of attendance and I think it's getting worse but I don't think it's necessarily the students' fault. Given the funding situation, I don't know many students who don't work as well ... The general opinion is that students at this university are full time students doing part time jobs, I think for many of them it's the other way round.

In contrast, Paula indicated clearly that, while she was sympathetic to students who did not attend because of employment, this was a mistake on their part and something that they were responsible for:

> Attendance isn't fantastic and at some point it definitely tails off. Some students have good reasons; others get their priorities a little bit mixed up, maybe due to financial reasons they end up prioritising their job over and above their studies and there comes a point where you have to ask them to re-consider.

These differences led me to create a further sub-category, i.e.

3   *The debate over employment*

Another specific issue where I thought it might be helpful to create a sub-category was the monitoring of attendance. In sections of the transcripts used earlier in this chapter, Fern briefly mentioned monitoring as a response to non-attendance, while Susan expressed concerns about students being monitored when they might have good reasons not to attend. As Susan's response referred to responsibility, although again without using the word, my fourth sub-category was:

4   *Monitoring of attendance*

Thinking slightly more conceptually, it occurred to me that two comments that appeared at first to have nothing in common actually revealed an important difference. Fern said that her response to low attendance was simply to teach those who did attend, implying that it was not her responsibility to change her approach. In contrast, Rachel's response to some traditional students not reading in preparation for seminars was to vary her method of delivery between mature and traditional students – clearly taking responsibility for the quality of teaching sessions in response to different circumstances. Noting this contrast led me to create two further sub-categories:

5   *Methods of adapting to difficulties*

6   *Not changing because of difficulties*

Finally, there were some comments about students' attitudes that were relevant beyond the specific issues and difficulties that were discussed in the interviews.

So, for example, Fern attributed student non-attendance to a lack of interest which, if correct, would clearly have substantial implications for both students and the university. Similarly, Susan's belief that students were not just motivated by assessments was a positive statement with very broad implications. So two sub-categories were again created to accommodate contrasting views:

7 *Positive student attitudes*

8 *Inappropriate/negative student attitudes*

So now I had a list of eight sub-categories. There were several subjective decisions that were made in order to create them: some concerned my interpretation of respondents' comments and there was also an important choice to have one sub-category about employment, rather than to have two contrasting sub-categories, i.e. 'Difficulties due to employment – students held responsible' and 'Difficulties due to employment – students not held responsible'. The reason for creating a single sub-category was that I wanted to identify with one code how many respondents discussed the issue of employment. This was another decision that could have been made the subject of a methodological memo.

Although sorting codes into sub-categories is a task that you have already undertaken in Chapter 5, Exercise 8 gives you some more practice with this more complex list of sub-categories.

Exercise 8

Read through the following codes that were placed in the category of responsibility. Then look at the list of eight sub-categories that follows and decide which sub-category each of the codes should appear in:

Some students very motivated: Fern

Some students not interested: Fern

Reason for non-attendance – lack of interest: Fern

Reason for non-attendance – employment: Fern, Susan, Rachel, Paula, Thomas

Reason for non-attendance – some students only interested in passing assessments: Fern

Response to non-attendance – monitoring attendance at seminars: Fern

Response to non-attendance – teaches those who are there: Fern

Students not just motivated by passing assessments: Susan

Reasons for non-attendance – boring subject matter: Susan

Reason for non-attendance – subject not taught in an interesting manner: Susan

Reason for non-attendance – teaching sessions at an inconvenient time: Susan, Thomas

Response to non-attendance – monitoring attendance at seminars, but may not be appropriate: Susan

Preparation for seminars dependent on good direction: Susan

Need to break up lectures to prevent students from becoming bored and distracted: Susan

Mature students more likely to read: Rachel

Mature students tend to take learning more seriously: Rachel

Some traditional students read: Rachel

Can no longer expect students to have prepared for seminars: Rachel

Need different teaching methods for mature and traditional students: Rachel

Lack of preparation makes seminars more difficult: Rachel

Reason for non-attendance – students are paying so think they should choose whether to attend: Rachel

Danger of students not attending but taking assessments: Rachel, Laura

Accepts responsibility for students' reaction: Lewis, Laura

Staff should provide an environment where students can contribute: Lewis, Laura

Lecturers' job to motivate students: Lewis

Some very hard-working students: Laura

Must manage seminar differently when some students have not prepared: Laura

Students may not attend lectures if they have PowerPoint slides in advance: Paula

Need to meet students' expectation to be entertained: Paula

Seminars can be set up to ensure students participate: Paula

Attendance sometimes good: Paula

Students who miss teaching because of jobs have wrong priorities: Paula

Monitoring attendance can lead to broader discussion of wellbeing: Paula

Staff should not be responsible for monitoring attendance: Thomas

Seminar becomes a lecture when students have not prepared: Thomas

Students need to have jobs: Thomas

Students can work long hours in jobs: Thomas

Sub-categories

1 *Attendance and learning: students held responsible*

2 *Attendance and learning: staff/university held responsible*

3 *The debate over employment*

4 *Monitoring of attendance*

5 *Methods of adapting to difficulties*

6 *Not changing because of difficulties*

7 *Positive student attitudes*

8 *Inappropriate/negative student attitudes*

Please complete the exercise before looking at how I would have tackled it below.

The manner in which I distributed these codes between the sub-categories is shown below:

Attendance and learning: students held responsible

Reason for non-attendance – lack of interest: Fern

Reason for non-attendance – some students only interested in passing assessments: Fern

Reason for non-attendance – students are paying so think they should choose whether to attend: Rachel

Attendance and learning: staff/university held responsible

Reason for non-attendance – boring subject matter: Susan

Reason for non-attendance – subject not taught in an interesting manner: Susan

Reason for non-attendance – teaching sessions at an inconvenient time: Susan, Thomas

Preparation for seminars dependent on good direction: Susan

Accepts responsibility for students' reaction: Lewis, Laura

Staff should provide an environment where students can contribute: Lewis, Laura

Lecturers' job to motivate students: Lewis

The debate over employment

Reason for non-attendance – employment: Fern, Rachel, Paula, Thomas

Students who miss teaching because of jobs have wrong priorities: Paula

Students need to have jobs: Thomas

Students can work long hours in jobs: Thomas

Monitoring of attendance

Response to non-attendance – monitoring attendance at seminars: Fern

Response to non-attendance – monitoring attendance at seminars, but may not be appropriate: Susan

Monitoring attendance can lead to broader discussion of wellbeing: Paula

Staff should not be responsible for monitoring attendance: Thomas

Methods of adapting to difficulties

Need to break up lectures to prevent students from becoming bored and distracted: Susan

Can no longer expect students to have prepared for seminars: Rachel

Need different teaching methods for mature and traditional students: Rachel

Lack of preparation makes seminars more difficult: Rachel

Must manage seminar differently when some students have not prepared: Laura

Need to meet students' expectation to be entertained: Paula

Seminars can be set up to ensure students participate: Paula

Seminar becomes a lecture when students have not prepared: Thomas

Not changing because of difficulties

Response to non-attendance – teaches those who are there: Fern

Positive student attitudes

Some students very motivated: Fern

Students not just motivated by passing assessments: Susan

Mature students more likely to read: Rachel

Mature students tend to take learning more seriously: Rachel

Some traditional students read: Rachel

Some very hard working students: Laura

Attendance sometimes good: Paula

Inappropriate/negative student attitudes

Some students not interested: Fern

Mature students more likely to read: Rachel

Mature students tend to take learning more seriously: Rachel

Danger of students not attending but taking assessments: Rachel, Laura

Students may not attend lectures if they have PowerPoint slides in advance: Paula

I should make the usual qualifying comment that you should not be concerned if the outcome above is somewhat different from yours, because the exercise involved a large number of subjective decisions. For example, I decided that Rachel's comment that mature students were more likely to read should be seen as representing both a positive student attitude (on the part of mature students) and a negative one (on the part of traditional students, although Rachel did also note that some traditional students read). You might have placed this code only into the positive attitudes category, only into the negative attitudes category or even into the 'Attendance and learning: students held responsible' category. All these decisions could be justified and this would be another point at which it would be useful to write a methodological memo, which could be referred back to when assessing the validity of the conclusions drawn from the data. There tend to me more difficult judgements to make when undertaking this type of task for conceptual themes than when considering illustrative issues.

Step 4: using the conceptual theme to explain differences between respondents and to build theory

Even when analysing a conceptual theme, some of the findings that emerge are likely to be simple ones, which identify similarities and differences. So, for example, the findings relating to the sub-category 'The debate over employment' were:

- A number of respondents identified employment as a factor that prevented students from attending teaching sessions.

- There were different opinions as to whether students should be blamed for missing teaching sessions due to employment.

However, the use of conceptual themes also provides the opportunity to explain the relationships between different parts of the data. Again, this is a process that can be best illustrated by using an example. I examined where the conceptual theme of responsibility could be used to explain broad differences in attitudes between my respondents. It occurred to me that there were three pairs of sub-categories where one included codes that placed responsibility for any difficulties with attendance and learning on students and the other incorporated codes suggesting that responsibility lay elsewhere. These sub-categories are listed below in their pairs, with the one where the codes suggested that responsibility lay with the student appearing first in each case:

Attendance and learning: students held responsible and

Attendance and learning: staff/university held responsible

Not changing because of difficulties and

Methods of adapting to difficulties

Inappropriate/negative student attitudes and

Positive student attitudes

Here a table was particularly helpful in looking for patterns of responses between different lecturers. The six sub-categories were re-arranged and numbered so that the three listed first were the ones incorporating codes that located responsibility largely with the student, i.e.:

1 Attendance and learning: students held responsible

2 Not changing because of difficulties

3 Inappropriate/negative student attitudes

4 Attendance and learning: staff/university held responsible

5 Methods of adapting to difficulties

6 Positive student attitudes

Table 6.3 shows which respondents made comments that were placed into each of these six sub-categories. The sub-categories are referred to by number to save space:

Table 6.3   Checklist of comments made in key sub-categories

Respondent	1	2	3	4	5	6
Fern	x	x	x			x
Susan				x	x	x
Rachel	x				x	x
Lewis				x		
Laura			x	x	x	x
Paula			x			x
Thomas				x	x	

From this table, we can see that Susan provided the clearest example of a respondent who tended to locate responsibility away from the student, although Laura and Thomas also appeared to lean towards this position. In contrast, Fern was more likely to hold students responsible for their own learning.

So the conceptual theme of responsibility provided greater understanding of the data at two levels:

- It helped to explain some of the different views that were expressed about elements of teaching and learning. For example, it suggested reasons for non-attendance being attributed either to student centred factors such as lack of interest or to broader factors such as the timing of teaching sessions. It could also offer an explanation as to why one respondent continued as before despite low attendance at teaching sessions, while another adjusted their approach to seminars because some students did not read in preparation.

- It could explain the pattern of responses between different respondents: views expressed across a range of areas were affected by whether or not the respondent held the student primarily responsible for their own learning.

You might question whether these findings could be considered as theory, given the description of its role provided by Charmaz (2006: 128): 'A theory can alter your viewpoint and change your consciousness. Through it, you can see the world from a different vantage point and create new meanings of it'. However, I was able to demonstrate that the conceptual theme of responsibility helped to explain and understand data across a number of issues. So the analysis produced microtheory as defined by Gribch (2007: 186), i.e. concepts were used to identify common aspects of phenomena. It is important to remember that every piece of microtheory, no matter how small or apparently mundane, makes an important contribution to our understanding of the social world.

Summary

Unlike other elements of data analysis discussed in this book, it is difficult to provide clear guidance as to how the researcher can identify a conceptual theme. Such a theme might be identified in the process of, or after, analysing illustrative issues. Conceptual themes are likely to underlie discussions of several illustrative issues and, if coding is being used as a method of data analysis, codes may be drawn from across the interview transcripts. They are often not specifically discussed by respondents, but represent an underlying idea or principle. They are likely to explain relationships between different elements of the data and can contribute to the building of theory, usually microtheory.

Many of the elements of analysing a conceptual theme, such as using codes and creating sub-categories, are similar to those used to analyse illustrative issues. Tools which may be particularly helpful are data memos – which the researcher can use to note emerging ideas – and tables, which can help to identify patterns of response.

The identification of conceptual themes depends heavily on the ability of the researcher to 'see' something that may lie below the surface of what is said. Like most skills associated with qualitative data analysis, it is one that tends to develop with time and practice. Analysis often involves a substantial element of interpretation, so it is particularly important that the researcher keeps a record of key decisions and reasons for making them. Space did not allow the inclusion of methodological memos in this chapter, but a number of points have been identified where they would have been useful.

Although there are likely to be as many processes of analysis as there are conceptual themes, this chapter has provided one example of a four stage process: a theme was identified and a category created for it, relevant codes were then moved into this category from across a range of illustrative issues, the codes were divided into sub-categories and a table was used to establish patterns. Some of the findings in relation to the conceptual theme identified similarities and differences between respondents, but others were able to explain relationships within the data, showing the influence of ideas about responsibility on the comments that were made about a range of issues.

While some datasets only include illustrative issues to examine, the researcher should be equipped to search for conceptual themes, and to analyse them if they are identified, in order to ensure that they take the opportunities that are available to contribute to a body of theory.

Further reading

For a good discussion of the process of using codes as tools to build theory see Boeije, H. (2010) *Analysis in Qualitative Research*. London: Sage.

An example of how data can be organised into categories, and these categories refined as the analysis progresses, is provided in Maykut, P. and Morehouse, R. (1994) *Beginning Qualitative Research: A Philosophic and Practical Guide*. London: The Falmer Press. Although the authors discuss the use of manual cards as tools for data analysis, the process could easily be adapted for use with a word processor.

As noted earlier in the chapter, a wide range of tables that may be useful when analysing data are discussed in Miles, M. B. and Huberman, A. M. (1994) *Qualitative Data Analysis*, 2nd edn. London: Sage (1st edn, 1984).

7

Alternative approaches to analysing qualitative data

Introduction

Chapters 4–6 demonstrated the process of analysing data collected from seven interviews, from first reading the transcripts to arriving at findings. Choices were made that meant, by definition, that other possible approaches were not used. This chapter provides an insight into some of the alternative methods of analysing qualitative data.

Given the very wide range of methods of qualitative data analysis, further decisions had to be made as to which approaches could be demonstrated in this chapter and which could be mentioned only briefly or not at all. The guiding principle was to focus on those approaches that are most feasible for the first-time researcher to use.

Examples of approaches that are important for the qualitative researcher to be aware of, but which they may not wish to use until they become more experienced, are feminist analysis (Grbich, 2007: 98–99), phenomenological analysis (Wertz, 2011: 142) and intuitive inquiry (Anderson, 2011: 244–245). While these three approaches are very different from the ones discussed in earlier chapters, the first approach to be demonstrated in this chapter has much in common with the methods used previously. Using the same sources of data – i.e. interviews with seven lecturers at a case study university – it will be shown that thematic analysis can be conducted using deductive, apriori codes rather than inductive, empirical ones. These codes will be applied to discussion of the barriers to study facing mature students.

Themes will also be central to the next type of approach discussed and demonstrated – thematic narrative analysis. Narrative analysis is most often associated with life history interviews, where the respondent is encouraged to discuss their life, or parts of it, as a narrative. However, there are also examples where it has been used to examine accounts that people give of changes to the workplace, and this is the approach that will be used here; the narratives of three lecturers about the transition of their institution from a polytechnic to a university will be analysed thematically.

Structural narrative analysis moves the focus away from the content and towards the manner in which the narrative is constructed. This approach will be used to demonstrate how the same three respondents sought to construct their accounts to limit the blame attached to the university for perceived negative changes that had occurred since the time when it was a polytechnic.

The focus on structure is also characteristic of discourse analysis. Any written or spoken words can be subjected to this form of analysis, which has similarities to both conversation analysis and critical discourse analysis. Discourse analysis will be used to show how the seven lecturers constructed different aspects of the role of the guidance tutor.

Finally there will be a brief discussion of the specialist computer software that is available to assist with qualitative data analysis. Although it is unlikely that the first time researcher will feel confident to use software packages such as NVivo and ATLAS.ti, a brief discussion of the strengths and weaknesses of such packages is included, because any reader who wishes to develop their research skills further will, at some time, need to make a decision as to whether to use them.

Deductive coding and analysis

The inductive approach demonstrated in earlier chapters began with the analysis of data and moved on to the production of findings and the building of theory. A different approach is taken when conducting a deductive research study, where the existing theory and literature is the starting point and the data collection and analysis are then planned to test a hypothesis or answer a specific research question arising from the literature (as discussed in Chapter 2). Deductive research involves making the codes used in the data analysis part of the research design; such codes are referred to by Gibson and Brown (2009: 132–133) as apriori codes, because they reflect the interests that the researcher brings into the study or themes that are considered important in the existing literature on the topic concerned.

Although the method of data analysis discussed in earlier chapters was inductive, it was argued in Chapter 2 that most research lies somewhere between an entirely inductive and an entirely deductive approach. This was the case for the research conducted at the case study university, where it was possible to take one part of the data – that related to barriers facing mature students in higher education – and use a deductive approach to coding and analysing it, examining the existing literature in order to determine the codes.

It was noted in Chapter 4 that a number of lecturers discussed in positive terms the experience of teaching mature students, but also acknowledged that this group faced some extra barriers. The process of creating and using apriori codes about these barriers is discussed below, focusing on the differences with the use of empirical codes (which were discussed in Chapters 5 and 6).

Choosing apriori codes

A literature search identified a number of apriori codes that were likely to be helpful when examining the barriers to success in higher education faced by mature students. Three of these codes, and some of the literature on which they were based, are identified below:

Dispositional barriers – a number of academic sources suggested that this would be an important code. For example, Burton et al. (2011: 26–27) note that many mature students feel unprepared and do not understand what study in higher education involves. Carney and McNeish (2005: 1–3) found that mature students faced particularly large challenges in a number of areas, including unfamiliarity with the education system. These challenges could easily become barriers.

Financial problems – this was chosen as a code on the basis of sources such as Tones et al. (2009: 506–507), who note that economic and family responsibilities often create difficulties for mature students in Australia.

Differences – the literature suggested that there could be particular difficulties for specific groups of mature students entering higher education. For example, Bowl's (2001: 144–145) research among female mature students found that the concerns that they had included inadequate funding, lack of childcare, difficulties with the benefit system and their institutions failing to respond to the needs of students with dependent children.

Using apriori codes

Having created these and other apriori codes, the next step was to establish where they could be applied to the interviews with the seven lecturers from the case study university. There are three possible outcomes of applying apriori codes to data; each of these outcomes was demonstrated in the case of one of the above codes:

Outcome 1: the code can be applied as it was originally devised

The **dispositional barriers** code was found to be relevant to apply to three of the transcripts, with lack of confidence being the specific disposition that was discussed. The comments that Fern and Rachel made in this area were noted in Chapter 4: Rachel said mature students might lack confidence and so be more likely to bring their work for a lecturer to look at and Fern discussed her satisfaction when she had seen mature students overcome their lack of confidence. Similarly, Thomas drew on his own experience to speak at some length about the lack of confidence felt by many mature students, saying, 'it's a disease you get and it's incurable'.

So the apriori code was applied without any adjustment, reflecting the close match between the issue discussed in the literature and the one that arose in the data.

Outcome 2: the code can be adjusted

There were also three transcripts that the apriori code **financial problems** could be applied to. Thomas highlighted the financial costs and other difficulties that mature students might face:

> It's a huge investment for mature students, not just in money but in the difficulties that they have to overcome to get here and stay in childcare.

Fern blamed a reduction in the number of mature students on problems caused by changes to the system of student finance:

> ... you don't have that now because of course they can't afford to take the loans out, mature students, they have to work. You know, no government grants, there's no support for them so they've all gone, nearly all gone.

Similarly, Paula argued that changes to funding systems had reduced the numbers of mature students, although she also felt that changes to the university's method of marketing had played a part:

> I think it's partly to do with funding and partly to do with the degrees and, and the way in which our marketing is done.

So here was a case where an apriori code needed to be divided in order to represent differences between respondents. While Thomas discussed the financial problems faced by mature students in a similarly broad manner to the existing literature, Fern and Paula focused specifically on changes to financial systems that could prevent mature students from entering university. My response was to divide the **financial problems** code into **financial problems – shortage of money** and **financial problems – funding system.** Other forms of adjustment that sometimes need to be made to apriori codes are to change the wording of them to fit better with the issues discussed by respondents or to join two similar codes together.

Outcome 3: a code could not be applied to the dataset at all

This was the outcome for the **differences** code: none of the respondents referred to different groups of mature students.

Reflections on the use of apriori codes

These three different outcomes for the apriori codes reflect discussions that appear in the literature about their use. Barbour (2008: 204–205) suggests that the researcher should be constantly reviewing their list of codes and asking themselves, for example, whether a code is too broad and should be broken down further or whether two codes are, in fact, describing the same concept and should be merged together. Similarly, Gibson and Brown (2009: 133) note that some apriori codes may prove not to be relevant as data begins to be analysed. It is also possible that the researcher may decide to add another code to their list, if they decide that a theme that is not mentioned in the literature is important in the data. So the list of apriori codes should be treated as flexible and capable of being changed.

However, despite all the adjustments that may need to be made to apriori codes, they can still play a useful role in directing the researcher towards themes that are important in the literature, ensuring a clear link between the findings section of the output and the literature search section (see Chapter 10). The findings in relation to the three codes used as examples above were:

- Dispositional barriers were identified by a number of respondents; in all cases the barrier mentioned specifically was a lack of confidence.
- Financial problems were also a factor discussed in several cases, both a shortage of money in general and difficulties brought about by changes to funding systems.
- Despite the specific difficulties noted in the literature for groups of mature students such as women, these difficulties were not referred to by respondents.

Narrative analysis

Narrative analysis is frequently used in subject areas such as the study of literature, to analyse the type of story told through prose or poetry (see, for example, Herman and Vervaeck, 2001). Elliott (2005: 3–4) notes that, although analysing narratives is a literary tradition, in recent years it is an approach that has spread to the human and social sciences. The stories that people tell represent the manner in which they make sense of events; narrative analysis does not seek objective truth but to capture people's own understanding of their lived experience (Josselson, 2011: 225–226). Bryman (2008: 553) notes that narrative analysis is not restricted to life history interviews (which were discussed in Chapter 2) and cites the work of Brown (1998, cited in Bryman, 2008: 558) to illustrate that it can be used to analyse organisational change such as the introduction of a new information support system in a hospital.

Similarly, the data that will be used here to illustrate the process of narrative analysis is the accounts of changes with time which were given by three of the respondents of longer standing at the case study university, focusing particularly on change since 1992. 1992 was a crucial year for 'new' universities in the UK, because it was then that they ceased to be polytechnics which were partly funded by, and responsible to, local government and instead became universities, where funding and accountability are linked entirely to central government (Clark, 2009).

Before conducting narrative analysis, it is necessary to consider a number of distinctions between forms that it may take. Josselson (2011: 226) distinguishes between a faith approach, which involves re-presenting the speaker's own narrative, and a suspicion approach, where the researcher looks for hidden motives beyond the literal and conscious meaning (Josselson, 2011: 226). The questioning of the motives of the speaker has something in common with critical discourse analysis (see below). However, in practice, analysis often tends to move between these two extremes, taking the respondent at face value but also seeking to critically analyse their response and understand why this might be their stated position. The analysis that follows will lean more towards a faith approach, as the questioning of the motives of the speaker is something that a new researcher may not feel confident to do.

Josselson (2011: 226) makes a further distinction. Narratives can be considered on their own – sections of the text of one narrative are compared to other parts of the same narrative. An alternative approach, if there are multiple narratives, is to make comparisons between different respondents, by creating categories and codes with which to compare similar sections of different narratives. It is this second approach that is demonstrated here.

A number of writers (e.g. Elliott, 2005: 39–46; Grbich, 2007: 127–134) draw a distinction between those approaches that focus on the content of the narrative and those where the principal concern is the structure and the language. This distinction is also evident in Riessman's (2006: 186–188) typology of four different types of narrative analysis, i.e.:

- thematic analysis;
- structural analysis, which continues to consider content but also considers the mechanisms by which the speaker seeks to make the story more persuasive;
- interactional analysis, which emphasises the construction of the story through dialogue between the speaker and the listener; and
- performative analysis, which considers how words and gestures convey a story to an audience, and the audience's reaction.

The two types of narrative analysis that will be demonstrated here are thematic and structural analysis. Interactional analysis and performative analysis would both be impossible to undertake, because the interviewer listened to the brief narratives without asking questions and no records were kept of the respondents' gestures. The narratives of the three respondents appear below, followed by a discussion of how I analysed them. The account of Fern is slightly different from the one that appears in the Appendix, because the exact words have been used, reflecting the concern within structural analysis to focus on the language with which the narrative is constructed.

Fern said:

Oddly because the expansion of higher education went with becoming a university, erm it was more like a university in some ways when it was a poly [polytechnic] because we weren't as pressured. In the traditional universities you have time for research, you have time to teach small numbers. So when I came here it was small numbers and I had time to do research and erm but the difference was that I'm like in an old university where there's an expectation to do research, in this, being a polytechnic there was no expectation at all. I did it because that was my choice, so I always behaved as if I was in an old university even though I was in a new university. So for me it didn't, it didn't really make much difference because I wasn't heavily – the workload, you know the workload wasn't light but it wasn't, you know, it seemed do-able and erm, but I did notice that there were people around me who didn't do research; they just were teachers, which is what they were employed to be. That's no criticism of them but whereas over the years I've obviously, as we've become a university it's been ever so more slightly research. But to be fair umm, not a huge emphasis and erm, I was always the same – I always personally chose to do research so erm, so I suppose you know, it's not changed a lot really, I don't know. And the numbers didn't help us. It made it seem more like a, like a more work-a-day when you have seventy students. So, I'm not sure, not a very clear answer.

Lewis said:

I think, well this will seem like an odd reply in a sense, but I think polytechnics were closely linked with their local communities as well. It was a polytechnic and it was funded in part by the city council, and I think actually that gave it a closer link to people in the region, I think we used to get more mature students and more err working class background students, you know I think that there was a wider participation from different sorts of students when it was a polytechnic and I liked that. I understand the university has to compete on a competitive market for the students but I know why that's changed but I do think that's a change, you know, for the worse. I hardly see – I see very, very few mature students coming through the programme and when I started we ran almost whole programmes with just mature students on. So that's a change but I think is disappointing, umm other changes are more exciting. Err there's a lot of investment in us as a university and that's exciting and that's good, that's positive you know, we can see the university, you know, is taking real steps forward as well to be a leading university. I think that we are a good new university, so I'm really, umm, you know, avoiding the word proud but actually I am proud to be a part of a university that is doing good things as well.

Thomas said:

Oh yes, erm, when I first came here erm, the polytechnic, I think the polytechnic knew what it was: it was a polytechnic and it was a good polytechnic. And when it because a university erm, it tried to be the best university it could but I've always thought it would have been better if it had stayed a polytechnic. I'm not saying the university got ideas above its station or anything like that, it may just be a martyr case, I might be like, overly romantic or something, I don't know – maybe it's the same in every organisation. It was, in this case it was better to work in when it was a polytechnic, absolutely better, umm I think that the changes which took place might have taken place anyway – I don't know – but certainly since it became a university there has been a steady chipping away of, erm, of the quality of what we do. I can't give the time to the things I was to do in the way which I could, I am working: for example, I couldn't do what I wanted to on Sunday because I was writing a lecture for here for Monday afternoon right, it's last minute preparation and every year I have had to deliver material that I've never delivered before. For years there hasn't been a sort of comfort zone where you can take your time and think 'right, I've got it all set now' every, this year I'm teaching two new subjects I've never taught before and err, erm it's stressful. There's not the time, there's not the time to give err to research I would like to do. We have to research, we have to publish. And I do, do that, err, err I work closely with one particular colleague here in doing that, but we haven't got the time. The pressure is on all the time; teach, research, administration. And those requirements are going up, they're changing the rules about administrative processes which require us to do things we've never done before.

The first point to note about the above accounts is that I was not surprised by the different factors that were emphasised. As the aim of narrative analysis is to capture respondents' own understanding rather than objective truth (Josselson, 2011: 225), the different focuses of the accounts – on research, student diversity and quality – was to be expected. Recounting a narrative inevitably involves selection of material (Riessman, 2006: 186) and there were elements in the narrative of each of the respondents that suggested that they were aware how subjective their account was. Lewis acknowledged that his account might seem 'odd', Fern made clear that many of her colleagues would not focus so much on research and Thomas suggested that his recollection of the time when the university was a polytechnic might be 'overly romantic'.

Thematic narrative analysis

A thematic approach to analysing the data would use codes and categories to identify similarities and differences between the accounts. Space does not allow a demonstration of how such analysis could be conducted, but it is hoped that you are now sufficiently familiar with the process of thematic analysis to see that the following findings could be identified:

- One theme that ran through the accounts was an element of regret about the change from being a polytechnic to a university. Fern suggested that staff felt under less pressure when the institution was a polytechnic; Thomas agreed and suggested that quality of work had fallen as the pressure had increased. Lewis regretted the loss of links to the local area and the reduction in the number of mature and working-class students.

- Although all three respondents sought to explain these negative changes, there was no consensus as to the reason for them. Fern felt that high numbers of students were responsible for the more pressurised environment, while Thomas argued that the pressure was due to the university losing its identity. Lewis suggested that competition for students had played a role.

- There was also a lack of consensus as to whether negative changes had been balanced by more positive ones. Lewis spoke enthusiastically about investment and 'good things' that were happening. Fern discussed the university becoming 'ever so slightly' more focused on research; the other sections of her narrative indicated that she saw this as a positive development, because she attached great importance to research. However, Thomas suggested that the focus on research was a negative change, creating time pressures for staff who were also required to teach and perform administrative tasks.

Structural narrative analysis

A structural analysis of the narratives would take a different form, focusing on the manner in which the respondents sought to make their accounts persuasive. It could follow the thematic analysis and address a question raised by the above findings: who did respondents hold responsible for negative changes? Or, to be more specific, how far did respondents hold the university itself responsible for negative changes that had occurred since it changed from being a polytechnic? I conducted structural narrative analysis to answer this question using a four-stage process:

1 Identifying the comments made by each respondent where the theme of responsibility was referred to, either directly or indirectly.

2 Reading these comments carefully and determining the narrative that was being presented in relation to responsibility.

3 Showing how the narrative was presented in order to make it persuasive.

4 Comparing the structure of the narratives of the three respondents.

To begin with Lewis, I identified the following as the section of his account that referred implicitly to responsibility for negative changes:

> I understand the university has to compete on a competitive market for the students but I know why that's changed but I do think that's a change, you know, for the worse.

After careful reading of this statement, my interpretation was that Lewis was suggesting that the university should not be blamed for the reduction in the number of mature students because the changes to its marketing/admissions policy had been forced on it. Considering next the language that was used to make this narrative persuasive, the lack of choice that the university faced was conveyed by the use of the phrase 'has to'. In addition, the suggestion that the university was responding logically to external pressures was made through the use of the phrases 'I understand' and 'I know why.'

In the case of Fern, the key statement about responsibility appeared to be:

> Oddly because the expansion of higher education went with becoming a university, erm it was more like a university in some ways when it was a poly [polytechnic] because we weren't as pressured ...

Again, I read this statement carefully to determine the nature of the narrative, which appeared to be that negative changes were the result of a broad national policy – increasing the numbers in higher education – rather than the more specific local development of changing from a polytechnic to a university. Fern's comment had something in common with that of Lewis, in that she suggested that changes at the institution were forced on it by external policy-related factors. In examining the language that she used to construct this argument, one phrase that I identified as being particularly important was that the expansion of higher education 'went with' the change to being a university. This phrase illustrates the subjective nature of narratives: an alternative understanding of this historical period would be that the expansion in numbers in higher education occurred over a number of years (Blanden and Machin, 2004: 232), while the polytechnics became universities at one point in time (1992). So the use of the 'went with' phrase constructed a narrative in which these two changes occurred together, with the negative developments being attributed to the increase in numbers.

There were several parts of Thomas' narrative that referred to the issue of responsibility for negative changes; careful reading suggested to me that, unlike Lewis and Fern, he held the university responsible for these changes, but sought to limit the blame that he attached to it. The first point at which Thomas appeared to refer to the responsibility of the university was in the following two sentences:

> Oh yes, erm, when I first came here erm, the polytechnic, I think the polytechnic knew what it was, it was a polytechnic and it was a good polytechnic. And when it because a university erm, it tried to be the best university it could but I've always thought it would have been better if it had stayed a polytechnic.

The key phrase seemed to be 'it would have been better', which I interpreted as suggesting that the polytechnic had a choice over whether to retain its original status or become a university. This interpretation, if correct, again highlights that narratives are subjective – by law, polytechnics had no option but to become universities (Clark, 2009).

Responsibility for negative change – i.e. the greater pressure faced by staff – was more obviously assigned to the university in the final sentence of Thomas's narrative:

> And those requirements are going up, they're changing the rules about administrative processes which require us to do things we've never done before.

My interpretation here was that 'they' referred to senior people within the university and that Thomas was suggesting that pressure on staff had continued to build ever since the change from being a polytechnic.

However, while Thomas did not regard the university as blameless for negative changes, there were also sections of his narrative that I interpreted as attempts to persuade the listener that the amount of responsibility attached to the institution should be limited. The linked devices that he used were:

1 He sought to guard against a particularly negative interpretation of his comments when he said: 'I'm not saying the university got ideas above its station or anything like that'. To suggest that negative changes had come about because of conceit or over-ambition on the part of the university would have been extremely critical. Although Thomas did not suggest what the university's motivation was, he eliminated one of the most negative possibilities.

2 He was prepared to accept that his interpretation of events might be incorrect. As noted previously, he acknowledged that his memories of the polytechnic might be 'overly romantic'.

3 He acknowledged that the changes that he attributed to choice on the part of the university might be universal, which would weaken the assumption of blame, when he said, 'I don't know – maybe it's the same in every organisation.'

4 He further acknowledged that his assumption of cause (the change from being a polytechnic to being a university) and effect (greater pressure on staff) might be inaccurate when he said, 'the changes that took place might have happened anyway'.

So the conclusion to my structural analysis was that Lewis and Fern believed that the university was not to blame for negative changes and structured their accounts to seek to persuade the listener that such changes were the inevitable consequence of a broader policy context. In contrast, Thomas believed that the university was responsible for decisions leading to negative changes, but qualified this criticism by guarding against a particularly negative interpretation of his comments and acknowledging the possibility that his own understanding might be incorrect.

In this example, a very simple structural analysis has been undertaken following a thematic analysis, but it is important to be aware that structural narrative analysis can be more complex and completely independent of a thematic approach. Both Grbich (2007: 127–130) and Flick (2009: 347–349) suggest multi-stage processes for the structural analysis of more complex narratives. The structural approach to narrative analysis has much in common with discourse analysis (Josselson, 2011: 226) – a point that will be demonstrated in the next section.

Discourse analysis

It was noted in Chapter 1 that Dawson (2009: 119–125) discusses four approaches to data analysis. Elements of three of these – thematic analysis, comparative analysis and content analysis – were present in the analysis undertaken in Chapters 4–6, although the thematic approach was predominant. The fourth approach identified by Dawson, discourse analysis, is more distinctive. Like structural narrative analysis, the focus is not so much on what is said but how it is said.

Discourse analysis differs from conversation analysis, which is a study of the methods by which individuals achieve social practices such as greetings and giving directions (Greco, 2006: 42). While conversation analysis is concerned only with 'naturally' occurring everyday conversations, discourse analysis can be applied to a wider range of forms of the written and spoken word, including research interviews and newspapers articles (Bryman, 2008: 499). Discourse analysis is defined by Muncie (2006: 74) as:

> Detailed exploration of political, personal, media or academic 'talk' and 'writing' about a subject, designed to reveal how knowledges are organised, carried and reproduced in particular ways and through particular institutional practices.

Bryman (2008: 500) notes that one characteristic of discourse analysis is anti-realism, i.e. the denial of the existence of an external reality waiting to be discovered by the researcher. Instead, it is constructionist, examining how discourse constructs a particular depiction of the matter that is being discussed.

Muncie (2006: 75) argues that discourse analysis involves study of the maintenance of power relations, showing how power is achieved through the use of words. However, for others such as Wooffitt (2005: 137), analysis that is concerned with issues of power should be referred to as critical discourse analysis:

> Critical discourse analysis ... is concerned to analyse how social and political inequalities are manifest in and reproduced through discourse.

For Wooffitt (2005: 13–18), discourse analysis, when used without the word 'critical', refers to study of the manner in which language is used to construct descriptions, stories and accounts. Here Wooffitt's definitions will be accepted.

It was noted in Chapter 2 that critical approaches to social research set aims that are concerned with studying structures of power and the manner in which they are maintained. It is clear that critical discourse analysis fits within this framework, focusing specifically on the use of language. Two examples of research that employed critical discourse analysis are Mautner's (2008) study of the use of language in newspaper reports designed to maintain the subservient position of East European migrants and Gill's (1993) analysis of the language used by male disc jockeys and programme controllers to justify the lack of women employed to broadcast at radio stations.

Critical discourse analysis can present major difficulties with regard to validity and ethics. In particular, presenting research findings to respondents as a check on validity – as suggested in Chapter 6 – is likely to be problematic. In the above two examples, it is unlikely that the newspaper reporters or the radio station employees would agree that their words and phrases were chosen to construct a view of reality that justified continued oppression of a disadvantage group. This in turn raises ethical questions about possible damage to research participants, which must be balanced against the wider benefits that the research may bring about.

Considering the question of validity in discourse analysis more generally, Muncie (2006: 75–76) notes that it is an approach that depends on the researcher 'reading' a text in a particular way; it is difficult to demonstrate that this reading is superior to that of another person, who might choose to interpret the text differently. However, this is not a problem unique to discourse analysis: all forms of qualitative analysis involve interpretation and the researcher must always acknowledge the possibility that alternative interpretations are possible. Reflexivity (see Chapter 1) is important when using discourse analysis, as it is whenever working with qualitative data.

If it had been decided to demonstrate critical discourse analysis in this chapter, the interviews with the lecturers at the case study university might have been analysed to determine whether the language that they used to discuss students sought to maintain and reinforce their own position of power. However, I decided that it was not appropriate to demonstrate an approach that involved questioning the motives of the speaker, as it may take time before new researchers are ready to address these types of questions. Instead I will demonstrate how I used discourse analysis to consider the role that language played in constructing the lecturers' understanding and depiction of the guidance tutor role (a role that involves the provision of pastoral support to students).

As with narrative analysis, it is important to use the original transcript when conducting discourse analysis, rather than the type of edited version that has been used in Chapters 4–6. However, beyond this, there is little practical guidance available as to how discourse analysis should be conducted. As Muncie (2006: 75) notes:

> It is easier to trace the theoretical underpinnings of discourse analysis than to identify and describe the formal processes of actually carrying out such research. This is partly due to the often intuitive and reflexive nature of the skills involved.

McMullen (2011: 209–211) is one of the few authors to describe the process of discourse analysis – he suggests the following steps:

1 Read the transcripts.

2 Make undirected notes on key words and the approach of the speaker.

3 Begin to apply concepts used by discourse analysts such as positioning of oneself and others, interpretative repertoires, patterns and variability.

4 Identify key concepts.

5 Note the manner in which respondents construct reality with particular reference to these key concepts.

However, for the first-time user of discourse analysis, it might be more helpful to use a simplified version of this process, which first identifies themes, before considering the language used to construct these themes. This process is similar to the one used earlier for structural narrative analysis and involves the following steps:

1 Read the transcripts.

2 Identify themes in the data.

3 Identify the language that is used to construct each theme.

4 Identify commonalities in the use of language in relation to each theme.

I took the first two of these steps in relation to the guidance tutor role and identified the following thematic findings:

- A number of respondents indicated that guidance tutoring was a heavy burden when considered alongside the other tasks that they needed to undertake.

- However, several commented that guidance tutoring was a rewarding task, which could facilitate more personal relationships with students.

- A number noted that guidance tutors needed to be aware of the appropriate boundaries to their role.

I will now show in detail how I carried out the distinctive third and fourth steps of the process, identifying words and phrases by which these themes were constructed and the commonalities that existed between respondents. I began by annotating the section of Lewis' transcript relating to guidance tutoring, marking key words and phrases that I considered to construct the themes of burden, reward and boundaries:

> I like guidance tutoring, I think it's an important part of err the job that we do. I think erm, it's difficult in this faculty because we have around *45 students* [BURDEN] each member of staff, and that's *too many*. [BURDEN] Umm it's too many, erm it's too many for them to be able to make appointments and to see you so some of the students do get to know you so, you, you it's hard to make contact, and it's too many to get to know people really well. So I know a small proportion of those students err, pretty well, and another proportion okay and some frankly I won't see from one year end to the next. So I think it's an important role, I'm committed to

being a guidance tutor – I mean I've been promoted but I don't want not to be a guidance tutor; I think I should still be a guidance tutor. I like doing that, *I like helping people with their problems* [REWARDING] err but I also think there's a limit to what guidance tutors do, err and we can help and advise *about academic issues* [BOUNDARIES] and so on but we also have to be very clear that sometimes *that's not our job* [BOUNDARIES]. You know, if students have *real emotional problems* [BOUNDARIES] or something then we have to refer them on, and I'm not sure we always do because *it's much easier to be sympathetic* [BOUNDARIES] and like, you know listen to a student but it might be *bad advice* [BOUNDARIES] and so on.

This exercise was then repeated for the other six lecturers and commonalities were sought in the manner in which the perception of burden, reward and boundaries were constructed. To take first the example of burden, there were three main methods of construction:

1   Stating an approximate number of students that each member of staff was required to be a guidance tutor to. This method was used by Lewis who, as noted above, said: 'we have around 45 students each member of staff and that's too many.' Susan made the same point with a slightly different figure: 'The most difficult part of it is having nearly 50 guidance tutees – that's phenomenal, managing that many is too many.'

2   Using words and phrases that did not involve a numerical estimate but still indicated very large quantities. Susan's use of 'phenomenal' in the quote above is one example of this. Rachel exaggerated by saying that some students needed to be seen 'hundreds of times' and Fern, when asked how much guidance tutoring she had to do, said 'gallons of it'.

3   Giving accounts that highlighted the difficulty of balancing guidance tutoring responsibilities with other parts of the jobs. Laura constructed the idea of burden by describing a problematic scenario in which the need to support a student was in conflict with the need to prepare teaching:

sometimes if they're passing and they see that you're there, even though you're kind of working and it's not necessarily a convenient time, if someone comes with a problem you do have to sort of fit them in. So it is sometimes a bit of a juggling act if you've got a lecture in fifteen minutes and someone comes with a really difficult thing that they need to talk about.

Susan also discussed a scenario, but reinforced the theme of burden by showing that the lack of time to see guidance tutees increased the length of her working day:

I find that I move my other commitments to do outside of work so my work–life balance goes because you can't tell your student 'oh I'll see you at eight o'clock tonight'. So you see your student during the day, so the writing of lectures will get moved. I'll do that at night to make sure that I can accommodate students during the day.

Notice how the choice of words by Susan emphasised the long hours that resulted from balancing guidance tutoring with other responsibilities: she discussed writing lectures 'at night' when she could have said 'in the evening'.

While Laura and Susan used familiar scenarios, Thomas provided a specific example of recent communication with students, where their wish to meet him for tutorials was impossible to fulfil immediately because of his teaching timetable:

> I don't think we have enough time, I think err, actually. I mean I've had three emails today; three emails this morning for students wanting academic tutorials and I can't because I'm teaching all day. I can only see them on Thursday, because tomorrow I'm teaching all morning and we have meetings all afternoon, so I can't see them on Wednesday either; I'll have to see them on Thursday.

So the use of discourse analysis demonstrated three methods by which the respondents sought to persuade the interviewer of the heavy burden that they faced in meeting their commitments to guidance tutoring alongside other elements of their work: using numbers, using words and phrases to indicate large quantities, and providing scenarios/anecdotes to demonstrate the difficulties of fitting guidance tutoring around other responsibilities. The storytelling element demonstrates again the similarities between discourse analysis and structural narrative analysis.

Exercise 9

This exercise focuses on identifying commonalities in the language used to construct the theme of guidance tutoring as a task where appropriate boundaries are required. The words and phrases that Lewis used to indicate the need for boundaries are presented again below, together with the comments of some of the other respondents in relation to guidance tutoring. Your first task is to identify the key words and phrases used by Rachel, Susan, Laura and Paula to construct the idea of a role that must have boundaries. You should then make a list of the common elements in the approaches of these five respondents.

> **Lewis:** We can help and advise *about academic issues* and so on but we also have to be very clear that sometimes *that's not our job*. You know, if students have *real emotional problems* or something then we have to refer them on, and I'm not sure we always do because *it's much easier to be sympathetic* and like, you know listen to a student but it might be *bad advice* and so on.

> **Rachel:** I think I know where now to draw the line and when you need to say to them 'you actually need to go and use some of the other facilities in the university'...

> **Laura:** It's sometimes challenging in that we're not trained as counsellors and there's a lot of – where do you draw the line and say to someone 'I think you should go to the university's sort of counselling service' kind of thing?

Because obviously you want to help people and you want to be able to do your best for them, but you know a lot of people's problems are kind of quite complex and there's often nothing you can do, except listen to them and sympathise with them, but you do sometimes feel you're getting quite difficult problems. It's quite a lot of responsibility as well if you've got someone telling you their life's falling apart or that they're having particular problems and you're – you feel certainly a degree of responsibility to help them and help them sort it out, but when do you say 'it's more than I can cope with?' But it is quite tricky sometimes.

Susan: I don't find it difficult; I find it concerning that I'm often put into situations where students have got significant problems and, although you can redirect them to other agencies within the university to support them, your contact with them is still crucial. So while you're trying to encourage them to get help and support somewhere else for example, what you say in that short, brief time can have quite significant connotations for them, so that can get difficult.

Paula: Sometimes it can be very rewarding – yes, yes you feel umm privileged sometimes with the information the students are telling you and sharing with you. Erm it can be a very difficult role, because we're not – I'm not – and we're not expected to be trained counsellors so we have to know when to refer on and yet we have to know when to, not to be too stand-offish and appear uncaring. We can't be too sympathetic or too empathetic so it – sometimes there is a fine line to be drawn and sometimes we're dealing with very disturbed, very vulnerable erm students. And it would be very easy to get out of your depth and I think it's a role that sometimes can be underestimated, but yes it can be very rewarding.

Please complete the exercise before looking at how I would have tackled it below.

While adding the usual qualification that there are no correct answers in qualitative data analysis, and that the outcome of your analysis could be just as valid as mine although it is different, I suggest that there were four methods by which the respondents sought to construct the role of guidance tutor as one that needed boundaries:

1 Using the metaphor of a line that should not be crossed. Rachel used this directly when she said: 'I think I know where now to draw the line'. Paula used the same metaphor but implied that it might be more difficult to determine where the line should be located when she discussed 'a fine line to be drawn'. Laura demonstrated that she was even less certain when she asked a rhetorical question: 'where do you draw the line ...?' However, while they differed as to their level of certainty about locating the line, the use of this metaphor was a method by which all three respondents constructed the idea that a boundary existed.

2 Emphasising the extent of problems that students might face. Paula described some students as being 'very disturbed, very vulnerable', Laura spoke of problems being 'quite complex' and 'difficult', Lewis discussed 'real emotional problems' on the part of students, while Susan spoke about 'significant' problems. All these words and phrases sought to construct the problems that could be faced by students as major ones: the use of the words 'very' and 'real' – which could have been excluded – emphasised the extent of the difficulties.

3 Emphasising the limitations of lecturers' expertise. Lewis made clear that guidance tutors provided support for 'academic issues' – clearly linking the role to the course that the student was studying – and stated that other forms of support were 'not our job'. Both Laura and Paula constructed the lecturer as being ill prepared for a counselling role by pointing to a lack of training in this area: Laura commented that 'we're not trained as counsellors', while Paula noted that lecturers were not expected to be 'trained counsellors' when she could have just said 'counsellors'.

4 Suggesting that there would be negative consequences if the appropriate boundary was not respected. Lewis argued that the outcome of failing to respect boundaries could be providing 'bad advice' to students and Paula discussed the danger that a lecturer could 'get out of their depth'. There was a less direct reference to this danger from Susan, who suggested that it was 'concerning' that lecturers were sometimes faced with such serious student problems, implying that they might unintentionally exacerbate the difficulties.

As a footnote, and going beyond the task that you were asked to complete for the exercise, it was clear that the lecturers were anxious not to present their need to keep to appropriate boundaries as a lack of concern for students. In four cases, they also used words and phrases that indicated their desire to be supportive:

• 'It's much easier to be sympathetic' (Lewis).
• 'Your contact with them is still crucial' (Susan).
• 'You want to help people and you want to be able to do your best for them' (Laura).
• 'We have to know when to, not to be too stand-offish and appear uncaring' (Paula).

So the discussion of boundaries was used by the respondents to construct themselves as people who wanted to help their guidance tutees but who were aware that they could cause damage if they tried to resolve complex needs in areas that they were not trained for.

It may become clear at this point that discourse analysis, like structural forms of narrative analysis, is unlikely to lead to practical recommendations. If such recommendations had been the required outcome, further thematic analysis could have examined questions such as what respondents found rewarding about guidance tutoring and how this element of the task could be developed further. Instead, the focus on the language used to construct the ideas of burden and boundaries, and the links to lecturers' perception of themselves as guidance tutors, meant that a contribution could be made to an understanding of the lecturers' perspective without pointing to actions to bring about practical change. The question of when social research should lead to recommendations is returned to in Chapter 10.

Computer assisted qualitative data analysis (CAQDAS)

It is not recommended that the researcher conducting qualitative data analysis for the first time should use specialist computer software. The reason for this is that grasping basic principles of analysis is a demanding task in itself, without adding a decision as to whether the use of such software will help or hinder the process. However, the widespread availability and use of programs mean that, as a researcher grows more experienced, they will need to decide at some point whether to use them and, if so, under what circumstances. This section aims to inform this decision by giving a brief overview of some of the arguments that have been advanced in favour of, and against, the use of specialist software.

Computers have long been established as critical to quantitative research because of their ability to handle large amounts of data and to perform complex statistical processes. No quantitative researcher would consider analysing a large dataset without using a statistical package such as Excel or SPSS/PASW. The value of computer packages for qualitative study is less easy to determine because so much depends on the interpretation of the researcher, rather than on the use of the widely accepted formulae used to calculate statistics such as chi-square.

Even when using written texts, CAQDAS may be of more obvious value to the quantitative than the qualitative researcher. Programs that can search for words or combinations of words, and count the number of times that they occur, can be particularly useful when undertaking content analysis. Programs in this category include widely used qualitative packages such as Atlas.ti and NVivo (Gibson and Brown, 2009: 179) but also programs created specifically for the purpose of counting such as the Linguistic Inventory and Word Count.

Gibson and Brown (2009: 176–177) make the important point that, even when computers are used, it is still the researcher who undertakes qualitative data analysis. Similarly, Blismas and Dainty (2003: 458) note that computers cannot replace the intuition and judgements of the researcher. However, the use of computers can have an impact on the management of data and even the direction that analysis takes.

Advantages of using CAQDAS

Advantages that have been suggested for the use of specialist software are that it is more efficient than analysing data manually, that it facilitates more complex forms of analysis and that it enables the researcher to think more clearly about the data. Computers undoubtedly have advantages in terms of efficiency, eliminating many physical tasks such as writing codes on transcripts and cutting and pasting chunks of text (Bryman, 2008: 565). An appropriate piece of software such as NVivo can enable a researcher to view all parts of a dataset very simply rather than hunting through large numbers of manually or electronically stored documents (Blismas, 2003: 458; Gibson and Brown, 2009: 178). Bazeley (2007: 3) notes that it is not just transcripts that NVivo and similar programs can store, but material such as published documents, rough notes and conceptual maps.

Specialist software is valued for its code and retrieve functions: the researcher can apply codes to text while working through transcripts and then retrieve these codes later (Bryman, 2008: 565). Bazeley (2007: 3–7) argues that computer programs can deal with more complex systems of coding than a researcher would otherwise be able to cope with, because of the efficiency with which codes can be retrieved. A computer can ensure that every example of a code or category is found, while other methods of working risk one or more being 'missed' due to human error.

Specialist software programs are capable of complex forms of analysis such as searching for negative cases, for example cases where two codes that are expected to appear together do not (Bazeley, 2007: 3). At the most advanced level, NVivo has functions that can assist with theory building by showing how codes are developing and the relationship that they have with each other (Gibson and Brown, 2009: 180–181).

Finally, Bryman (2008: 567) suggests that CAQDAS may help the researcher to improve their thinking about, and analysis of, their data. As NVivo and similar programs arrange codes in 'trees', the researcher may be encouraged to think about the connections between them. The use of software may also make it easier for a researcher to be reflexive, because there will be a record of how they analysed their data and it will be easier for them to see, for example, how representative a quotation is.

Disadvantages of using CAQDAS

The efficiency which is frequently suggested to be one of the advantages of using specialist software has also been argued to be a disadvantage. Bazeley (2007: 8–9) suggests that computer programs may be used out of convenience, when manual approaches would be more appropriate (Bazeley, 2007: 8–9). Similarly, efficiency may lead to inappropriate forms of analysis: the ease with which similar sections of transcript can be grouped together may encourage the researcher to concentrate on quantifying their findings, rather than considering the detail that is one of the hallmarks of qualitative research. Alternatively, the ease with which data can be separated and put back together may encourage the fragmentation of material and the viewing of sections of transcript outside their original context; segments may be removed from the whole, meaning a loss of perspective (Bryman, 2008: 566). However, criticisms of this nature have caused program designers to write software that facilitates closeness to the data: for example, by improving screen displays and enabling segments of text to be retrieved in their original context (Bazeley, 2007: 8).

More fundamentally, Blismas and Dainty (2003: 458) argue that computer packages limit the type of analysis that can be conducted because of their capabilities. For example, NVivo assumes that data will be analysed through the use of codes and that these codes will be analysed in a hierarchical manner. While a researcher could give themselves more flexibility by using more than one package, this would impact on the improved efficiency which is a key reason for using CAQDAS.

Specialist software may be unsuitable in some situations. One example is the analysis of focus group data, because of the importance of analysing interactions between respondents (discussed further in Chapter 8): such interactions may be 'lost' as data is moved around. In addition, researchers working in teams may find it difficult to adopt a co-ordinated and consistent approach to coding (Bryman, 2008: 567), a difficulty which the author is familiar with.

So these are some of the benefits and costs that have been argued to arise from the use of specialist software. Perhaps the best advice that can be offered to the researcher who is becoming more confident in applying the principles of qualitative data analysis is to experiment with the use of a program and to judge for themselves whether their work is enhanced.

Summary

This chapter has introduced a range of approaches to qualitative data analysis which differ from those that were demonstrated in Chapters 4–6. In some cases, these have been approaches which the new researcher may not feel confident using but should be aware of as part of the range of options that will be available as they become more experienced. Approaches that fall into this category are as diverse as critical discourse analysis and Computer Assisted Qualitative Data Analysis (CAQDAS).

In other cases, approaches have been suggested that provide a realistic alternative for the new researcher to the inductive, primarily thematic approach that was discussed in Chapters 4–6. Deductive or apriori codes are used when the researcher wishes data analysis to be driven by existing theory and literature in relation to their chosen subject area. Codes are selected that ensure that the researcher searches initially for themes that have already been established to be important. However, the researcher should be open to unexpected ideas emerging and will almost certainly have to adjust the list of codes in the light of themes that emerge from the data.

Narrative analysis can take many forms but the two that may be most feasible for a new researcher to use are thematic and structural narrative analysis. Thematic narrative analysis can follow the familiar pattern of comparing accounts, using codes and establishing themes. The distinctive nature of this type of analysis is that the data takes the form of one or more narratives, which can be whole life stories or accounts of matters as specific as organisational change.

Structural narrative analysis moves the focus to the method by which the speaker seeks to make their account persuasive through their choice of subject matter and language. It is an approach that highlights the subjective nature of narratives. Structural narrative analysis has much in common with discourse analysis, where the focus is on the construction of a particular depiction through the spoken or written language that is used to discuss it. In this chapter, structural narrative analysis and discourse analysis have both been demonstrated by first identifying themes and second examining the language that was used to construct them. Such an approach does not fit easily with some of the literature about the principles or practice of these two methods of data analysis, but seems the most practical option for a new researcher wishing to examine the role of language for the first time.

It is hoped that, at the end of this chapter, you are more aware of the range of options that the qualitative researcher can choose from when analysing interview data and more confident to use some of these approaches. Many of the methods can also be used when examining focus group material, but the analysis of this type of data has some unique features, which are considered in the next chapter.

Further reading

For reasons discussed above, this chapter includes no step-by-step guide to using CAQDAS packages. For examples of such guides, I recommend:

Edhlund, B. E. (2011) *NVivo Essentials: The Ultimate Help when You Work with Qualitative Analysis*. Stallarholmen: Form & Kunskap.

Or:

Friese, S. (2011) *Qualitative Data Analysis with ATLAS.ti*. London: Sage.

For more discussion of narrative analysis, discourse analysis and other approaches, I recommend:

Wertz, F. J., Charmaz, K., McMullen, L. M., Josselson, R., Anderson, R. and McSpadden, E. (2011) *Five Ways of Doing Qualitative Analysis*. New York: The Guilford Press.

A particularly helpful feature of this book is that it provides an example of the analysis of a complete life narrative using a range of approaches.

8

Analysing focus group data

Introduction

By the time you reach this stage of the book, you should feel more familiar and comfortable with some of the techniques that can be used to analyse qualitative interview data. This chapter will demonstrate where similar techniques can be applied, and where different skills are needed, in the analysis of focus group transcripts. The data used for examples will be a focus group of academic staff, which I facilitated, on the subject of teaching seminars. This focus group has been discussed in several previous chapters. It was introduced briefly in Chapter 1 with a discussion of the objective and of the participants, the reasons for choosing focus groups as a data collection technique were discussed in Chapter 2 and the skills needed to prepare for and moderate a focus group were covered in Chapter 3.

Where research involves data collection from more than one focus group, there is the opportunity to undertake an extended thematic analysis, looking for similarities and differences between the groups. However, as a starting point for the new researcher, this chapter will concentrate on the analysis of a single focus group.

One simple practical problem that is likely to occur more often with focus group data than individual interviews is that issues and themes may be returned to at different points of the discussion, meaning that it is more difficult to bring together all the relevant material for analysis. In addition, focus groups tend to take more time than interviews, so there will usually be a longer transcript to search for relevant material.

However, these are relatively straightforward practical difficulties to deal with. A more complex question is whether the analysis of focus groups should be fundamentally different from the analysis of individual interviews, to reflect the distinctive features of the data, particularly the interactions between respondents. This question has received little attention in the literature on focus groups (Duggleby, 2005: 834; Onwuegbuzie et al., 2009: 5).

Some of the suggestions that are made for analysing focus group data are similar to those for analysing interview data: Barbour (2007: 117–119) discusses the use of codes and Onwuegbuzie et al. (2009: 6–7) suggest the use of the constant comparative method where there is more than one group. Indeed, Wilkinson (2011: 169) argues that the distinctive methodological feature of focus group research is the data collection rather than the data analysis. However, a different view is advanced by Krueger (1998b: 20), who suggests that, in order to realise the full potential of focus group data, a distinctive method of analysis is required:

> There is danger in assuming that the focus group transcript should be analyzed in the same way as the transcript of an individual interview ... Focus group interviews produce data derived from a group process in a focused manner. As a result, participants influence each other, opinions change, and new insights emerge.

This chapter will take a middle course between these two opposing views, using some of the skills discussed in Chapters 4–7, but adapting them where necessary to take account of the unique features of focus groups.

Morgan (2010: 719) suggests that some analysis of focus group data emphasises questions of 'how' – i.e. analyses interactions between respondents – while in other cases the focus is on 'what', i.e. the subject matter of the discussion. Duggleby (2005: 835) makes a helpful distinction between the analysis of individual data (which is primarily concerned with 'what' is discussed), group data (again, concerned with 'what') and group interaction data (where the focus in on 'how' discussion takes place). In the sections that follow, each of these three forms of analysis will be discussed and demonstrated. There will then be consideration of whether the approaches can be brought together, i.e. whether 'how' something is discussed can help to enhance understanding of 'what' is said.

Individual data analysis

As was noted in Chapter 1, the term content analysis, when not being applied specifically to the analysis of documents, means working through the transcript systematically in order to determine how often certain themes are discussed and to consider what is said in relation to each theme (Dawson, 2009: 122–123). This form of analysis can be applied to transcripts of interviews and also to the contribution of one focus group respondent on a theme. The extra dimension that the group offers is that the strength with which a respondent holds a view may become clear if they are faced with alternative perspectives. While an interviewer would rarely directly present an opinion opposing that of the respondent, other members of the focus group may disagree with an individual, leading them to either defend or modify their position. Barbour (2007: 31) warns against viewing attitudes as fixed when reading focus group data because individuals may be persuaded in the course of discussion: the researcher should expect to find inconsistencies in some of the views expressed because these views develop as a result of interaction with others.

In seeking to identify the views, and the strength of views, of a focus group member in relation to an issue or theme, I suggest taking three steps:

1 Select the sections of the transcript where the respondent addressed the subject.

2 Read the comments in sequence, identifying the views expressed but also considering whether these views developed (hardened or modified) as the discussion progressed.

3 If the views appeared to develop, seek to identify the cause of the change by considering the context of each comment and, in particular, the contributions of other group members that may have been influential.

The example that I will use here concerns the views of a focus group member referred to as Amy about the process of student learning and whether it can be measured. An examination of the transcript showed that there were two occasions on which she mentioned this issue. The first followed an exchange quoted in Chapter 3, where I as the moderator sought other opinions after Evan had expressed a strong view:

> **Moderator**: ... so, going back to Kevin's question, how do we measure whether a seminar's worked?
>
> **Evan**: You can't.
>
> **Moderator**: Well, others might think that you can.
>
> **Evan**: Measurement was eighteenth-century thinking.
>
> **Amy**: I tend to agree: it's very difficult to determine how much students have learnt.

The second occasion, which involved two contributions from Amy, occurred after Kevin had spoken about trying to add value to students' previous learning through seminar work. He suggested that it was necessary to have an understanding of what students had learnt prior to a seminar in order to measure their learning during the seminar. There followed an exchange between Amy and Melissa:

> **Amy**: I'm not certain about the idea of adding value. Isn't a seminar just there to support the lecture material and to make sure that students engage with the ideas so that they reinforce their learning? Does it really matter where students have come from so long as the seminar supports the lecture?
>
> **Melissa**: I think I find out whether things have worked or not in tutorials for dissertations. Where you're not constantly telling them to do stuff; do, do, do. Be active, active, active. I just say, 'think, go away, wander around and think, just think about it, mull it over'. And it's then when they come back and you can actually have that intellectual dialogue which is quite challenging when you think, 'oh, yeah, they have got it from all of these units of study'. Do you know what I mean? So it's very difficult to grasp that as evidence isn't it? But I think that's where you think, 'oh, that's good, that worked'. You know that something is ...
>
> **Amy**: I suppose it is useful to see what changes students' way of thinking: I guess that's a way of measuring what types of teaching have worked.

The second stage of the process of individual data analysis was to examine the three comments that Amy made on this subject in sequence and to determine whether there was any change of perspective evident. Her first statement clearly indicated that she agreed with Evan that it is impossible to measure learning. Her second (at the start of the second extract) reinforced this point in a slightly less direct way: she questioned the idea of 'adding value' which, as Kevin had suggested, is clearly crucial to the idea of measurement. However, Amy's third comment appeared to indicate a change of thinking: she acknowledged some value in discovering which forms of teaching are effective, although the use of the phrases 'I suppose' and 'I guess' suggested that she was still doubtful.

So, having accepted that Amy had changed her way of thinking, albeit with some reservations, the third stage of the process was to consider the context of the comments made and to try to identify what had brought about the change. As the only person who spoke between Amy's second and third comments was Melissa, it was clear that it was her contribution that had made the difference: identifying the most influential comment would have been more difficult or even impossible if several people had spoken.

However, determining the specific words of Melissa that had influenced Amy was more difficult and involved a large element of interpretation. The best indication appeared to be that Amy interrupted Melissa shortly after she had used the word 'worked' and used the phrase 'what types of teaching have worked' in her own contribution. So changing the emphasis from students' learning to the effectiveness of lecturers' teaching appeared to be the factor that moved Amy towards accepting the value of trying to make measurements.

The finding arising from this analysis was that Amy doubted the feasibility or value of measurement when discussing students' learning, but appeared to be persuaded that it could be useful in assessing the effectiveness of methods of teaching. This finding was presented cautiously because of the large amount of interpretation that is often required when analysing interactions between respondents.

Group data analysis

This section will demonstrate how thematic analysis can be undertaken when considering focus group data at the level of the group. The process involves four steps:

1 Identifying which themes were discussed by which respondents through the use of codes.

2 Placing these codes into categories then considering whether the codes or categories need to be adjusted.

3 Where there is a code (or category of codes) attached to the comments of a sufficient number of respondents to make thematic analysis possible, bringing all the comments together.

4 Identifying commonalities and differences in the comments that were made.

When a similar coding process was discussed in relation to interviews in Chapter 5, it was suggested that categories could be identified by reading through the relevant sections of the transcripts, before any specific codes were created. This approach could also be taken with regard to focus groups, but would be more difficult because of the tendency of groups to move rapidly between, and often return to, different issues. The use of a three-column table where codes can be placed (see below) is often the first step by which the researcher begins to identify where different issues were discussed and which of the focus group members commented on them.

I will demonstrate how I used this process with two excerpts from the transcript of the lecturers' focus group, the first of which is shown below. At the start of the discussion, I asked an introductory question, requesting that the respondents described a type of seminar that they used with their students. These were the first few contributions that arose from this question:

Excerpt 1

Neil: Giving the students one particular reading in advance and three questions to think about in advance of the seminar. So the seminar is structured around those three questions at the beginning; it gives you a sense of who's done the reading and who hasn't. Ask them what they thought of it in general, how they approached any difficulties with it so you can then follow up on those difficulties and answer these questions. And then essentially structure the seminar around the questions which specifically refer to parts of the readings even in terms of page numbers so they can very clearly see how the seminar discussion relates to the particular reading. Then also make clear how the reading links to assessment questions that they may be doing. I quite like that sort of approach because it's very focused and structured and draws on their preparation but also they can see how that preparation is important not only for the seminar, but also the assessment. But of course the difficulty is, the classic one where some of them have read it, some of them haven't and those who have read it are supplementing the learning of others who are there to benefit from others and almost taking notes from other students as they're going along. But in general I do use that approach quite a lot.

Moderator: Any questions or comments? Shall we go on to Nick?

Nick: I suppose a different approach in contrast to Neil is one that I used with the first-year students focused around some photographs of people at work. I asked them to discuss what that depicts about work, how those photographs help them to understand work, critically analysing the depictions of work and using what they've done in the lectures to understand the photo graphs that they are looking at. A weakness of it is being really clear about learning outcomes and I'm not sure I always am frankly, and then we might get into a discussion around the picture itself or photography or something like that when what I'm trying to focus on is the nature of the work. So I think it's an issue about keeping people focused and keeping the learning outcomes to the forefront of my mind which I don't always do. It would be fair to say it's a weakness. But as a strength we got a good group discussion going, definitely.

Leanne: Could I just make a comment? It's interesting that you talk about learning outcomes and when I sat down and wrote about different kinds of seminar, I did question how often I think about learning outcomes. To be honest I think sometimes we're doing things in a hurry and we don't. I don't know if other people find that; whether they think 'this is what I'm going to achieve from this'.

Neil: I think a lot of them get two minutes thought beforehand; thinking that I would like students to come out of the session with two key things. And hope that they do, but whether that matches onto learning outcomes I'm not so sure.

In this short excerpt we can already see one of the distinctive features of focus groups and the richness of data arising from interactions: Neil did not explicitly refer to outcomes in his original comment, but added to his earlier answer when this factor was mentioned by Leanne, providing a fuller view of his approach.

In order to take the first step in analysing this data, i.e. identifying themes through codes, I used a three-column table (Table 8.1), slightly modified from the type suggested by Liamputtong (2011: 83), in which I summarised each contribution and used codes to identify factors that I thought might become themes:

Table 8.1   Codes for first excerpt from focus group on seminars

Respondent	Summary of comments	Codes
Neil	Gives students something to read and three questions to answer around the reading. Gives indication of who has read and who has not, but concerned that some students may benefit from others. Students shown how reading links to seminar questions and to assessment.	Requires reading Non-preparation, noting Fairness Links to assessment
Nick	Gives students photographs and asks them to critically analyse the depiction of work. Needs to keep learning outcomes in forefront of mind and can easily become sidetracked – a weakness. Can generate good discussions.	Provides materials Learning outcomes Discussion generated
Leanne	Sometimes prepares in a hurry. Doesn't always consider learning outcomes or what will be achieved by a seminar.	Time to plan Intended outcomes Learning outcomes
Neil	Thinks about outcomes briefly but not sure that they match learning outcomes.	Time to plan Intended outcomes Learning outcomes

Hopefully this table is self-explanatory, but please refer back to Chapter 5 if you would like a reminder of the process of creating and applying codes. Exercise 10 gives you the opportunity to create a similar table.

Exercise 10

Excerpt 2 shows a slightly later stage of the discussion, which began with Leanne outlining her method of seeking to ensure that students prepared for seminars. You are invited to complete a three-column table, similar to the one above, for this part of the discussion. (There is no need to include the question that Neil asked Leanne in the table.)

Excerpt 2

Leanne: What I did in the latter part of my second-year undergraduate unit was to set a particular piece of reading for students for each seminar. As they came in I actually had prepared a sheet which at the top said your name, your course and what you've read. And asked each of the students in turn to actually sign to say that they'd read something, to write out what it was they'd read. So I did set something and they could either read that or they could read something related to it from the reading list which was fine. Then I would set questions – similar to what Neil would do – and the feedback that I got around that was incredible. But I guess it's the keen students who are there – who are doing the reading, who are filling in the feedback forms – who just found that very helpful. I have to challenge myself; sometimes I think you can get into a bit of a negative mind set – 'students don't read' – well it's true that some of them don't, but I've been prompted in doing this by those who are reading and feel let down because we take the easy option. We take the easy option because we don't give them reading or we take the easy option because we try to keep the session going even when many have not read. So they've really enjoyed having a very structured kind of approach. And I think that notion that you must sign here, sign your name next to what you've read means that the students come prepared because I'm asking them to verify that they've done it.

Neil: What do you do with those that come and sign even if they haven't read?

Leanne: I think they don't come, but I haven't noticed numbers falling because I think the good students come anyway. I'm sure some of them pretend that they have read and they still sign and they look at what other people have read and they copy that down, but they may not do that the next time round because they'll know it's quite uncomfortable. I also say bring it with you. And they bring it with them and have highlighted it and can say, 'oh right, well let's have a look then'.

Neil: Yes, because in terms of referring to particular parts of it, page numbers you know, look at this, this is how this illustrates this and they've got it in front of them. But I think one of the things I find with that is it works much better with smaller groups; if you've got 15 or 20 it can be very difficult to have that structured approach where you watch everybody and whether they're participating or not.

Ian: Again, just to add, I would say the participation level is quite different: for instance first-year students tend not to come to seminars prepared but second years tend to come very well prepared and they are all very much engaged. So I think the first year is where the challenges lie.

Leanne: I think that Ian's made an important point because it's setting the culture – I think it's about a culture of engaging. It might be reading or it might be contributing or it might be just being involved; it should start from induction. How we quite do that is another matter but I do think it's about establishing a culture from the early stages.

Please complete the exercise before looking at how I would have tackled it below.

As usual, it should be noted that my response to this exercise is not the 'correct' one, but you might find it helpful to compare your table to Table 8.2:

Table 8.2   Codes for second excerpt from focus group on seminars

Respondent	Summary of comments	Codes
Leanne	Requires students to sign to say that they had read. Enthusiastic students appreciate this. Not fair to enthusiastic students to assume that no one will read. Requiring signature encourages students to read.	Non-preparation, taking action against Fairness Not having negative expectations
Leanne	Weaker students either do not attend or pretend to have read (but uncomfortable and may read next time).	Non-preparation, taking action against Non-preparation, impact on attendance
Neil	Difficult to check that larger numbers have read.	Non-preparation, taking action against
Ian	Second-year students more likely to prepare than first-year students. Need to take action in first year.	Differences between students at different levels Non-preparation, taking action against
Leanne	Need to create culture of preparation among first-year students.	Student culture

The second step of the suggested process of analysis involves putting the codes into categories and then considering whether any adjustments should be made. This step could be taken once a three-column table has been drawn up for every part of the transcript but, given the length of focus group discussions, it is probably advisable to begin the process of categorisation at an earlier stage. It is clearly advantageous to identify as soon as possible where codes should be merged, split or otherwise adjusted.

Looking for categories in which to place codes involves a search for commonalities. These can sometimes be easy to see: it should be obvious from Tables 8.1 and 8.2 that a number of codes could be put together in a category with the heading 'Non-preparation for seminars'. In other cases, the researcher may need to read through the codes and sections of the transcript several times and think more conceptually. For example, when I read Extract 1 and Extract 2 again, although none of the respondents used the word 'purpose', some thinking suggested that the purpose of seminars was a concept that underlay a number of codes, i.e.

Links to assessment (coded against comment of Neil)

Learning outcomes (Nick, Leanne, Neil)

Intended outcomes (Neil, Leanne)

So a 'Purpose of seminars' category was introduced. Once a category has been created and the codes to go into it are listed, more conceptual thinking is then needed to determine whether there should be any adjustments made to the codes: for example whether any should be merged or sub-divided. In the above example, I gave some thought to the possibility of merging 'learning outcomes' and 'intended outcomes' into one 'outcomes' code. I eventually decided that these two codes should remain separate because learning outcomes are quite closely linked to assessment in the literature on teaching and learning (see for example, Kuh and Ewell, 2010), but the lecturer may intend to achieve outcomes that cannot be directly assessed.

The third and fourth stages of the suggested process of analysis – bringing together the comments to which a code has been applied and looking for similarities and differences between them – would often be left until the entire transcript had been coded. However, for illustrative purposes, I will show how I reached initial findings about learning outcomes based on the early part of the transcript of the lecturers' focus group.

Bringing together the comments to which a code is applied is a routine task, albeit one that must be carried out carefully because of the likelihood of some issues arising at several different stages of the focus group discussion. Clearly, comments that have the same code applied to them will have some similarities but the researcher should also consider whether there are differences. Excerpt 1 included three comments that the learning outcomes code was applied to in Table 8.1:

- Nick said that he was concerned that he was not always clear about the intended learning outcomes of his seminars.

- Leanne similarly feared that she did not give enough attention to learning outcomes.

- Neil said he thought briefly about what students should get from seminars, but was not sure whether his intended outcomes could be considered to be learning outcomes.

These comments were marked by their similarities: all three implied that learning outcomes should be set for seminars, but doubted whether they were clear as to what these learning outcomes were. However, examination of the section of the transcript between Excerpt 1 and Excerpt 2 showed that the comments of three other respondents about learning outcomes contained an important difference. Kevin, Ian and Melissa not only suggested that it was appropriate to have learning outcomes for seminars but also that they made the nature of these learning outcomes clear. For example, Ian said:

> … it's about giving an introduction and telling them [*students*] what we have done, what we've been doing and where we are trying to get to and linking their activities to learning outcomes.

So, in examining the six comments about learning outcomes, one notable difference emerged. Three respondents were confident that they made clear the learning outcomes for their seminars, while three were not. However, of course there was also one key commonality: underlying the comments of all six respondents was an assumption that it was desirable for seminars to have learning outcomes. This result demonstrates that the use of codes can be effective in drawing findings from focus group data. The three-column table is a particularly helpful tool when beginning the analysis.

Avoiding reaching findings that lack validity

Before considering the third form of analysis of focus group data, group interaction data analysis, it is appropriate to pause to consider validity: a concept that was introduced in Chapter 1 and which becomes particularly important when considering the accuracy of research findings, as will be discussed in Chapter 9. There are two specific threats to validity that apply more to focus groups than to data collected through other methods: taking comments out of context and assuming incorrectly that there is a consensus.

As the interaction between focus members is one of the distinctive features of this form of data collection, the danger of misinterpreting comments when they are read out of context is even greater than is the case for interviews. However, the simple remedy is to read through the relevant sections of the transcript to ensure that the interpretation that has been placed on contributions is consistent with the discussion that they were part of. I used this method to check the validity of the findings relating to learning outcomes that were discussed in the last section. Careful reading of Excerpt 1 – to examine the comments of Nick, Leanne and Neil in context – confirmed that it was reasonable to interpret their contributions as meaning that they thought it appropriate to set learning outcomes for seminars, but were not always clear as to what these learning outcomes were.

A more substantial difficulty, specific to findings about commonality in focus groups, is establishing when there is a consensus. Barbour (2007: 130) warns against assuming too easily that agreement has been reached by the group and suggests that some discussions do not reach any sort of consensus. The factor that makes it particularly difficult to establish when there is a consensus is that there are likely to be several areas where not every focus group member makes a comment, in contrast to semi-structured interviews, where the use of an interview guide can ensure that every respondent is asked about a specific issue. The focus group moderator would destroy the 'flow' of the discussion if they sought to ensure that every respondent expressed an opinion on every subject.

It can be impossible for the researcher to establish whether lack of comment indicates that a focus group member agreed with the prevailing view, that they disagreed but did not want to enter into a debate or that they did not have an opinion (or at least not a strong one). Using again the example of the focus group about seminars, three members of the group – Yvette, Amy and Evan – made no comment in the early stages of the discussion about learning outcomes, which could have led me to assume that they agreed with the apparent consensus that it was appropriate to have learning outcomes for seminars. However, the issue arose again later in the discussion and Evan expressed the view that being too specific about learning outcomes could fragment the learning process. So to make an assumption that there is unanimous agreement on an issue where not every focus group member has contributed would clearly be a mistake.

One method of dealing with the difficulty of establishing the extent of agreement, suggested by Onwuegbuzie et al. (2009: 8), is to record the number of focus group members who express support for a point of view, the number who state their disagreement and the number whose view cannot be determined. This ensures that a comprehensive record is kept, which does not make inaccurate assumptions.

Group interaction data analysis

Returning to Morgan's (2010: 719) distinction between the 'what' and the 'how' of focus group data analysis, analysing interaction between group members tends to focus on 'how' issues are discussed. The manner in which focus group members interact with each other, in particular how they try to persuade others of their point of view where there is an element of disagreement, can say much about their relationships.

Morgan (2010: 718) notes that conversation analysis and discourse analysis have dominated the study of interaction in focus groups. The use of discourse analysis for interview data was demonstrated in Chapter 7, but a slightly different process can be used for focus groups. A key factor here is relationships within the group, so it is helpful to make interactions the focus of analysis. However, a focus group discussion should be interactive from start to finish, so an important practical question is which part of the transcript to consider first. My suggestion is that there is most to gain by identifying and examining areas of disagreement because there are so many different ways in which this can be expressed.

One possible process for using discourse analysis to examine disagreements between focus group members, in order to arrive at findings about the nature of group relationships, involves the following steps:

1 Reading the transcript carefully and identifying an area of disagreement.

2 Looking at the language used to construct the disagreement and what it infers about relationships.

3 Making comparisons with other areas of disagreement to assess the validity of the initial findings.

These three steps are discussed and demonstrated below.

Step 1: reading the transcript carefully to identify an area of disagreement

Identifying an area of disagreement is easier when respondents speak to each other in a simple and direct manner. If someone uses a phrase such as 'I disagree' or 'I think you're wrong', this is an obvious section of the transcript to select for study. However, there are many less direct methods of expressing disagreement, for example by using phrases such as 'Another perspective on the issue is ...' or 'I think it's also important to remember that ...'. Indeed, studies have been made of the manner in which opposing points of view are expressed in different cultures (e.g. Cordella, 1996; Edstrom, 2004). The researcher must be sensitive to the local context in order to identify less obvious methods by which disagreement may be expressed. When they have identified an exchange that they think reflects disagreement, they should seek to confirm this by examining other parts of the transcript to establish whether the respondents involved had differing points of view.

This advice is perhaps best illustrated with reference to an example from the focus group discussion on seminars. One area where I decided that there was some level of disagreement was Leanne's approach of requiring students to sign to say which reading they had undertaken in preparation for a seminar, which was discussed in Excerpt 2. In response to a question from Neil as to how to deal with students who might sign even though they had not read any material, Leanne said:

> … I'm sure some of them pretend that they have read and they still sign and they look at what other people have read and they copy that down, but they may not do that the next time round because they'll know it's quite uncomfortable. I also say bring it with you. And they bring it with them and have highlighted it and can say, 'oh right, well let's have a look then'.

Neil's response was to say:

> Yes, because in terms of referring to particular parts of it, page numbers you know, look at this, this is how this illustrates this and they've got it in front of them. But I think one of the things I find with that is it works much better with smaller groups; if you've got 15 or 20 it can be very difficult to have that structured approach where you watch everybody and whether they're participating or not.

Careful reading suggested to me that Neil was questioning the effectiveness of Leanne's method when dealing with larger groups; the phrase 'very difficult' was the one that alerted me to an element of disagreement. I looked for supporting evidence for this interpretation by reading contributions from Neil elsewhere in the transcript and noted that, in his first comment in Excerpt 1, he said that his approach to seminars 'gives a sense of who's done the reading and who hasn't', which implied that this was all that he wanted, rather than asking students to provide evidence by signing a piece of paper. So I was confident that I had identified an area of disagreement for further analysis.

Step 2: looking at the language used to construct the disagreement and what it infers about relationships

The second stage of the process is linked to the first. If focus group members use very blunt language to express disagreement, then not only are these disagreements easy to identify, but the language used also says something about the relationships between the respondents. However, it is important not to reach unjustified findings: respondents who make their disagreement with each other very obvious may feel hostility towards each other but, alternatively, may trust each other not to interpret disagreement as personal dislike.

Similarly, using cautious language when disagreeing could indicate that respondents are considering each other's feelings, which is usually an indication of positive relationships, but could also indicate something negative such as fear of causing upset. The types of devices that a respondent might use to disagree in a cautious manner include:

- Indicating specifically which part of another respondent's perspective is disagreed with and emphasising the areas of agreement.
- Acknowledging that, although they disagree with another respondent's perspective, both views are reasonable and one is not inherently more valuable than the other.

- Avoiding the use of personal pronouns such as 'I' or 'you' and choosing phrases such as: 'There seems to be more evidence to support a view that ...'

Again, the disagreement between Neil and Leanne is used as an example. My analysis of the language that Neil used to construct his response to Leanne suggested that he was eager not to make his point too bluntly and was showing consideration for her feelings. Four elements of his contribution (which was quoted above) pointed me towards this finding:

1 Neil demonstrated that he understood the nature of Leanne's approach. By specifying 'page numbers' he indicated how it could be checked that a student had undertaken reading.

2 He emphasised the subjective nature of his view by saying 'I find', which highlighted the differing nature of the experience of individuals, rather than suggesting that Leanne was simply incorrect.

3 He stated where he felt that an approach like Leanne's could be effective, i.e. working with smaller seminar groups.

4 He then highlighted the specific situation where he felt that Leanne's approach would be ineffective, using numbers to emphasise the size of the group concerned, i.e. 15 or 20.

Step 3: making comparisons with other areas of disagreement to assess the validity of the initial findings

The danger of making assumptions about a consensus was noted earlier in the chapter. Similarly, it should not be assumed that one, or a small number of, disagreements gives a comprehensive picture of the nature of relationships within a focus group. The researcher should examine as many disagreements as possible, ideally all of them, in order to develop a full picture. Even then, they should consider whether there are respondents who have not been involved in disagreements and avoid assuming that they fit any pattern that has been observed among other focus group members.

The exchange discussed above between Neil and Leanne could have been generalised inappropriately and an assumption made that this was a group where consensus was valued, with members being very cautious about the manner in which they expressed disagreement. However, when Melissa advocated making explicit the skills to be developed through seminars, Evan was very blunt in his disagreement, saying: 'I'm suspicious of that, I'll be quite unequivocal about it, I'm suspicious about it.' Further examination of the transcript was necessary to determine the frequency with which Neil's method of disagreement, Evan's method or other methods were employed and consideration given to how much could be inferred about the nature of the relationships within the group as a result.

So study of group interactions within a focus group, particularly where there are areas of disagreement, may demonstrate a complex and varied pattern of relationships. As with the forms of discourse analysis that were discussed in Chapter 7, there may be questions about the usefulness of analysis of this kind. It is clearly very important if the main purpose of the research is to examine the nature of relationships between group members but its value is less obvious when the focus in on the subject matter of the discussion – in this case, opinions about seminars. Two points can be made in response to concerns of this nature. The first is that findings about interactions may inform other forms of analysis. In particular, the extent to which respondents are willing to openly disagree with each other is highly relevant when assessing whether a consensus can be assumed. If respondents have tried to avoid highlighting disagreement, this magnifies concerns that those who have not spoken on a subject may have a differing view from the majority. Second, the analysis of the nature of interaction may contribute to the analysis of the subject matter, as will be demonstrated in the next section.

Combining analysis of the 'how' and the 'what'

As a new researcher, you may feel that analysing the strength of individuals' views, looking for commonalities and differences between respondents through a thematic analysis, and inferring something about the nature of the group through the manner in which members interact are sufficiently challenging tasks when dealing with focus group data for the first time. However, it is sometimes possible to take this analysis a stage further by considering how the nature of the interaction between the group members can contribute to understanding the subject matter of the discussion.

Morgan (2010: 719) suggests that, if one topic produces longer contributions than another, there is every reason to consider why these two subjects produce such different responses. The length of contributions in different areas of discussion is an obvious starting point for analysis that combines consideration of 'what' is discussed with 'how' it is discussed. I will demonstrate how I identified an area where there were particularly long contributions, then looked for an explanation by examining the content of what was said, the context and the language used. An experienced researcher may begin by looking for different types of language in different parts of the transcript, but length of contributions is an easier place to start.

Close to the midpoint of the focus group about seminars, discussion returned to a topic that was mentioned in Excerpt 2, i.e. the appropriate expectations of students at different stages of study. There were some comments about the type of material that students could be expected to read in the first year, with Yvette saying: 'If they don't read, they're not going to be able to write.' I noted that this comment was followed by three long contributions. Melissa, Eric and Leanne all described seminars that they had delivered in which students were not required to read academic material such as journal articles in advance (although, as was discussed earlier, Leanne had also discussed other seminars where students were required to indicate that they had read). Sections of these three accounts are presented below:

> **Melissa**: ... Ian and I gave first-year students sections of key landmarks in relation to policy and said right, pick one of those and do a Google search. It's really quick and they may go beyond that and do a more academic search around it and find more literature. So what most have is very basic factual information from a quick Google search and then at least that's some way into the subject area where they can begin to swap examples of different policies. But then you always encourage them 'Yes, you've done that but did you go any further?' ...

> **Eric**: ... In the first year, particularly during the courses that I've run for a number of years, instead of giving students reading, I have produced comprehensive handouts. I have given them to students and just asked them to construct the discussion around what they see as the important points ... but in the third year what I try to do is offer them two alternative views, two pieces of reading and try to get them thinking about different viewpoints on a particular topic. And it's trying to move them on. And I have to be honest, there's problems with every approach; there isn't one right way to do things.

> **Leanne**: ... A seminar that I think works well at the beginning of a unit of study rather than later on in it was one that I used as my first seminar on my second year unit. So we hadn't got onto any particular content; we had barely started the lectures. I asked them to come into the seminar room unprepared and I gave them a sheet of A4 paper and said, 'You're each in the next 15 minutes going to draw what society looks like'. And they were slightly taken aback but they all did it and after that they all had to stick their drawing to the wall. And then each student in turn had to talk about what theoretical position their drawing represented. It was quite a nice seminar because it allowed them to talk about their engagement with theory as they could best remember it. I wouldn't have done it at the end of the unit ...

In considering the reasons for the length of these contributions, discourse analysis again proved helpful. The three respondents may have spoken at some length about their own seminars simply to provide examples that others could follow. However, a careful look at the language used suggested that a more likely explanation was that they felt a need to justify an approach that did not involve reading academic material in preparation for the seminar. The main reason for this interpretation was that each speaker used a phrase to suggest that their approach was only an interim measure and that the aim was to move students towards more challenging forms of learning:

> **Melissa**: 'You've done that but did you go any further?'
>
> **Eric**: 'It's trying to move them on.'
>
> **Leanne**: 'I wouldn't have done it at the end of the unit.'

The nature of these comments pointed to a tentative finding of a group norm that reading academic material should be required in preparation for seminars and that deviation from this norm needed to be justified. As usual when using discourse analysis, this may seem like a particularly subjective explanation. However, in addition to the immediate context – Yvette's comment about the importance of reading – further examination of the full focus group transcript provided other reasons for suggesting that the three respondents felt some need to justify their approach:

- At the start of the discussion (see Excerpt 1), Neil provided the first example of a seminar and used one where students were required to read academic material in preparation. This may have set the terms for the contributions that followed.

- In contrast to the comments highlighted above, Evan felt no need to justify requiring students to read academic material before a seminar, saying later in the discussion: 'Well I do require reading. That's it. I won't budge on that.'

- Eric's final comment quoted above – 'there's problems with everyone; there isn't one right way to do things' – appeared to be arguing for a plurality of approaches and rejecting an assumed norm of best practice.

So here was an example where the nature of the interaction did not say so much about relationships between group members, but instead pointed towards a finding about one of the key themes discussed, i.e. that requiring students to read academic material in advance appeared to be an assumed norm for seminars.

Summary

The distinctive features of focus group data have caused some to argue that specific methods of data analysis are required, while others have suggested that the methods used with individual interviews can also be effective in the case of focus groups. This chapter has taken a middle path between these two approaches, using many techniques that are similar to those used to analyse interview data, but adapting and developing them to take advantage of the unique opportunities that focus groups present.

Helpful distinctions are made in the literature between the analysis of individual data and group data, both of which are concerned with 'what' is discussed, and the analysis of group interaction data, where the focus is on 'how' it is discussed. If these forms of analysis can be combined, so that the 'how' sheds light on the 'what', then the richness of focus group data can be exploited to the full.

When considering individual data, the interactive nature of focus groups sometimes makes it possible to determine not only what a respondent's opinion is, but also how strongly this opinion is held. If a respondent speaks several times on one issue, it is possible to bring together all their comments and to establish whether there are changes in their view as the discussion progresses. If there is a change, identifying possible causes, i.e. the contributions of other focus group members, can give a fuller picture than might be provided in an individual interview.

The analysis of group data can involve many techniques that are also used with individual interviews, such as making summaries of contributions, using codes to reveal themes and identifying similarities and differences between respondents. However, the identification of similarities may present particular problems because it is unlikely that every respondent will comment on every issue. There are often major risks in assuming a consensus, because it may be that some group members are unwilling to express a view different from that of the majority. Thorough reporting, including identification of the numbers not expressing an opinion on a subject, reduces the likelihood of presenting misleading findings.

Examining group interactions is likely to require the use of conversation analysis or discourse analysis and may be particularly revealing in the case of disagreements between respondents. Where areas of disagreement are identified, the words and phrases with which opposing views are expressed may say something about the nature of the relationships between focus group members. However, it is important to examine disagreements across the full transcript because the nature of relationships will, of course, vary between individuals.

Combining the 'how' and the 'what' by considering whether the form of contributions says anything about the subject matter is the most challenging aspect of focus group data analysis, in addition to being potentially the most rewarding. It is an area where it is difficult to provide guidance but an obvious starting point is to look for the length of contributions in relation to particular issues. Discourse analysis techniques may then be helpful in establishing why contributions on a particular subject are either shorter or longer than the norm; the outcome may represent an important finding in relation to the topic under discussion.

Whatever the method(s) of analysis used for focus group data, it is important to check the validity of any findings, usually by examining the full context of contributions. Methods of checking validity will be discussed further in the next chapter, together with some of the unique features of writing about focus group data.

Further reading

The two sources that discuss in greatest detail the question of how to analyse focus group data, and which I have found particularly helpful, are:

Duggleby, W. (2005) 'What about focus group interaction data?' *Qualitative Health Research,* 15: 832–840 and

Morgan, D. L. (2010) 'Reconsidering the role of interaction in analyzing and reporting focus group data', *Qualitative Health Research*, 20: 718–722.

For a broader discussion of the use of focus groups and the data that they provide, I suggest reading:

Barbour, R. (2007) *Doing Focus Groups*. London: Sage.

or

Liamputtong, P. (2011) *Focus Group Methodology*. London: Sage.

9

Writing about research (1) – methodology and findings

Introduction

Chapters 4–8 demonstrated the process of moving from transcripts of interviews and focus groups to research findings. The next, crucial stage is to communicate these findings to the people who will be reading your work. Gibson and Brown (2009: 194) provide the following helpful definition of writing about research:

> Writing, more generally defined, is a means of thinking through one's ideas, of trying to set different formulations into a workable form that does justice to one's data.

The exact format of research output depends on the type of document that is being produced. However, all forms of output are likely to include the following sections:

1 Discussion of the existing literature on similar subjects to the research.
2 Discussion of the methodology and methods used in the research. (This is usually referred to as the methodology section, although it also includes discussion of the methods – see Chapter 2 for a discussion of this distinction.)
3 Discussion of the research findings (sometimes referred to as the results).
4 A conclusion showing how the existing literature contributes to understanding the findings and vice versa.

The space devoted to each of these sections will vary considerably between different forms of output. Some of the most frequently used forms are:

- Research reports for the workplace, professional bodies, pressure groups or other organisations. Here the emphasis is usually on the research findings so the existing literature tends to be referred to only briefly, with a similarly short methodology section and the majority of the space devoted to discussion of the data. The conclusion then concentrates on the implications of the findings for policy and/or practice.
- Undergraduate dissertations: for the undergraduate, the literature is likely to form the majority of the content of the dissertation and will usually be divided into two or three chapters. The methodology and findings sections can either be a chapter each or combined into one chapter. The conclusion should then demonstrate the implications of the findings for the issues discussed in the literature chapters.
- Master's dissertations are likely to include more substantial discussions of both the existing literature and the research findings than undergraduate dissertations. The methodology usually forms a separate chapter and the findings may be divided into two chapters.

For a doctoral thesis, the research findings are likely to be the major part of the output and to be divided into several chapters. The literature search will also be much more substantial than in undergraduate or Master's dissertations and should cover a very wide range of sources. The methodology section is particularly important to a thesis, as methodology and methods are likely to be key areas of assessment of the work. The conclusion must not only tie together literature and research findings, but also include a substantial reflection on the impact of the chosen methodology and demonstrate how the thesis makes an original contribution to knowledge.

The section of the output on the existing literature and the conclusion will be discussed in Chapter 10. This chapter considers the methodology section and the presentation of the research findings. However, before writing either of these sections, the researcher should check the validity of their findings.

Checking validity

The concept of validity was introduced in Chapter 1 and reflects the extent to which the findings accurately reflect the data (Jupp, 2006a: 311). Some specific issues about the validity of focus group data were considered in Chapter 8, but the measures discussed here are useful when considering either interview or focus group data. They are necessary because in a data analysis process that involves many stages – such as reading transcripts, producing codes, identifying themes and reaching findings – it is possible that the views expressed by respondents can become unintentionally distorted. Patton (2002: 457) argues that data should be allowed to 'tell their own story', but it has been noted on several occasions in previous chapters that decisions made by qualitative researchers during data analysis are often subjective; such decisions affect the findings that are eventually communicated to the reader.

There are a number of measures that you, as a qualitative researcher, can take to ensure that the written account of the findings accurately represents your data:

1 Read the findings and then read back through the transcripts. This is a good and simple method of checking that the story you are telling through your findings accurately reflects what was said by the respondents. Can the patterns that you believe you have found be seen when you look back at the original data? If not, you will need to re-consider your analysis or parts of it.

2 A further step is to check whether the respondents are satisfied with the findings, as recommended by Miles and Huberman (1994: 275–277) and Steinke (2004: 185). There are difficulties associated with this step – for example, respondents may disagree with each other about the accuracy of the analysis – but it can provide an indication of whether you have unintentionally misrepresented the views that were expressed.

3 Silverman (2006: 47) argues that the validity of conclusions drawn by qualitative researchers are sometimes doubted when they have made no attempt to deal with findings that do not fit the patterns that they believe they have identified. Similarly, Miles and Huberman (1994: 271–275) suggest that the researcher should actively look for findings that do not fit with their chosen explanation and consider whether rival explanations may in fact be more accurate. It is useful to consider a hypothetical situation: if someone was seeking to discredit your findings and suggest alternative interpretations of the data,

how much evidence would there be that their interpretations were correct and that yours were wrong?

4 Triangulation means checking the findings against the results produced by another method (Bryman, 2008: 379). So, at the simplest level, if your main data collection was through semi-structured interviews, you could then conduct a focus group or distribute some questionnaires to a similar group of respondents. If this alternative method of data collection yielded similar results, you would be much more confident that your findings were accurate. The time and resources available for a research study often make triangulation difficult or impossible, but this should be acknowledged in the methodology section as a factor that could influence the validity of the findings.

5 A friend or colleague who is familiar with the subject matter of the research could be asked to read the transcripts and the findings, then to comment on whether the findings are justified. This may raise issues about confidentiality and certainly requires a very supportive friend or colleague. However, it can also be an extremely valuable measure: justifying findings to someone else can act as a very effective safeguard against any bias that you may have unintentionally introduced.

6 Alternatively (or additionally), you could find someone who does not know much about the subject, then tell them about the data and the findings, to get a detached view as to how well the two fit together. Again, another person's view – even that of someone who is not familiar with the subject area – can provide protection against bias.

7 You can exercise reflexivity, which is an important attribute of the effective qualitative researcher and one which is closely linked to questions of validity. It is discussed in the next section.

Reflexivity

The concept of reflexivity is another one that was introduced briefly in Chapter 1. In recent decades, there has been a movement towards social scientists discussing their own role in collecting and analysing data and producing findings, in acknowledgement that their decisions are likely to have an impact on the outcome (Fontana and Frey, 2008: 140–141). Steinke (2004: 186–187) suggests that a comprehensive and very detailed account of decisions made during the research process is required to ensure that the quality of the researcher's work can be assessed by others. So researchers should be reflexive not only in order that they can assess the validity of their findings and conclusions themselves, but also so that someone reading their research output can do the same. The methodology section is the one where key decisions, and the reasons for making them, should be discussed.

The effective reflexive researcher records key decisions as they are made. While I have not followed specifically the advice of Gibson and Brown (2009: 195) to keep a research diary, in previous chapters I have provided methodological memos at some points and noted at others that such memos could have been written. For example, in Chapter 4 a methodological memo was used to explain the exclusion of a small number of issues from the summary of the interview with a lecturer given the pseudonym of Fern. In Chapter 6 it was suggested that a methodological memo could have been used to explain why a single sub-category was created for codes about students not attending teaching sessions because of employment commitments, rather than having two separate sub-categories – one for codes suggesting that students were responsible for this clash of commitments and one for codes suggesting that they were not. A good methodology section for a Master's dissertation or PhD thesis should discuss decisions such as these, and the reasons for making them, to enable the reader to decide whether the findings of the research should be considered to be valid.

The methodology section

The process of data analysis is an important topic to discuss in the methodology section of any research output. Where space allows – typically in a Master's dissertation or PhD thesis – this section should cover the approach to looking for themes and patterns in the data, methods of interpreting the data and how the findings were reached (Boeije, 2010: 194).

However, the methodology section should also include discussion of all the stages of the research process. In each case, there should be a description of the actions taken, identification of the most important decisions and the reasons for taking them and the researcher's assessment of the shortcomings of the methodology. The steps discussed, in addition to the data analysis, should include:

- The decision as to whether to conduct the research using an inductive or a deductive approach. If the research was primarily deductive, the research question or questions to be addressed, or the hypothesis to be tested, should be identified; if there was a primarily inductive approach taken, or an approach that fell somewhere between the two, the objectives of the research should be discussed.

- The decision to use qualitative methods rather than quantitative ones. This decision could be made on philosophical grounds (for example, it was necessary to understand the perspective of those involved), practical grounds (for example, data could only be collected from a small number of respondents) or both. Where mixed methods have been used, this decision should also be justified – typically by suggesting that such an approach draws on strengths of both quantitative and qualitative methods.

- The chosen research design should be described and it should be demonstrated why this design was considered appropriate. In the case of deductive studies, it should be shown how the design addressed the research question(s) or facilitated the testing of a hypothesis. An inductive approach often involves a flexible research design, but there should still be discussion of major decisions about the direction of the research, why these were taken and how they contributed to meeting the research objectives.

- The choice of data collection method(s) and the reasons for choosing it/them should be identified. For example, focus groups may have been chosen rather than semi-structured interviews because the researcher wanted to examine shared understandings within the group. Depending on the number of words available for the methodology section, further details that might be added are the nature of the topic guide, the time period for the interviews or focus group discussion(s) and their mean duration (Boeije, 2010: 195).

- If a theoretical sampling approach was taken, there should be discussion of the types of criteria that were used to select sample members and a demonstration that these arose from analysis of the early data. In the case of other methods of selecting respondents, it should clearly be stated whether the people or other units (e.g. newspapers) who/which data was collected from formed a population or a sample. If a sample was chosen, there should be a discussion of, and justification for, the choice of sampling method (for examples see Chapter 2).

- The most important ethical issues that affected the research should be discussed. The researcher should demonstrate that these issues influenced the planning and conduct of the research: for example, enough information was provided to participants to ensure that all consent was informed.

It will now be demonstrated how this advice about writing the methodology section could be put into practice in the case of the interview research at the case study university that was discussed in Chapters 3–7 of this book. Space only allows the demonstration of the type of methodology section that might be appropriate for a research report or an undergraduate dissertation. Substantially more discussion would be required if working at postgraduate or doctoral level: for example, there would be consideration of the extent to which the inductive approach used had characteristics of grounded theory, and advantages and disadvantages of using semi-structured interviews for the study would be considered in detail. There would also be reflections on the decisions that were made the subject of methodological memos and how these might have affected the outcomes of the research.

Example of a methodology section

The research took a largely inductive approach because the researcher was committed to examining the data without the constraints imposed by needing to test theory; this meant that data was analysed before considering its relationship to existing knowledge in the subject area (Moses and Knutsen, 2007: 22). However, the researcher's experience of working in higher education, and his awareness of current debates in this area, were reflected in the research objectives that were set for the study, i.e.:

1 to identify the motivation of lecturers for their choice of career;

2 to identify feelings about, and practical difficulties associated with, different elements of the job;

3 to discuss different types of students and the experience of teaching them;

4 to identify feelings about reflective practice and methods by which it was put into practice; and

5 to discuss changes with time in relation to the above factors.

The choice of a qualitative methodology was theoretically and practically driven: there was a commitment to seek to understand the perspective of those being studied (Bryman, 1988: 61–63) and there were also only small numbers of respondents available to take part in the research, making the collection of quantitative data impossible. The research design was a case study, which was a decision made largely on pragmatic grounds of the lack of resources to collect data across a range of institutions. As Yin (2003: 13) notes, the context is crucial to case study research; it is important to note that the research was conducted in the Faculty of Social Sciences of a single former polytechnic based in the United Kingdom, in an era where student numbers were stable after a rapid expansion in the 1980s and 1990s. The findings are intended, therefore, to make a small contribution to theory rather than to be generalised to other institutions that may be operating in very different circumstances.

Interviews were an appropriate method of data collection because some of the research objectives required the examination of personal narratives (Hennink et al., 2011: 110), both of the processes by which respondents entered higher education and the changes that they had observed while employed in the sector. The interviews were semi-structured to ensure that some areas were covered in every interview: for example, the mechanisms by which respondents undertook reflective practice and their motivation for doing so. The interviews usually took approximately 40 minutes to complete.

A major weakness of the research was that the respondents were selected by a convenience sample. This approach was taken out of necessity because there were a limited number of lecturers who were available and willing to give up their time to be interviewed during the short period of data collection. Indeed, only seven could be interviewed, despite the number working in the Faculty of Social Sciences being considerably larger. It would have been preferable to have used purposive sampling, choosing those members of the faculty who had the most experience of working there and were best able to reflect on changes with time.

The approach taken to analysing the data was primarily thematic, as there was a concern to identify commonalities and differences in the experiences and views of the respondents.

The major ethical factor to be considered was confidentiality. As the intention was to use the data both for a research project and a methods textbook, substantial amounts of information about the respondents and the views that they expressed was to be published, so it was important that they were aware that it might not be possible to conceal their identity. All signed a declaration indicating that they were willing for identifying information to appear in the output, satisfying the principle of informed consent. As an extra safeguard, respondents were sent copies of the proposed book chapters and asked if there was anything that they wanted to be changed before publication.

Writing about qualitative findings

When considering the section of the research output that deals with the findings, it is important to remember that there is no 'correct' way of writing about them that is better than all others (Richards, 2009: 195). The key requirement is that the findings section accurately represents the views, ideas and experiences of the respondents. The research objectives should influence decisions about the issues and themes that are given most emphasis in the discussion of the findings.

In Chapters 5 and 6, thematic findings from interviews at the case study university were identified using bullet points, for example:

- All respondents agreed that reflective practice was important.
- A small number of respondents discussed incorporating student feedback into their reflective practice.

The choice of words to express trends – for example, 'all' and 'a small number'– were discussed in Chapter 5. However, while identifying trends within the data is important, if qualitative researchers were only to do this then their findings would be similar to those of quantitative studies, but with smaller numbers of respondents. Instead the interest of the qualitative researcher in perspectives and the individual should be reflected in the research output. Broader trends can often be effectively illustrated by using individual examples and direct quotations.

Using individual examples

Individual examples can show how a theme is manifested in the case of one respondent. They are different from case studies, which are an approach to a whole research project, as was discussed in Chapter 2. The extent of information provided in any example can vary considerably: sometimes it can involve giving a brief account of all or part of a respondent's life; in other cases there can be a detailed description of a respondent's point of view. There are a number of reasons why research output might include detailed information about an individual or their perspective:

1 To illustrate or explain an element of the researcher's discussion of the findings. For example, Aburabia-Queder (2011) writes about the experiences of women from the Palestinian-Bedouin minority in Israel who left their home villages and studied in higher education institutions in different parts of Israel. She argues that it was important

to the women to be accepted by their fellow students. The nature of this acceptance is shown by discussing the experiences of a number of individuals, including a student given the pseudonym of Tamara, who told her friends about the importance of Bedouin gender norms and religion. As a result, her friends respected these values and did not kiss her when they greeted her, also warning others who were to meet her against using a kiss in greeting (Aburabia-Queder, 2011: 191–192).

2   To emphasise an argument advanced by the researcher. Pells (2011: 599–600) supports her argument that a siege mentality exists in post-genocide Rwanda by using the case of Sylvie. Sylvie's one-year-old nephew died suddenly during the night and, while there was no evidence to corroborate the claim, she and her family believed that the baby had been poisoned – poisoning being thought to be the favoured method of murder in the village.

3   To present contrasting experiences or perspectives. Gordon et al. (2010: 968–970) discuss different approaches to dealing with diversity among university educators in Australia, using examples to illustrate each one. One type of approach, which they refer to as compensating students, is exemplified by exploring the views of an educator given the pseudonym of Joanne, who felt that students with disabilities or health difficulties faced extra difficulties in learning. She gave these students extra time to complete work and provided them with additional support. This is contrasted to an approach that focused on utilising the diversity within the student group, illustrated by discussing the perspective of a teacher trainer referred to as Meg. Meg felt that it was important to show student teachers how diversity could become a tool to enhance teaching so asked bilingual students to take the role of 'experts' in a discussion of the needs of students who did not have English as their first language.

Using quotations

Morgan (2010: 718) makes the case for including quotations in the reporting of qualitative data:

> … quotations provide valuable evidence for the credibility of the analysis, because they generate a direct link between the more abstract contents of the result and the actual data; in addition, they are also the strongest connection between the reader and the voices of the original participants.

Most qualitative studies make use of direct quotations from respondents; important decisions have to be reached about where to include quotations and which ones to choose. This is something that many students find difficult; a common mistake is to write about findings using too many quotations that are held loosely together by a very brief commentary on the part of the writer. Quotations should be interspersed with the researcher's own discussion of the findings.

There is no set length for an effective quotation. The researcher should use as few words as possible: sometimes a word or phrase is sufficient, but on other occasions a quite substantial section of text is needed to convey meaning effectively. The researcher should always be clear in their own mind why a quotation is being included in the discussion of the findings. There are a number of possible reasons, some of which are similar to reasons for discussing individual cases:

- The researcher may not be able to effectively re-phrase or summarise what was said. Keogh and Wang (2010: 15), discussing the benefits that students saw to the use of clickers enabling them to vote on quiz questions put to them during a lecture, find it simpler to quote some of the students than to find different words to record the points that were made:

  > The student group commented that beginning the clickers portion of the class 'allows a moment of transition', 'breaks up the class' and provides a 'chance to focus, to think about and apply the information' under discussion.

- A point may need explaining. Goddard and Myers (2011: 560) describe the method by which a school for excluded young people in the USA used dispute resolution to overcome arguments. To explain what is meant by dispute resolution, an educator from the school is quoted:

  > 'We tell the students that you need to sit down and tell the person that committed the crime or did harm to the community what it is they did wrong and how you feel about it. We go through hard dialogue ...'

- One or more quotations may illustrate particularly effectively a point that is being made. Martel et al. (2011: 243) discuss the programmes provided to Aboriginal offenders in Canadian prisons to encourage them to stop offending by reminding them of their cultural heritage. The hostility of Aboriginal staff to the involvement of non-Aboriginal people in delivering such programmes is illustrated with a quotation:

  > 'It's non Natives giving programmes on how to be a Native ... showing us how to be a Native. How would they understand these concepts?'

- Contrasts between respondents may be effectively highlighted. Kramer (2011: 385), examining the interest of some people in their genealogy, argues that some of her respondents did not feel this interest required any explanation and quotes one who said: 'I've had an instant connection with anyone I've met that shares my bloodline.' She uses a further quotation to contrast this position with that of other respondents who felt that they needed to explain their interest: 'We inherit our looks, our behavioural patterns, diseases, our strengths and our weaknesses. We are the sum of those who went before.'

Boeije (2010: 201) suggests that the following points should be regarded as good practice when using quotations:

- Do not use a quotation more than once, even when it illustrates several points.
- Illustrate a point using no more than one or two quotations.
- Add an indicator for quotations such as the site where it was taken from, a pseudonym and/or an indicator of relevant information such as gender or age. However, no indicator should be used that threatens the anonymity of respondents, if this has been promised.

One danger of using quotations is that the researcher will simply choose those that best support their arguments (Silverman, 2007: 61) or reflect their initial expectations (Schmidt, 2004: 255). Another danger is that the researcher will misrepresent a respondent's views through a quotation. Consider this section of the interview with the lecturer referred to as Fern at the case study university:

> **Interviewer**: Since you began the job, how have your expectations and hopes changed?

> **Fern:** Not a bit. I've always enjoyed doing the job; I suppose there is more bureaucracy and we have more students. So it is a different job than it was when I started, just because of mass higher education, it's changed. So I suppose from that point of view it's a bit less satisfying; there's a difference between marking 40 essays and marking 150. Marking 40, you can just about maintain your enthusiasm for it, but I think with fairly high numbers it can be quite difficult.

This could be reported in the following manner:

> Fern said that the job had changed for the worse: '... there is more bureaucracy and we have more students ... it's a bit less satisfying, there's a difference between marking 40 essays and marking 150. Marking 40, you can just about maintain your enthusiasm for it ...'

However, this would obviously be misleading. Fern clearly stated that she still enjoyed the job, although it had become more difficult in some ways, but this quotation ignores the overall positive nature of her response and makes Fern sound dissatisfied with her role. The manner in which the researcher selects and presents quotations involves subjective judgements, but a key principle is that they represent the findings as fairly and accurately as possible. The choice of quotations should be checked for validity in the same manner as other elements of the discussion of the research findings.

Presenting focus group data

While much of the advice given above can be applied to focus groups as much as to interviews, it is important that the reporting of focus group data also reflects the interactions that are the unique feature of this form of data collection. The issue of how to record the extent of any apparent consensus was discussed in Chapter 8. Another key question is how to use quotations in a manner that captures the nature of interactions. Morgan (2010: 719–721) notes that some authors writing about focus groups suggest that it is essential to quote full exchanges rather than individual responses. However, he then suggests that this approach is, in many cases, inefficient and that a quotation from a focus group can be either introduced or followed by a summary of other relevant contributions. If Morgan's advice were followed, findings from the focus group discussed in Chapter 8 could be presented in the following forms:

> Ian warned against assuming that students who made limited verbal contributions to seminars were not learning, saying: 'in seminars I have found that even those

who are quiet have done well with their assessment.' Three other respondents reinforced the point that there should not be an expectation for every student to make a substantial contribution to seminar discussions.

Kevin advocated the introduction of an interactive element in all forms of teaching but agreed when Melissa suggested that this was more difficult when teaching larger groups: '… it's obviously more challenging with 300 than it is with 50.'

Writing about qualitative findings – example 1: student employment

There now follow two examples of writing about qualitative findings: the first takes the form of a demonstration of how I wrote about data; the second sets you an exercise. The analysis of interview data conducted in Chapter 6 identified the conceptual theme of responsibility for students' learning, which appeared to underlie discussion of issues such as attendance and preparation for seminars. Through use of a coding process, a contrast was demonstrated between those respondents who tended to hold students responsible for their learning and those who were more inclined to locate responsibility with academic staff or with other factors. This concept of responsibility also underpinned discussion of students missing teaching sessions due to employment. The codes that were produced in relation to employment are shown below, together with the respondents to whom they applied:

Reason for non-attendance – employment: Fern, Rachel, Paula, Thomas

Students who miss teaching because of jobs have wrong priorities: Paula

Students need to have jobs: Thomas

Students can work long hours in jobs: Thomas

From these codes, the findings that were noted in Chapter 6 were:

- A number of respondents identified employment as a factor that prevented students from attending teaching sessions.
- There were different opinions as to whether students should be blamed for missing teaching sessions due to employment.

Before writing a paragraph about these findings for my research output, I noted that the only two respondents to have commented in any detail on the issue of employment were Thomas and Paula. So I read again the relevant passages from their interview transcripts:

There is a problem of attendance and I think it's getting worse but I don't think it's necessarily the students' fault. Given the funding situation, I don't know many students who don't work as well … The general opinion is that students at this university are full time students doing part time jobs, I think for many of them it's the other way round. (Thomas)

… attendance isn't fantastic and at some point it definitely tails off. Some students have good reasons; others get their priorities a little bit mixed up, maybe due to financial reasons they end up prioritising their job over and above their studies and there comes a point where you have to ask them to re-consider. (Paula)

I then wrote the following paragraph for the research output:

A number of respondents identified employment as a factor that prevented students from attending teaching sessions, although there were differing views as to how far students should be held responsible for this. Thomas noted that most students had a job and spoke sympathetically about those who had to work long hours, suggesting that this was a result of 'the funding situation'. However, Paula argued that students gave priority to employment when they 'get their priorities a bit mixed up', often as a result of financial difficulties.

In this paragraph, some small but significant additions have been made to the bullet pointed findings. The first is that, after identifying that several respondents discussed employment, the end of the first sentence makes the connection to the broader theme of responsibility, demonstrating that this paragraph is linked to other findings. Second, the views of Thomas and Paula are developed as individual examples, to present contrasting perspectives. Finally, the two very short quotations were chosen to highlight the contrast further: the phrase 'the funding situation' (used by Thomas) clearly located responsibility away from the student and pointed to a situation beyond their control, while the phrase 'get their priorities a bit mixed up' (used by Paula) indicated that difficulties were a result of choices made by the student, for which they should be held responsible. However, this second quotation also makes clear the gentle nature of Paula's criticism, as she chose to say 'a bit mixed up' rather than 'wrong'.

Writing about qualitative findings – example 2: motivation for reflective practice

This exercise refers to the issue of motivation for undertaking reflective practice, which was discussed in Chapter 5 and where the trends identified were:

- Most respondents identified stronger internal than external pressure to undertake reflective practice.
- Some expressed surprise at the lack of external pressure to be reflective.
- All identified motivation that was associated with personal satisfaction and the quality of the job that they did.
- Some also discussed motivation associated with the experience of students.

Space does not allow the inclusion of the comments of all seven respondents in relation to motivation, but the relevant sections of some of the transcripts are shown below:

Interviewer: And how important to you is reflecting on your own practice?

Fern: Oh I've always been interested in student feedback. I always want to know how it's gone and I don't like if I feel I haven't been on top form or I haven't explained things right: that really annoys me. So I do think, I do feel it over in my mind what I've done and how I've done; how I've answered questions and that kind of thing. I think I do it almost all the time, I don't think 'another lecture over, on with the next'; I always want to feel it's gone well and if it hasn't gone well then why hasn't it gone well? And so if I'm understanding what reflective practice actually does, then it's my natural condition.

Interviewer: And what is your motivation to be reflective of your practice?

Fern: Pride.

Interviewer: Pride?

Fern: Yes I want to do a good job; I would not wish to produce poor research or produce poor teaching.

Interviewer: So what would you say your motivation to be reflective of your practice was? Would you say internal?

Lewis: It's driven internally by wanting to be good at what I do. And thinking that I should be good at what I do. But lecturing is communicating effectively with students. So what should also drive me is if I've failed to communicate something. That's usually very clear from students' puzzled looks or students coming up to me afterwards and saying, 'I don't understand that.' And that's not a student's responsibility; it's my responsibility. If I'm not communicating effectively that's not their problem, it's my problem, so I need to change. So it's really important.

Interviewer: What motivates you to do reflective practice? Is it internal or external?

Thomas: It's internal, absolutely internal. This might sound silly but when I started work someone taught me if you're going to do something then you should do it the best you can. And I've tried to live by that, even in a work situation.

Interviewer: Would you say there is any pressure from the university to be reflective?

Thomas: No. That's what I find strange. We have timetables so we've got to be in rooms at particular times but what we do in those rooms nobody checks up on. Nobody listens to my lectures; nobody asks to see my PowerPoint slides. We're given the autonomy to do this. The oversight is on how many lectures we have to do, what do we publish, where do we publish: those things are quantifiable but the quality of our delivery is never tested. The only oversight is we have this system of peer review where one of our colleagues will sit in on a lecture or a seminar. It's supposed to be done every year but I've never done it for two years, it just never happens – we're too busy, we just don't do it.

Exercise 11

Based on the bullet points and the sections of the transcript provided above, consider how you would write up the findings in relation to motivations for reflective practice. Use individual examples and quotations where appropriate.

Please complete the exercise before looking at how I would have tackled it below.

My discussion of the findings is shown in the next two paragraphs:

Most respondents identified stronger internal than external pressure to undertake reflective practice. Indeed, some commented specifically on the lack of external pressure to reflect. Thomas said that he found it 'strange' that there was so little pressure; he identified only one formal mechanism of reflective practice: a system of peer observation that he had not put into practice for two years. He contrasted the oversight of lecturers' writing and publishing with the lack of external pressure on them to improve their teaching.

All respondents discussed internal motivation associated with a desire for personal satisfaction with the quality of the job that they did. For example, Fern used the word 'pride' and expressed the need to feel that teaching sessions had gone well, while Thomas said that he had always wanted to do the best job that he could in any work situation. Lewis discussed the desire to be good at his job but was also one of a small number of respondents who identified motivation associated directly with students. He thought that he should reflect as to whether he had communicated effectively with students: 'But lecturing is communicating, that's what it is, and it's communicating effectively with students. So what should also drive me is if I've failed to communicate something.'

This is another exercise where there is a large subjective element, so you should not be concerned if the material that you have written is quite different from mine; I would suggest simply comparing the decisions that were taken to arrive at the two accounts. My first decision was not to elaborate on the first bullet point, that respondents identified more internal than external pressure to reflect, because both internal pressure and the lack of external pressure were discussed in more detail in relation to further points. Thomas' comments were used as an example to illustrate the perceived lack of external pressure and to show why some respondents found this surprising. The word 'strange' was quoted because it appeared to summarise his feelings particularly effectively.

Personal motivation to be good at the job could be illustrated quickly by using all three respondents as examples: the brief information given demonstrated the similar types of comments that were made on this subject. It was particularly important to indicate that Lewis was thinking about students rather than himself when he talked about the motivation to communicate clearly, to support the interpretation that his focus was not just on personal satisfaction (an interpretation discussed further in Chapter 5). The first sentence chosen for the quotation made students the focus and the second emphasised that the needs of students provided Lewis with motivation.

Summary

This chapter has discussed two sections that are likely to be included in any form of research output: the methodology and the results/findings section. Validity should be a major concern when writing both these sections: the researcher should be satisfied that the findings fairly reflect the data and, by including as much information as possible about key decisions, enable the reader to make a judgement on this matter. The account of what was done and why should be included in a methodology section that covers every part of the research process, including data analysis.

The findings section of a piece of qualitative research output should discuss the trends in the data, illustrated by individual cases and quotations. The researcher should have clear reasons for the inclusion of these cases and quotations and should check that the chosen material reflects the data fairly. Among the reasons for discussing individual cases are that they illustrate or explain particularly effectively an element of the researcher's discussion, that they provide emphasis to part of the researcher's argument or that they give contrasting examples of views or experiences. All of these could also be reasons for choosing material to quote; an additional reason for using a quotation is that there is no effective method of re-phrasing the words of a respondent.

The two sections commonly included in research output that are not covered in this chapter are those that deal with the existing literature and the links between the literature and the research findings. These sections will be discussed in Chapter 10.

Further reading

There is a helpful section on writing about qualitative data (including mistakes to avoid) in Richards, L. (2009) *Handling Qualitative Data*, 2nd edn. London: Sage (1st edn, 2005).

For a discussion that incorporates issues of structure and style, but also practical questions such as finding the best time of day at which to write, see Henn, M., Weinstein, M. and Foard, N. (2009) *A Critical Introduction to Social Research*, 2nd edn. London: Sage (1st edn, 2006).

For a more advanced discussion, suitable for a student writing a Master's dissertation or a thesis, I recommend Halliday, A. (2007) *Doing and Writing Qualitative Research*, 2nd edn. London: Sage (1st edn, 2002).

10

Writing about research (2) – making links to the literature

Introduction

Most forms of research output include a discussion of the existing literature, a section on methodology, a discussion of the research findings and a conclusion. Chapter 9 dealt with methodology and findings; this chapter will consider the section dealing with the literature and the conclusion. These parts of the output are important because the researcher must demonstrate how their own findings contribute to what is already known about their chosen topic.

It should be noted that there are occasions when literature can be cited in the findings section, if there is a very clear and specific link between a particular finding and previous published work. For example, Sheard (2011) undertook research into women's participation in the night-time economy, their consumption of alcohol and their fear of violence. When discussing her own findings about concerns over substances being added to drinks, she makes a brief reference to a previous study where women suggested that this risk could be reduced by drinking quickly:

> ...some women would consume their drink in one go or considerably faster than they would ordinarily have chosen to do rather than leaving their drink unattended .... This issue is reported in Burgess et al. (2009) whereby a participant had heard from friends that it was recommended to drink 'as fast as possible' ...

(Sheard, 2011: 628)

However, more substantial links between the existing literature and the researcher's own study are usually demonstrated by writing a section on the relevant literature early in the research output and then, in the conclusion, demonstrating the contribution that the researcher's own findings make to this literature. This is a skill that many students find difficult to learn. Dissertations are frequently submitted that include a good account of the existing literature and a good discussion of the research findings, but do not make effective links between these two elements of the output.

Charmaz (2006: 165) suggests a role for the literature when using an approach to research called grounded theory (see Chapter 2):

> The literature review and theoretical framework can serve as valuable sources of comparison and analysis. Through comparing other scholars' evidence and ideas with your grounded theory, you may show where and how their ideas illuminate your theoretical categories and how your theory extends, transcends, or challenges dominant ideas in your field.

The key principle here is important, regardless of whether a grounded theory approach has been taken or whether the researcher's findings can be described as theory. For the researcher to demonstrate that the findings that that they have produced are useful, they must show how their work contributes to the ideas that are discussed in the existing literature.

This chapter will demonstrate how literature can be selected and written about in a manner that makes clear the relevance and importance of the researcher's own findings. It will then show how a conclusion can make the links with the literature specific, demonstrating the contribution that the researcher's findings make to key discussions and debates. I will provide a brief example of a literature search and conclusion that I wrote in relation to some data that was analysed in Chapter 6, then invite you to do the same for material that was discussed in Chapter 5.

The literature review

Silverman (2006: 340) suggests that a literature review should serve two purposes:

- To demonstrate that the research is building on the topics, methods and theories frequently used in the subject discipline.
- To demonstrate that the research is building on previous studies.

The purposes of a literature review are described in more detail by Henn et al. (2009: 281), who suggest that it should address the following questions:

- What research has been carried out which is relevant to my own study?
- What were the main conclusions to be drawn from the previous research?
- What were the methods employed by previous research?
- In which ways (conclusions and methods) are previous studies similar?
- In which ways (conclusions and methods) are previous studies different?
- Where are there gaps in knowledge?

The focus on the methods used in previous studies is most appropriate at postgraduate level: the literature search sections of undergraduate dissertations or research reports are likely to be concerned mainly with the findings of earlier studies. However, the above questions are helpful when considering the purpose of the literature search section.

There are many useful guides to searching literature including practical questions such as the types of research engine that are available (see, for example, Lester and Lester, 2006; Johnson et al., 2010). This chapter is not concerned with the process of searching but with the next stage of selecting the most appropriate sources and discussing them in a manner that demonstrates the importance of the researcher's own findings.

Finding an appropriate theoretical background

It is always necessary to consider the relationship between the researcher's own findings and previous studies. For most forms of output, with the exception of research reports, the findings should also be located in a body of theory. Finding the most appropriate theoretical background in which to locate their own study is more likely to be problematic for the inductive than the deductive researcher. As was noted in Chapter 2, the deductive researcher tends to begin by examining the existing literature before designing a study to fit with this literature, so the appropriate background is selected at an early stage. In its purest form, a deductive approach involves finding an appropriate theory to test, an approach that Glaser and Strauss (1967: 10) criticise because it limits the scope of the enquiry.

However, the greater freedom experienced by the inductive researcher must be balanced against the difficult decisions they may face as to how to locate their findings or microtheory in a broader theoretical context. (Microtheory, as was noted in Chapter 6, is the simplest level of theory and uses concepts to identify common aspects of phenomena.) In some cases, the body of theory in which to place a study is fairly obvious. For example, microtheory produced by Mok et al. (2010), about the impact of technology on the distance over which people maintain interpersonal contact, fitted clearly into a broader theoretical framework of 'glocalisation', i.e. people having close relationships that go beyond the local neighbourhood. However, in other cases, the inductive researcher may face one of two difficulties in seeking to find an appropriate theoretical background in which to locate their research: choosing between existing theories (if there are many with links to the subject of the research) or 'borrowing' a theoretical background (if there are no theories with obvious links to the topic).

To take an example where there are several linked theories, a researcher collecting data from people who stole possessions from unlocked cars might build some microtheory about the reasons for these crimes being committed. They might then look at a Criminology textbook and find an almost bewildering range of broader theories which could form the context for discussing this microtheory. For example, Newburn (2007) discusses the following theories and concepts that may help to understand why crime is committed:

- Classicism
- Biological positivism
- Psychological positivism
- Anomie and stain theory
- Cultural and subcultural theory
- Labelling theory
- Control theories
- Radical and critical criminology
- Realist criminology
- Contemporary classicism
- Feminist criminology
- Late modernity, governmentality and risk

It would be an impossible task for the researcher to compare their microtheory to all of these broader theories, so they would need to select those that seemed to have the clearest links, i.e. those that are most concerned with opportunist crime. The chosen theories would probably be:

- Routine activities theory (part of the contemporary classicism approach) which argues that an increase in crime is due to an increased number of targets for crime with fewer people to guard these targets (Newburn, 2007: 286–287).
- Control theories which examine why some people resist the urge to commit crimes while others do not (Newburn, 2007: 228–242).

In other cases, a researcher may be faced with the opposite problem, i.e. there is no body of theory that obviously fits with their findings or microtheory. This is a difficulty that I faced when writing my PhD thesis, where I had collected data about the circumstances in which a young person (16–17 years old) could successfully live independently in their own property. A search of the literature revealed that there was very little written about independent living among this age group, meaning that there was no obvious body of theory in which my findings could be located. So instead I had to use theories as to why young people became homeless and adapt them to apply to the question of why some fail in independent living. The four theories or explanations for youth homelessness that I chose were:

- Explanations that blame the young person's deviant behaviour for their homelessness.
- Explanations that blame the young person's family for their homelessness.
- Explanations that blame the young person's immaturity for their homelessness.
- Explanations that blame structural factors such as poverty and shortages of housing.

One of the most striking findings to emerge from my data was that the young people who expected to experience difficulties living in their own property, and those who were warned about these difficulties, seemed more likely to be successful than those who were unrealistic and expected living independently to be easy. I therefore concluded that explanations based on immaturity, although originally applied to the question of why young people became homeless, were also helpful in explaining why some lived successfully in their own accommodation while others did not (Harding, 2001). So my findings in relation to independent living were located within a body of theory that had originally been used to explain youth homelessness.

Some practical advice on writing about literature

In addition to the broader theoretical background, any literature search section must make reference to existing research findings in the area of study (Rudestam and Newton, 2007: 62). There are a number of practical pieces of advice that are likely to be useful in making the best use of the existing published material.

The beginning of the literature search should demonstrate the importance of the researcher's findings

Rudestam and Newton (2007: 62), writing specifically about undergraduate dissertations, suggest the following role for the chapter on the existing literature:

> This chapter of the dissertation provides a context for the proposed study and demonstrates why it is important and timely.

The standard of importance that a piece of research must satisfy varies according to the type of output being produced. While research at doctoral level needs to demonstrate that the findings make an original contribution to knowledge, students at undergraduate level do not need to make such a large claim for their work. It may be that their study is similar to one or more that have been conducted previously, so it can either add support to, or question, the findings from the previous research. Alternatively, the undergraduate student may take a subject that has been examined at a national or international level and provide a local perspective. For example, opinion polls in the UK have consistently suggested that a majority of the public support the restoration of the death penalty for certain crimes, but is this view reproduced among a group of social science undergraduates at one university?

The importance of the study should be established as early as possible in the literature search section. Research in the social sciences can be important for a large number of reasons, three of which are discussed below:

1 It can contribute to long running academic and/or theoretical discussions. For example, Valentova and Zhelyazkova (2011: 92) cite a number of authors to show that there has been a substantial debate as to whether the post-socialist states of Eastern Europe have followed individual social policy directions or whether they share commonalities and so should be considered a welfare state model. This sets the context for their comparative study of the consequences for women in East European countries of interrupting their careers to care for children.

2 It may help to explain or illuminate current social phenomena. Khan and Jarvenpaa (2010: 137) note the importance of Facebook as a means of organising social events in order to demonstrate the relevance of their own study, which analyses the types of social group behaviour that takes place on Facebook's events pages and walls:

> People are increasingly using social networking technologies such as Facebook.com and Evite.com to organise physical gatherings within social groups (Booher et al., 2007; Golder et al., 2007 ; Joinson, 2008) ... Despite popular use, little is known about how social groups use social networking technologies for social event coordination.

3 There may be a social issue that is of particular importance or is likely to be of growing importance in the future. For example, Wang et al. (2010: 79) demonstrate the value of their study of the living costs of older people with disabilities in Northern China by citing research showing the growth of the older population:

At the end of 2008, the number of older people reached 160 million, 12 per cent of the total population (BNS, 2009). It is predicted that the number will reach 200 million in 2014, 14 per cent of the total Chinese population (CWCA, 2007).

Detailed discussion should concentrate on the most relevant previous research

In the same way that, for most forms of output, the researcher should choose the most appropriate theoretical context in which to locate their findings, they should also select the most relevant previous research findings to cite and quote in their literature section. This may mean disregarding substantial numbers of studies if examining an area where there has been much previous research. The selection should be driven by the need to demonstrate the importance of the researcher's findings.

To take an example, Skovdal and Andreouli (2010) undertook research about children who adopted caring responsibilities in Western Kenya. They examined the manner in which social recognition of the children's role affected their response to their circumstances, with a particular focus on their resilience and sense of identity. The article written about the study begins with a discussion of previous research into the lives of African children which showed that:

- children in Africa play an active role in the household and this is part of their socialisation;
- children who give care in Africa tend to experience problems such as disruption of schooling, loss of friends and isolation;
- a minority of care-giving children in Africa suffer from mental health problems;
- there can be benefits to children of caring such as developing new skills, becoming more mature and developing the relationship with the person that they care for; and
- the ability of children who give care in Africa to cope with their situation is influenced by the extent to which they can participate in community life and access support.

So the literature search section demonstrates the physical and cultural context, what is known about advantages and disadvantages to children of being care-givers and the role that the community can play in making the experience easier or more difficult. It therefore shows how the researcher's own work extends this existing knowledge by examining the idea that it was not just physical support to the children that was important but also the status that the community could give them by recognising their role.

Of course, selecting the most relevant previous work for discussion will, by definition, mean deciding not to discuss other published material or to make only a passing reference to it. Berg (2009: 388–389) notes the danger of the researcher failing to make reference to classic works or recent studies that are of relevance to their subject. However, Silverman (2006: 341) argues that it is important to focus only on those studies that are relevant to the researcher's own research problem. Similarly, Rudestam and Newton (2007: 65) argue that, no matter how important an author or their research, it must only be discussed in proportion to its relevance to the topic under study. It is crucial that the literature search section concentrates on the most relevant existing work and does not become involved in a detailed discussion of areas that are not central to the researcher's own topic.

Where the researcher wishes to indicate that they are aware of literature, but does not want to discuss it in any detail, there is an academic skill to referring to sources only briefly. One example of an article that demonstrates this skill is Murdie and Teixeira's (2011) discussion of the literature relevant to their study of the impact of gentrification on Portuguese people in West Central Toronto. They demonstrate awareness of studies of ethnic minority populations in the USA without discussing them at length, so leaving space for the literature that is more relevant to their work:

> ... Lees (2007: 230) reported relatively little progress in this area of research, except for Black gentrification in US cities (for example, Boyd, 2005; Freeman, 2006; Moore, 2009) and a few case studies of the impact of gentrification on minority groups, especially in Chicago (for example, Betancur, 2002; Boyd, 2005; Nyden et al., 2006).

> (Murdie and Teixeira, 2011: 62)

Literature should usually be discussed thematically rather than source by source

An essential characteristic of a good literature search is that it is organised in the form of an argument rather than simply describing other studies (Silverman, 2006: 341). It is relatively easy to write about literature source by source and there are a limited number of situations where this is appropriate. However, more commonly, the need to write thematically means that a source may be referred to on several occasions in order to illustrate different parts of an argument. Writing in this manner is challenging; even experienced researchers are likely to have to produce several drafts of a literature search to ensure that they are presenting a clear argument and citing sources in the most appropriate places.

Ray et al. (2004) provide an example of a thematic literature search in which some previous work is cited several times in order to develop an argument. Before presenting the findings of their own study of the role that shame plays in motivating racist violence, their literature search cites a previous study (Retzinger, 1991) on several occasions as the argument develops. To take some examples:

- They first refer to Retzinger (1991) to introduce shame as the theoretical framework they will use to analyse some of their data (Ray et al., 2004: 350).

- They later use Retzinger's work to develop this theoretical framework by citing her argument that shame can make people feel helpless and passive (Ray et al., 2004: 354).

- Later still they use the work of Retzinger and another academic to show how shame can influence the moral justification that some racist offenders offer for their crimes (Ray et al., 2004: 354).

The role of the conclusion

The section of the research output which students often find most difficult to write is the conclusion. It is usually the final section that is written, at a time when the researcher is often tired and short of time. However, as it is also the last section of the output that will be read, it is crucial that it provides a clear message about the implications of the research and shows how the findings contribute to the debates that have been raised by the existing literature.

A good conclusion will include some reflection on the body of theory in which the research has been located (unless the output is a practical research report, as noted above) and on previous findings in areas similar to those investigated by the researcher. Some students are nervous about suggesting that their research contradicts existing published work, but it is important that they do this where appropriate: this is part of the process of academic debate. For example, a study by Newman-Ford et al. (2008) produced very different findings from an earlier one by Woodfield et al. (2006) in relation to gender differences in student attendance at teaching sessions. There were no reservations in highlighting these differences:

> This study failed to corroborate Woodfield, Jessop, and McMillan's (2006) finding that average attendance rates for women are superior to men. The findings showed that male students not only achieved higher rates of attendance than women, but also superior assessment marks.

> (Newman-Ford et al., 2008: 712)

The study of racist offenders by Ray et al. (2004), which was referred to above, acknowledged the value of existing theory about motivation for racist offending but also suggested that this theory could be developed further:

> Many of the findings of our research resemble those of others (Hewitt, 1996; Sibbitt, 1997; Webster, 1999): for instance that racist violence rarely conforms to the image of classic hate crime, that those who perpetrate it are likely also to be involved in other types of violence and criminality, and that the racist sentiments they hold are widely shared in their local communities. But we have tried to develop a way of understanding such violence that stresses its deep emotional roots in alienation, shame and rage.

> (Ray et al., 2004: 364)

Of course, the researcher should also acknowledge when their research supports existing theory or previous research findings. However, there are frequent occasions when the conclusion cannot simply agree or disagree with previous work: the contribution that a study makes to understanding the chosen subject area may be a complex one. For example, Adriaenssens and Hendrickx (2011) used their data collected in Brussels to examine two perspectives in relation to begging: a popular perspective that sees it as a lucrative activity organised by criminal gangs and an alternative perspective that sees it as an activity to provide the means to live. In the case of the Roma beggars studied, the authors were able to conclude that the popular perspective was incorrect and that begging was a means to maintaining existence. However, they were not able to reach such a clear conclusion in the case of indigenous people:

> For the indigenous people who beg the results are inconclusive: their earnings from begging surpass those of Roma and it is not certain whether it is possible for them to evade the poverty line by begging.

(Adriaenssens and Hendrickx, 2011: 36)

Recommendations

It is sometimes appropriate to include practical recommendations as part of a conclusion. In the case of research reports, these can be so important that they form a separate section of the output. However, in the case of other forms of output such as student dissertations, the decision as to whether it is appropriate to make practical recommendations will depend on the nature of the subject studied. Bachman and Schutt (2012: 314) make a helpful distinction between two aims of social research – to advance scientific knowledge and to shape social policy. Where research is designed to advance scientific knowledge, the making of policy related recommendations is unlikely to be appropriate:

> The idea is that developing valid knowledge about how society is organized or how we live our lives does not tell us how society *should* be organized or how we *should* live our lives.

(Bachman and Schutt, 2012: 314)

Ethnographic studies are among those that tend to be concerned with advancing scientific knowledge. For example, the conclusion of Parish's (2011) research among the West African diaspora in New York was that clients of antiwitchcraft shrines no longer saw the wealth of the Upper East Side as being a symbol of success but of moral decay. This is clearly a case where practical recommendations were not appropriate but scientific knowledge had been advanced as a result of the research.

In contrast, studies which aim to shape social policy are likely to include recommendations. For example, Ben-Shalom et al. (2011) examined the effectiveness of anti-poverty programmes in the USA. They noted that these programmes tended to focused on groups with specific needs, to give preference to people who were working and to provide specific benefits for items such as food and housing rather than cash (Ben-Shalom et al., 2011: 37). They recommended an alternative method of providing assistance:

> This ideal would provide cash benefits only on the basis of income and not on the basis of any other characteristic, and would therefore serve all poor families in similar economic circumstances equally.

(Ben-Shalom et al., 2001: 38)

While policy recommendations are much more appropriate for some forms of research than others, recommendations for further research can be made across a wide range of studies. If the output begins with a discussion of what was known about a subject prior to the researcher's own work, then discusses how the research findings contribute further to an understanding of the subject area, a logical next step is to indicate how future research could further develop knowledge of the subject. The word 'recommendation' does not need to be used specifically: the researcher simply needs to indicate how knowledge and understanding could be further advanced. To take an example, Nare's (2011) work begins by citing literature which discusses households in terms of the 'moral economy', i.e. an environment where actions are taken that do not have profit-making motives. She places within this theoretical framework her findings that the most important wish of migrant workers in Italy who were employed in domestic roles was to be part of this moral economy, 'feeling part of the family' in an environment where they were valued for more than their labour. Nare concludes by suggesting indirectly that more research is needed to determine whether the moral economy is a relevant concept to other areas of employment:

> A question that arises from this examination is whether such a moral economy is particular *only* to labour that takes place within private households and to what extent we find similar traits across other employment sectors.

(Nare, 2011: 408)

An example – writing the literature search and conclusion in relation to student employment

In Chapter 6, interviews with seven lecturers at a case study university were analysed using the conceptual theme of responsibility for learning. It was demonstrated that there were different perspectives in relation to the question of who was responsible if employment commitments prevented students from attending teaching sessions. The findings were presented in Chapter 9, pp. 180–181.

I will now use these findings to demonstrate how literature and research findings can be presented effectively in a piece of research output and drawn together in a conclusion. The piece of output appears below. Space does not allow the inclusion of a methodology section but there is a discussion of the existing literature on this topic (the first four paragraphs), followed by the paragraph presenting the findings that was produced in Chapter 6 and then a conclusion. Once you have read this, I will show how I followed the advice that I have given in this chapter:

Student attendance, employment and responsibility

Research in the UK has shown that increasing numbers of students are in term-time employment (Callender, 2008: 360), with the percentage measured at 40 per cent by Robotham and Julian (2006: 109–110). Australian studies have found even higher employment levels (Hall, 2010: 440). Although there are difficulties in measuring the impact of employment on achievement, a number of studies suggest that students' academic work is adversely affected by job commitments (for example, Humphrey, 2006: 275; Callender, 2008: 373). Countries such as Germany and the Netherlands have recognised the damage that can be caused to students by employment and have introduced legal limits to the number of hours that they can work (National Audit Office, 2002: 16).

Broadbridge and Swanson (2005: 239–240) suggest that role theory can help to explain the impact of pressures created by student employment: students find difficulties in adopting a number of roles to meet the demands of work, university life and home. Hall (2010: 447) suggests that seeking to balance work, student and social roles can lead to a reduction in the hours devoted to leisure activities and sometimes to an acceptance by students of lower grades for academic work.

Previous studies have produced mixed findings as to whether students should be held responsible if employment is cited as a reason for not attending teaching sessions, i.e. if combining all the roles that they are expected to perform is simply impossible. A series of studies in the UK (for example, Robotham and Julian, 2006: 109–110; Callender, 2008: 373–374) have suggested that students' motivation for working is to meet essential living costs. So employment is clearly a necessity for many, not a result of irresponsible spending. Employment has been identified as one factor that can have an impact on attendance (Newman-Ford et al., 2008: 700). However, other research has indicated that students may use employment as an excuse not to engage in group activities (Greenbank et al., 2009: 47) and the study of Woodfield et al. (2006: 16) suggested that absenteeism was often a sign of a lack of application on the part of the student rather than any external pressure.

Hall (2010: 447–448) argues that universities have a responsibility to support students in dealing with the pressure created by their multiple roles, including those as employees, by taking measures such as introducing online submission of assignments. Greenbank et al. (2009: 51–52) suggest that there are responsibilities for both students and universities: students should look for forms of employment that can complement their studies and should be supported by universities in looking for these types of jobs. However, the extent to which academic staff are willing to take responsibility for supporting students may vary: Curtis (2007: 388) notes that some lecturers are sympathetic to the needs of students to work while others expect a full-time commitment to studying.

A number of respondents from the case study university identified employment as a factor that prevented students from attending teaching sessions, although there were differing views as to how far students should be held responsible for this. Thomas noted that most students had a job and spoke sympathetically about those who had to work long hours, suggesting that this was a result of 'the funding situation'. However, Paula argued that students gave priority to employment when they 'get their priorities a bit mixed up', often as a result of financial difficulties.

The views of Thomas and Paula reflect different strands of thinking on this subject: those of Thomas were consistent with studies which have suggested that students work to provide necessities (for example, Robotham and Julian, 2006: 109–110; Callender, 2008: 373–374), while Paula's views were supported by research which has suggested that non-attendance is a choice on the part of students (Greenbank et al., 2009: 47; Woodfield et al., 2006: 16). The findings reflect the lack of consensus identified by Curtis (2007: 388) as to whether academics and universities should take responsibility for adapting to the multiple roles that students must perform because increasing numbers are in employment. A consensus would be easier to reach if there were clearer evidence as to whether it is possible for students to be in employment without this affecting their attendance. Research that examined the extent to which students with jobs can make choices about attendance would help to bring about a shared understanding of where responsibility should lie.

Of course, this is a piece of research output in miniature and without a methodology section. However, it is useful to consider how I have followed the advice provided in this chapter:

- The first paragraph establishes the relevance of the subject to be addressed by noting the increasing numbers of students in employment, the impact this may have on achievement and that some countries have considered the issue so important as to limit the number of hours that students can work while they are studying.

- The second paragraph demonstrates that the findings are relevant to a broader theoretical question about the roles that students perform. As there is no specific body of theoretical literature about responsibility and learning, this was the area of theory that seemed to have most relevance to own findings.

- The third paragraph then discusses the most important previous research studies in relation to student employment and attendance, with a reference back to role theory to demonstrate the relevance of the theoretical background. The studies have been chosen according to their relevance: there is no reference to the disagreement between Woodfield et al. (2006) and Newman-Ford et al. (2008) in relation to gender and attendance (discussed earlier in the chapter), because gender was not an issue discussed by respondents. Instead, the findings that have been chosen concentrate on questions of responsibility: do students make choices as to whether to take employment and whether to attend teaching sessions? The fourth paragraph then extends this discussion by looking at suggested responses to problems created by student employment and the underlying assumptions that these suggestions make about responsibility.

- The four paragraphs that discuss the existing literature do so thematically rather than source by source. This means that some studies are referred to at more than one point in the discussion, most notably the key study of Callender (2008), which is referred to on three occasions.

- After the research findings are presented in the fifth paragraph, the concluding paragraph links them to both the theoretical background and previous studies. It is very important to make a reference back to role theory to demonstrate that the findings, in a small manner, extend existing theoretical debates: while there is theory about the multiple roles that students adopt, this research addresses a further question as to whether universities should take responsibility for helping students to cope with these roles, in particular the one as employee.

- The concluding paragraph also makes a recommendation for future research. The data did not make it possible to draw a firm conclusion as to who is, or should be, held responsible when students do not attend teaching sessions because of employment commitments. As a result, it is appropriate to suggest further research that may resolve the apparent disagreement between Thomas and Paula as to where responsibility should be placed.

Exercise 12

Using the literature to write about reflective practice mechanisms that involve colleagues

This exercise asks you to undertake a similar process to the one discussed in the previous section; you will be presented with some research findings and asked to 'add in' the discussion of the existing literature and the conclusion. The findings are again taken from the interviews with the lecturers at the case study university. In Chapter 5, the following finding was identified in relation to reflective practice:

- Several respondents discussed methods of involving colleagues in seeking to identify best practice. The methods discussed were both formal (e.g. peer review) and informal (e.g. watching the teaching of colleagues).

Expanding this slightly might produce the following findings section for a mini-research report on reflective practice mechanisms that involve colleagues:

> Several respondents discussed methods of involving colleagues in seeking to identify best practice. Some used formal processes involving colleagues either directly (e.g. peer review) or indirectly (e.g. comparing with practice in other parts of the faculty). However, others preferred to use informal processes such as watching the teaching of colleagues or discussing a teaching session with them.

You are invited to write a research report (approximately 400 words) which does not have a methodology section, but includes a literature search, the above paragraph of findings and a conclusion. You should use the five literature sources which are summarized below. Of course, this exercise can only represent the use of literature in miniature, but you should still seek to follow the process outlined in the previous example, i.e.

1 Establish the importance of the subject under discussion.
2 Identify the most relevant theoretical considerations.
3 Discuss previous work on the subject and related subjects.
4 Present the findings.
5 Conclude by linking the findings to the existing literature.

Literature source 1

Andreu et al. (2003: 31–32) note that student evaluations of teaching have been widely used as a method of improving practice in higher education. In other education systems such as schools, a critical friend technique is widely used; the authors discuss the application of this technique at one Spanish university. It is a two-stage process whereby a colleague offers a critique of a lecturer's work and the lecturer then undertakes self-reflection based on the ideas, suggestions and comments made. Andreu et al. (2003: 36) argue that teaching improved substantially as a result of this critical friend technique being introduced and suggest that, for it to achieve more than isolated examples of good practice, it should be formalised and built into universities' plans for improving quality.

Literature source 2

Schon (1987: 26–29) argues that there are many everyday activities that people do not need to think about very much. When one such activity produces an unexpected outcome, the response can either be to brush it aside or to reflect on it. If someone experiments on the spot with a new method of doing something and then notes what the outcome is, the process is referred to as reflection-in-action. However, Schon (1987: 31) also discusses the process by which a person reflects after an activity about decisions that they made and considers how they should alter their approach in the future, something that he refers to as reflection on past reflection-in-action. He argues that exercising this form of reflection on their work can turn people into professional artists.

Literature source 3

Boud (2010: 25) argues that courses of professional training now tend to include elements called reflection or reflective practice on the assumption that to reflect is good and that unreflective practice is bad. Boud (2010: 30) criticises professional courses for tending to encourage reflection on individual practice, which is inconsistent with a trend for professionals to work as teams.

Literature source 4

Bernacchio et al. (2007: 56–57) argue that reflective practice has become central to school reform and professional development of teachers in the USA. They note that mechanisms used for reflective practice include action research, peer observation and the critical friend method. They discuss a Critical Friends Group (CFG) used by five university colleagues to review syllabi and develop interventions in classroom practice in order to bring about a more equitable and accessible environment.

The process of reflection practised by the CFG involved a number of steps, including one member of the academic staff presenting their own syllabus and the other group members asking challenging questions to encourage them to think about it from new perspectives (Bernacchio et al., 2007: 58).

Literature source 5

Crow and Smith (2005: 493–496) suggest that commonly used methods of reflective practice such as individual reflection and written student evaluations do not provide any opportunity for dialogue. This problem can be solved by including colleagues in the reflection process; they suggest a number of mechanisms, including:

1 Peer observation: this should be followed by a debriefing in the form of a reflective conversation which considers the theories and values that underpin the teaching.

2 Reflective conversation with a mentor: an ongoing relationship with a mentor can facilitate discussion of how relationships with students develop over time.

3 Reflective conversation with a co-teacher: this involves lecturers working together to plan, deliver and assess teaching.

Please complete the exercise before looking at my version of the report below.

My research output about methods of reflection that involve colleagues

Boud (2010: 25) and Bernacchio et al. (2007: 56–57) both note the importance role that reflection plays in the training of professionals. Discussions of methods tend not to focus on the very rapid reflection which is needed to produce an experimental response to an immediate stimulus, something referred to by Schon (1987: 29) as reflection-in-action, but instead on the more considered reflection that can take place after an activity, referred to by Schon (1987: 31) as reflection on past reflection-in-action. Schon (1987: 31) argues that this form of reflection on their work can turn people into professional artists.

Commonly used methods of reflection are personal reflection (Boud, 2010: 30) and in, the case of higher education, reflections by the lecturer on student evaluations of their teaching (Andreu et al., 2003: 31–32). However, Crow and Smith (2005: 493–496) note that both these methods have limitations because they do not provide an opportunity for interaction. They advocate instead the involvement of colleagues through a number of mechanisms: peer observation or reflective conversations with a mentor or co-teacher. Other methods of involving colleagues in reflection include the use of a critical friend technique (Andreu et al., 2003: 31–32), action research and the creation of a critical friends group (Bernacchio et al., 2007: 56–58). Andreu et al. (2003: 36) argue that teaching improved substantially when the critical friend technique was introduced.

Several respondents at the case study university discussed methods of involving colleagues in seeking to identify best practice. Some used formal processes involving colleagues either directly (e.g. peer review) or indirectly (e.g. comparing with practice in other parts of the faculty). However, others preferred to use informal processes such as watching the teaching of colleagues or discussing a teaching session with them.

The use of reflective practice mechanisms that involved colleagues indicated that a number of respondents at the case study university acknowledged the arguments presented in the literature for the benefits of such an approach. However, the variety of practices involved, and some respondents not discussing any methods of involving colleagues in reflection, suggested that there was no standard institutional practice. Andreu et al. (2003: 36) argue that, for a critical friends process to achieve more than isolated examples of good practice, it should be formalised and built into universities' plans for improving quality. Similarly, it appeared that the case study university could go further in encouraging all lecturers to involve colleagues in reflecting on their teaching so that more could meet Schon's (1987: 31) definition of the professional artist.

Commentary on research output about methods of reflective practice that involve colleagues

As with every exercise in this book, you should not assume that you are wrong if your outcome is different from mine. Please remember also that you are rarely, if ever, likely to be asked to write such a short piece of research output, and that a methodology section should be included between the discussion of the literature and the findings. However, it is worth considering briefly how I followed the five-stage process discussed previously:

1 The first sentence establishes the importance of the topic by citing evidence that reflection is essential to developing effective practice among professionals. The reasons for arguing specifically that mechanisms involving colleagues are beneficial are left to the second paragraph, where a range of methods of reflective practice are discussed briefly.

2   The work of Schon is discussed in the second sentence in order to provide the theo-
    retical background into which the research best fits.

3   The second paragraph discusses the existing literature specifically on mechanisms that
    involve colleagues. It establishes the case for the importance of such mechanisms by
    citing both academic argument that interaction is crucial to effective reflection and one
    evaluation that points to the improvement of teaching. The paragraph also provides
    examples of the mechanisms used in order to illustrate to the reader what form reflection
    with colleagues might take. Although these mechanisms could have been discussed in
    detail, this was not essential and would have taken the report over the word limit.

4   The third paragraph presents the findings. The phrase 'at the case study university'
    has been added to make clear to the reader that the discussion is moving from the
    literature to one of the findings.

5   If space had allowed a more detailed discussion of the mechanisms discussed in the
    literature and those used by the respondents at the case study university, these could
    have been compared in the conclusion. However, given the word count, this was not
    feasible, so instead the paragraph sought to make links between the data and discus-
    sions about both theory (Schon, 1987: 31) and practice (Andreu et al., 2003: 36),
    ensuring that the reader could see the links between the different parts of the output.
    In addition, given the practical nature of the topic discussed, it was appropriate to
    make a recommendation.

Summary

The two main examples provided in this chapter – concerned with student
employment/attendance and reflective practice mechanisms that involve
colleagues – are artificial ones because it is unlikely that a researcher would
separate out such a small part of their findings to write about in this manner.
However, they have demonstrated the process of choosing and discussing the
most relevant parts of the literature at the start of the research output, then
linking the findings to the literature in the conclusion.

The researcher must make these links between their own findings and the
existing literature in order to demonstrate that their work makes a contribution
to what is already known about the subject. However, when taking an
inductive approach, the data is analysed before the literature is considered in
detail. So the inductive researcher does not know, when beginning to collect
and analyse their data, which body of theory their findings or microtheory will
be located in. Once they have their findings or microtheory, they may be faced
with one of two very different challenges – either needing to choose the most
relevant from a number of possible theoretical backgrounds or needing to
'borrow' a body of theory from a similar subject and apply it to their work.

Finding a theoretical background is essential for most, but not all, forms of
research output. However, the literature search section should always discuss

the most important previous research conducted in the area that the researcher is examining. This is likely to involve an element of selection: while searching for existing literature is largely a technical skill, choosing the most relevant sources (and the most relevant parts of these sources) requires careful judgement. It is essential to discard sources, or mention them only briefly, if they are not central to the researcher's argument.

While the literature search section discusses the most relevant previous work, it is the conclusion that makes explicit the links between the researcher's own findings and what is already known about the subject area. The conclusion is the most important part of any research output because it is here that the researcher demonstrates that the work they have produced is a single entity, all designed to answer the same question(s) or achieve the same objectives. If the research has examined a practical issue, it is often relevant to include recommendations for policy makers or others. In other cases, the nature of the subject area means that recommendations of this nature are inappropriate, but many types of study lend themselves to recommendations for further research, to advance the knowledge that is available through the existing literature and the researcher's own findings.

In the last two chapters, you have read about all the sections that usually appear in a piece of research output. The production of the output is not always the end of the story: researchers who are hoping to shape policies will often be substantially involved in disseminating and publicising their findings in an attempt to bring about change. However, it is my hope that you now feel confident to produce well written research output, linking existing literature to qualitative data which has been subjected to effective analysis.

Further reading

For a practical guide to finding, evaluating and writing about sources of literature, I recommend Deane, M. (2010) *Academic Research, Writing and Referencing*. Harlow: Pearson Education.

There is a short but helpful section, most relevant to postgraduate study, on the manner in which previous literature should be used in Berg, B. L. (2009) *Qualitative Research Methods for the Social Sciences*, 7th edn. Boston: Pearson (1st edn, 1989).

Appendix 1: interview with Fern

Interviewer: First I'm going to ask about your background. How long have you been in this particular job?

Fern: A large number of years now.

Interviewer: Right, okay. Have you had any other previous roles within this university?

Fern: I have progressed from a basic lecturer to a senior position.

Interviewer: Have you taught at any other universities?

Fern: Yes I've taught at one other.

Interviewer: Okay, why did you decide to enter into higher education?

Fern: Never wanted to do anything else.

Interviewer: But what were your reasons for doing that? Was it for your own satisfaction, financial reasons, flexible working?

Fern: Because I wanted to research and teach. I wanted to do the job and I didn't think about the money. It wasn't very well paid to start with. It never crossed my mind to do any other job to be perfectly honest.

Interviewer: In the beginning, what were your initial hopes and fears for the job?

Fern: I just wanted to be a good academic and I wanted never to have to leave. I didn't think about getting promoted; I just wanted to be a researcher and a teacher. My worry was perhaps I would have to leave because, like I say, I could never imagine doing anything else.

Interviewer: Since you began the job, how have your expectations and hopes changed?

Fern: Not a bit. I've always enjoyed doing the job; I suppose there is more bureaucracy and we have more students. So it is a different job than it was when I started, just because of mass higher education, it's changed. So I suppose from that point of view it's a bit less satisfying; there's a difference between marking 40 essays and marking 150. Marking 40, you can just about maintain your enthusiasm for it, but I think with fairly high numbers it can be quite difficult.

Interviewer: Okay, you say that you've been here for quite a few years, so were you here when it was a polytechnic?

Fern: Yes.

Interviewer: Have you noticed any changes since it became a university?

Fern: Oddly because the expansion of higher education went with becoming a university, it was more like a university in some ways when it was a polytechnic because we weren't as pressured. In the traditional universities you have time for research; you have time to teach small numbers. So when I came here it was small numbers and I had time to do research but, because it was a polytechnic rather than an old university, there was no expectation to do research. I did it because that was my choice, so I always behaved as if I was in an old university even though I was in a new university. So for me it didn't make much difference because the workload wasn't light but it seemed realistic. But I did notice that there were people around me who didn't do research; they just were teachers, which is what they were employed to be. That's no criticism of them but, as we've become a university, the emphasis has been slightly more on research. But to be fair, not a huge emphasis and I was always the same – I always personally chose to do research. So I suppose it's not changed a lot really. And the numbers don't help us. It makes it all seem more mundane when you have 70 students. So, I'm not sure, not a very clear answer.

Interviewer: How do you feel about recognition and appreciation?

Fern: Well I have that, personally. I think I have been recognised and appreciated so I feel fine about that.

Interviewer: Okay. And how do you feel about your workload?

Fern: It's always seemed heavy; I've always been at the top end of the scale for workload. But because I enjoy the job I suppose it doesn't feel like a burden. It feels heavy but I don't feel angry about it or anything. It is what it is which is on the high end, but always has been.

Interviewer: That's fine. Now some questions about different parts of your job. Do you design the units which you teach?

Fern: Oh yes.

Interviewer: And do you think that is a good thing? Being involved in designing the units which you teach?

Fern: I would hate to teach a unit I hadn't designed. Oh I would loathe that. That would take away all the integrity and independence, if you were given units to teach. I suppose that is a big thing that has changed over the years – having to specify what you're going to teach. You never used to; you just used to teach what you felt like teaching, broadly. You had titles for your units but, for the content, you could do what you felt you should do. So I suppose, in that sense, academic integrity has been lost as we had to decide a year in advance what we're going to teach. That's bad enough but if I had to teach a unit I hadn't written I would be pretty fed up.

Interviewer: What is your experience of teaching lecturers?

Fern: I enjoy lecturing, I've always enjoyed it. I'm starting to find them more tiring, physically being on my feet, particularly when they are three-hour sessions. Every unit, every lecture, even if it's not a new lecture, it is a new lecture to me in a sense that I always start them fresh again every time, so I don't have a set, I've never in my life had a set of lecture notes. So every time I've gone to give a lecture I start from scratch. I mean obviously I've been thinking ahead and have the PowerPoints from last year but I do go over it and think about it and read new texts and things just to refresh. I enjoy lecturing.

Interviewer: How about seminars?

Fern: Sometimes I like those less in a way because I'm not so much in control because obviously it's up to students to speak and if they don't speak then that's difficult. But over the years I think I have developed quite reasonable seminar skills; I do lots of exercises with students and do all different things. So I usually have enough materials and enough ways of stimulating students in a seminar to get a reasonable response from them. So I think I've got to like them over the years. I've always preferred lecturing to seminars, but I think the techniques have got better over the years. I still prefer the lectures to seminars but it's not so bad.

Interviewer: Okay. Are you involved in any other forms of teaching? Such as workshops or ...

Fern: Yes I do workshops; I do workshops with staff and PhD students. Some people are very good at workshops and very good at techniques of keeping people interested. And I know these techniques, and I think I've picked up on these techniques and therefore I don't mind doing them. But if you said to me 'a three hour lecture or a three hour workshop?' then I'd probably go for the three hour lecture. Because workshops are hard.

Interviewer: Have you been involved in guidance tutoring at all?

Fern: Oh yes.

Interviewer: Yes?

Fern: Gallons of it.

Interviewer: And how do you find that?

Fern: I don't mind doing it; we have a huge number of them now and the only reason we can cope with it is sometimes students don't turn up. They're supposed to come see us at least once a semester. But students don't tend to come to see you unless they've got problems. I think we've tried to solve that now by having group tutorials so at least we get to see them. But I suppose if they came individually a lot it would take up quite a lot of time. It's frustrating, though, because obviously if students are okay they don't bother to come and tell you and when they're miserable they can't come and tell you. It's no criticism of anybody but students in trouble who need support just don't ask for it; they run away and hide. So I suppose it is quite hard.

Interviewer: Do you find guidance tutoring rewarding?

Fern: Yes, the bit I like best is writing references for students who I know well. I don't like writing references for students I don't know. I don't know who they are or what they're doing; it's very frustrating. But when I've got to know a student and I know their interests and what they're hoping for I quite like supporting them to get what they want. To get their ambitions, I quite like that. But obviously I'm always happy to help students if they're in trouble so it's quite nice if you have a student who's really having a difficult time and you can support them through that.

Interviewer: Okay, we're going to move on to a little bit about research. You already mentioned it, is it very important to you personally that you ...

Fern: Absolutely! 100 per cent. Yes, most important.

Interviewer: Do you feel under pressure to do research from the university?

Fern: No more than I put myself under pressure.

Interviewer: So it's more from yourself?

Fern: Well I suppose, as a senior member of staff, if I didn't do research the university would look at me a bit oddly and think I was being paid money under false pretences. So if I wasn't doing research I would expect the university to demand that I did. But since I do it anyway, I demand that I do it. I would be annoyed if I wasn't put under pressure to do research.

That would mean they weren't taking me seriously, so no I don't feel under pressure but I do it.

Interviewer: If you personally need advice and guidance then where does that come from?

Fern: Not necessarily from people senior to me. I have a senior mentor-type person, but I ask different people at different times – it just depends on expertise.

Interviewer: And how do you manage to fit everything in that you have to do in a day? Time management?

Fern: In terms of time management I just do what I have to do. Some days I find I'm incredibly efficient and I'll just clear everything off my desk and I'll do about 1,000 things I need to do, but other days nothing seems to get done. And I just have the confidence that I have a sufficient balance of highly efficient days with less efficient days that I will get everything done and it has worked out at the end of the day. And I'm not the kind of person who waits until the last minute to do things; in fact I prefer to do things ahead of schedule. So I manage my time in the sense of if I'm feeling really bright and breezy, very fresh and optimistic then I'll do a really long day and I'll rattle everything out. But if I find I'm just getting nowhere then I'll just pack in and think it's just a waste of time and I'll come back when I'm fresh. So it's managing my energy levels more than my time; just doing time would be no good. I can use my time brilliantly sometimes and not so good at other times.

Interviewer: Okay, we are now going to focus on students. A question about the attendance and motivation of students.

Fern: I think that's difficult; I think now we're treating the preliminary degree as a career grade it's becoming a bit like school. In a sense you've got some kids who love to be there and other kids who can't be bothered because they're just going through the motions. And there used to be about 5–10 per cent of people went to university so I imagine you were effectively teaching that minority who really want to be there. But now you have some who are not too bothered; they're here to get a qualification and get on with their lives, and they're quite instrumental with that. But people don't attend because they're working; they don't come in because as soon as they know what the assessment is they go to do it and don't want to learn. They're not particularly interested in learning; they just want to get the assessment and that's it. So I think to a certain extent that I understand that's instrumental to students doing reasonably well. They don't have a breadth of education but they can technically get though the assignment. So I just let them get on with it and concentrate on those who really want to do it, you know. So really it's like the old university group inside the mass really, so you know I just focus – that not true, I don't just focus on those who are interested. But if a minority, like lectures aren't compulsory, we don't take down registers so there might be people not there. But we do take registers in seminars so we have more people there. If I find some people haven't turned up to class I don't worry about it because I teach those that are there and those who are there by definition are the most interested. So attendance is a problem, that cynicism of 'oh let's get through this', 'oh we've got to do this degree let's get through it'. There's still loads of interested students but, if they're not there, then they're either working or not interested.

Interviewer: Okay, what is your experience of teaching mature students?

Fern: Oh it used to be fabulous; in the good old days when there were grants we had loads and loads of mature students and sometimes up to a third of a course were made up of mature students. And there would be all sorts of people – we had vicars, we had retired miners – all sorts of people coming in. And lots of women who had returned to work after having children. And several of them struggled with it but some of them were really fabulous. In fact we had a couple of mature students just recently on the course; I wouldn't say more so than other students, but they were here because they wanted to be here. And they were desperate to learn and desperate to know, some of the brightest students we had were the mature students. And I thought it was marvellous taking somebody who had no chance of education and suddenly had the confidence to realise that they could come to learn and I think it's fabulous. I really, really enjoyed that; you don't have that now because of course they can't afford to take the loans out, mature students, they have to work. You know, no government grants, there's no support for them so they've all gone, nearly all gone.

Interviewer. Have you noticed this change since it became a university or just the whole ...

Fern: It's the loss of the grant. I don't think it's got anything to do with turning into a university; I suppose there's also the whole strict admissions and this kind of thing. But I don't think that's got to do with being a university because I think traditional universities used to take in more mature students all the time so I don't think it's got anything to do with being a university. I think that it's just to do with increased bureaucracy and the loss of grants.

Interviewer: Have you noticed any differences between the way that students like to be taught? Like more traditional students liking it one way and mature students a different way or?

Fern: I don't know ...

Interviewer: A difference in methods of teaching?

Fern: I don't think there's a difference in methods of teaching. I think all students now need the information; they want to know what the assessment is; they want to know what they need to do because they want to know how to get the marks. They really are quite instrumental, whereas the mature students never were here just to get the qualification – that was the icing on the cake. They were here to learn and to enjoy the process. I'm not sure that students enjoy the process any more; I don't know if students get a kick out of learning anymore; they do it because they have to do it otherwise they won't get the jobs they want. So whether it's to do with style of teaching, it's got to do with the content and the seminars, the attitude is just very, very different – take the information.

Interviewer: What is your experience of overseas students?

Fern: Loads of it through the years. Again it's about the same; there was a stage where the international students were quite exceptional: they had quite a struggle to get here and wanted to learn as much as possible. Whereas now we get loads of international students being sent by their government to get trained up, to get qualifications, and therefore they haven't got a hunger to learn. Well, that's not true, some of them do. But their priority is to get that qualification in the time scale because otherwise they'll have to pay the money back or lose their job so people are under that very instrumental pressure, so not doing it for the love of it. I think it's much the same; I don't think it's to do with being an international student but I think it's to do with being put through the grinder to get the qualifications. And I think that makes it difficult, but many of them are a delight to teach, very interesting; obviously they bring new experiences and different perspectives.

Interviewer: And what about language barriers?

Fern: That's very difficult because, if people just aren't experienced, they may not understand what you're saying. I have quite a fast delivery so I don't probably teach in a style that students would find useful. I work with PowerPoint but then I explain things and I think that I do that quite quickly, and therefore, if the language isn't there, I think that to pick up the meaning of what I am saying may be quite difficult. So I do try to repeat things rather than say it slowly; I try to say things two or three times. But yes, I think people seem to learn quite quickly when they get here and have to learn another language. But I know students who can barely speak and still manage to get through it somehow. I think a combination of low motivation, not really being very on top of a subject and not being able to speak – when you've got that combination it's pretty difficult, but I haven't often seen those combinations all together. For instance I have very able, very polite international students who barely speak English but, as I say, they can still get over it. It's a mixture really.

Interviewer: Okay we're going to move on to reflective practice now. What's your understanding of that?

Fern: It's about reflecting on how I do my teaching, how I practise my trade. Reflection is something that is required in every area of work these days.

Interviewer: And how important to you is reflecting on your own practice?

Fern: Oh I've always been interested in student feedback. I always want to know how it's gone and I don't like if I feel I haven't been on top form or I haven't explained things right: that really annoys me. So I do think, I do feel it over in my mind what I've done and how I've done; how I've answered questions and that kind of thing. I think I do it almost all the time, I don't think, 'another lecture over, on with the next'; I always want to feel it's gone well and if it hasn't gone well then why hasn't it gone well? And so if I'm understanding what reflective practice actually does, then it's my natural condition.

Interviewer: And what is your motivation to be reflective of your practice?

Fern: Pride.

Interviewer: Pride?

Fern: Yes I want to do a good job; I would not wish to produce poor research or produce poor teaching.

Interviewer: Have you got any final comments on being a lecturer?

Fern: I suppose it's going to get harder to have that creative atmosphere that I'm perhaps used to having. I think that there's more bureaucracy, more like teaching, more like school teaching. But I teach mostly postgraduates anyway, so I don't teach many of the large classes, but if I was teaching lots of huge classes I can imagine it would be pretty frustrating.

Interviewer: Okay, thank you.

References

Aburabia-Queder, S. 'Higher education as a platform for cross-cultural transition: the case of the first educated Bedouin women in Israel', *Higher Education Quarterly*, 65 (2): 186–205.

Adriaenssens, S. and Hendrickx, J. (2011) 'Street level informal economic activities: estimating the yield of begging in Brussels', *Urban Studies*, 48(1): 23–40.

Anderson, R. (2011) 'Intuitive inquiry' in Wertz, F. J. Charmaz, K., McMullen, L. M. Josselson, R. Anderson, R. and McSpadden, E. (2011) *Five Ways of Doing Qualitative Analysis*. New York: The Guilford Press.

Andreu, R., Canos, L., de Juana, S., Manresa, E., Rienda, L., and Tari, J. J. (2003) 'Critical friends: a tool for quality improvement in universities', *Quality Assurance in Education*, 11(1): 31–36.

Auerbach, C. F. and Silverstein, B. S. (2003) *Qualitative Data: An Introduction to Coding and Analysis*. New York: New York University Press.

Bachman, R. and Schutt, R. K. (2011) *Fundamentals of Research in Criminology and Criminal Justice*, 2nd edn. Los Angeles: Sage (1st edn, 2008).

Baildon, M. C. and Sim, J. B.-Y. (2009) 'Notions of criticality: Singaporean teachers' perspective of critical thinking in social studies', *Cambridge Journal of Education*, 39(4): 407–422.

Barbour, R. (2007) *Doing Focus Groups*. London: Sage.

Barbour, R. (2008) *Introducing Qualitative Research*. London: Sage.

Bazeley, P. (2007) *Qualitative Data Analysis with NVivo*. London: Sage.

Ben-Shalom, Y., Moffitt, R. and Scholz, J. K. (2011) *An Assessment of the Effectiveness of Anti-Poverty Programmes in the United States*. Institute for Research on Poverty Discussion Paper no. 1392–11. University of Wisconsin-Madison: Institute for Research on Poverty.

Berg, B. L. (2009) *Qualitative Research Methods for the Social Sciences*, 7th edn. Pearson International Edition, Boston: Pearson (1st edn, 1989).

Bernacchio, C., Ross, F., Robinson Washburn, K., Whitney, J. and Wood, D. R. (2007) 'Faculty collaboration to improve equity, access and inclusion in higher education', *Equity and Excellence in Education*, 40(1): 56–66.

Bilton, T., Bonnett, K., Jones, P., Lawson, T., Skinner, D., Stanworth, M. and Webster, A. (2002) *Introductory Sociology*, 4th edn. Basingstoke: Palgrave Macmillan (1st edn, 1981).

Blanden, J. and Machin, S. (2004) 'Educational inequality and the expansion of UK higher education', *Scottish Journal of Political Economy*, 51 (2): 230–249.

Blismas, N. G. And Dainty, A. R. J. (2003) 'Computer-aided qualitative data analysis: panacea or paradox?' *Building Research and Information,* 31(6): 455–463.

Bloor, M. (2011) 'Addressing social problems through qualitative research' in Silverman, D. (ed.) *Qualitative Research,* 3rd edn. London: Sage (1st edn, 1997).

Bloor, M., Frankland, J., Thomas, M. and Robson, K. (2001) *Focus Groups in Social Research.* London: Sage.

Boeije, H. (2010) *Analysis in Qualitative Research.* London: Sage.

Boud, D. (2010) 'Relocating reflection in the context of practice' in Bradbury, H., Frost, N., Kilminster, S. and Zukas, M. (eds) *Beyond Reflective Practice: New Approaches to Professional Lifelong Learning.* Abingdon: Routledge.

Bowl, M. (2001) 'Experiencing the barriers: non-traditional students entering higher education', *Research Papers in Education,* 16(2): 141–160.

Boyce, I. (2006) 'Neighbourliness and privacy on a low income estate', *Sociological Research On Line,* 11 (3).

Broadbridge, A. and Swanson, V. (2005) 'Earning and learning: how term-time employment impacts on students' adjustment to university life', *Journal of Education and Work,* 18(2): 235–249.

Bryman, A. (1988) *Quantity and Quality in Social Research.* London: Routledge.

Bryman, A. (2008) *Social Research Methods,* 3rd edn. Oxford University Press (1st edn, 2001).

Bryman, A. and Burgess, R. G. (1994) 'Developments in qualitative data analysis: an introduction' in Bryman, A. and Burgess, R. G. (eds) *Analysing Qualitative Data.* London: Routledge.

Burton, K., Golding Lloyd, M. and Griffiths, C. (2011) 'Barriers to learning for mature students studying HE in an FE college', *Journal of Further and Higher Education,* 35(1): 25–360.

Callender, C. (2008) 'The impact of term-time employment on higher education students' academic attainment and achievement', *Journal of Education Policy,* 23 (4): 359–377.

Carney, C. and McNeish, S. (2005) 'Listening to the needs of the mature student – a qualitative study', *Widening Participation and Lifelong Learning,* 7 (3): 1–8.

Charmaz, K. (2006) *Constructing Grounded Theory.* London: Sage.

Clark, T. (2009) 'The impact of reforms on the quality and responsiveness of universities in the United Kingdom', *Higher Education Management and Policy,* 21(2): 105–120.

Clough, P. and Nutbrown, C. (2012) *A Student's Guide to Methodology.* London: Sage.

Coffee, A. (2006) 'Participant observation' in Jupp, V. (ed.) *The Sage Dictionary of Social Research Methods.* London: Sage.

Cordella, M. (1996) 'Confrontational style in Spanish arguments: pragmatics and teaching outlook', *Language, Culture and Curriculum,* 9: 148–162.

Crow, J. and Smith, L. (2005) 'Co-teaching in higher education: reflective conversation on shared experience as continued professional development for lecturers and health and social care students', *Reflective Practice,* 6 (4): 491–506.

Curtis, S. (2007) 'Students' perceptions of the effects of term-time paid employment' *Education and Training,* 49(5): 380–390.

Davies, P. (2006) 'Research design' in Jupp, V. (ed.) (2006) *The Sage Dictionary of Social Research Methods.* London: Sage.

Davies, P., Francis, P. and Jupp, V. (2011) 'Glossary' in Davies, P. Francis, P. and Jupp, V. (eds) (2011) *Doing Criminological Research,* 2nd edn. London: Sage (1st edn, 2000).

Dawson, C. (2009) *Introduction to Research Methods*. Oxford: How to Books Limited.

De Vaus, D. A. (2002) *Surveys in Social Research*, 5th edn. London: Routledge (1st edn, 1986).

Denzin, N. K. and Lincoln, Y. S. (2008) 'Introduction: the discipline and practice of qualitative research' in Denzin, N. K. and Lincoln, Y. S. (eds) *Collecting and Interpreting Qualitative Materials* 3rd edn. London: Sage (1st edn, 1998).

Dey, I. (1993) *Qualitative Data Analysis: a User-Friendly Guide for Social Scientists*. London: Routledge.

Duggleby, W. (2005) 'What about focus group interaction data?' *Qualitative Health Research*, 15(6): 832–840.

Edstrom, A. (2004) 'Expressions of disagreement by Venezuelans in conversation: reconsidering the influence of culture', *Journal of Pragmatics*, 36(8): 1499–1518.

Elliott, J. (2005) *Using Narratives in Social Research: Qualitative and Quantitative Approaches*. London: Sage.

Fetterman, D. (1989) *Ethnography Step by Step*. London: Sage.

Fielding, N. G. (2006) 'Life history interviewing' in Jupp, V. (ed.) (2006) *The Sage Dictionary of Social Research Methods*. London: Sage.

Fielding, N. and Lee, R. M. (1998) *Computer Analysis and Qualitative Research*. London: Sage.

Finch, H. and Lewis, J. (2003) 'Focus groups' in Ritchie, J. and Lewis, J. (eds) *Qualitative Research Practice*. London: Sage.

Flick, U. (2006) 'Analytic induction' in Jupp, V. (ed.) (2006) *The Sage Dictionary of Social Research Methods*. London: Sage.

Flick, U. (2009) *An Introduction to Qualitative Research*, 4th edn. London: Sage. (1st edn 1998).

Fontana, A. and Frey, J. H. 'The interview: from neutral stance to political involvement' in Denzin, N. K. and Lincoln, Y. S. (eds) *Collecting and Interpreting Qualitative Materials*, 3rd edn. London: Sage (1st edn, 1998).

Gibson, W. J. and Brown, A. (2009) *Working With Qualitative Data*. London: Sage.

Giddens, A. (2001) 'Marx and Weber on class' in Giddens, A. (ed.) *Sociology: Introductory Readings* 2nd edn. Cambridge: Polity Press (1st edn, 1997).

Gilbert, M. (1994) 'Durkheim and social facts' in Pickering, W. S. and Martins, H. (eds) *Debating Durkheim*. London: Routledge.

Gill, R. (1993) 'Justifying injustice: broadcasters' account of inequality in radio' in Burma, E. and Parker, I. (eds) *Discourse Analytic Research*. London: Routledge.

Gillham, B. (2005) *Research Interviewing: The Range of Techniques*. Buckingham: Open University Press.

Glaser, B. and Strauss, A. L. (1967) *The Discovery of Grounded Theory: Strategies for Qualitative Research*. New York: Aldine de Gruyter.

Goddard, T. and Myers, R. (2011) 'Democracy and demonstration in the grey area of neoliberalism: a case study of Free Los Angeles High School', *British Journal of Criminology*, 51(4): 652–670.

Gordon, S., Reid, A. and Petocz, P. (2010) 'Educators' conceptions of student diversity in their classes', *Studies in Higher Education*, 35(8): 961–974.

Grant, R. and Sugarman, J. (2004) 'Ethics in human subjects research: do incentives matter?' *The Journal of Medicine and Philosophy*, 29(6): 717–738.

Grbich, C. (2007) *Qualitative Data Analysis: An Introduction*. London: Sage.

Greco, L. (2006) 'Conversation analysis' in Jupp, V. (ed.) *The Sage Dictionary of Social Research Methods*. London: Sage.

Green, N. (2008) 'Formulating and refining a research question' in Gilbert, N. (ed.) *Researching Social Life*, 3rd edn. London: Sage (1st edn, 1993).

Greenbank, P. Hepworth, S. and Mercer, J. (2009) 'Term-time employment and the student experience', *Education and Training*, 51(1): 43–55.

Hall, R. (2010) 'The work–study relationship: experiences of full-time university students undertaking part-time employment', *Journal of Education and Work*, 23(5): 439–449.

Haney, C., Banks, C. and Zimbardo, P. (1981) 'A study of prisoners and guards in a simulated prison' in Potter, D., Anderson, J., Clarke, J., Coombes, P., Hall, J., Harris, L., Holloway, C. and Walton, T. (eds) (1981) *Society and the Social Sciences: An Introduction*. London: Routledge and Kegan Paul.

Harding, J. (2001) 'Success and failure in independent living among 16–17 year olds', PhD thesis, University of Newcastle upon Tyne.

Harding J. (2006) 'Grounded Theory' in Jupp, V. (ed.) *The Sage Dictionary of Social Research Methods*. London: Sage.

Heaton, J. (2004) *Reworking Qualitative Data*. London: Sage.

Hemingway, A. (2007) 'Determinants of coronary heart disease for women on a low income: literature review', *Journal of Advanced Nursing*, 60(4): 359–367.

Henn, M., Weinstein, M. and Foard, N. (2009) *A Critical Introduction to Social Research*, 2nd edn. London: Sage (1st edn, 2006).

Hennink, M., Hutter, I. and Bailey, A. (2011) *Qualitative Research Methods*. London: Sage.

Herman, L. and Vervaeck, B. (2001) *Handbook of Narrative Analysis*. Lincoln: University of Nebraska Press.

Hesse-Biber, S. N. and Leavy, P. (2006) *The Practice of Qualitative Research*. London: Sage.

Homan, R. (1991) *The Ethics of Social Research*. London: Longman.

Humphrey, R. (2006) 'Pulling structured inequality into higher education: the impact of part-time working on English university students', *Higher Education Quarterly*, 60 (3): 270–286.

Humphreys, L. (1970) *Tearoom Trade*. London: Gerald Duckworth and Co Ltd.

Jackson, S. F., Cleverly, S., Poland, B., Burman, D., Edwards, R. and Robertson, A. (2003) 'Working with Toronto neighbourhoods towards developing indicators of community capacity', *Health Promotion International*, 18(4): 339–350.

Johnson, W. A. Jr., Rettig, R. P., Scott, G. M. and Garrison, S. M. (2010) *The Sociology Student Writer's Manual*, 6th edn. Boston: Prentice Hall (1st edn, 1999).

Josselson, R. (2011) 'Narrative research' in Wertz, F. J., Charmaz, K., McMullen, L. M., Josselson, R., Anderson, R. and McSpadden, E. (2011) *Five Ways of Doing Qualitative Analysis*. New York: The Guilford Press.

Jupp, V. (2006a) 'Validity' in Jupp, V. (ed.) *The Sage Dictionary of Social Research Methods*. London: Sage.

Jupp, V. (2006b) 'Reflexivity' in Jupp, V. (ed.) *The Sage Dictionary of Social Research Methods*. London: Sage.

Kavanagh, D., Richards, D., Smith, M. and Geddes, A. (2006) *British Politics*, 5th edn. Oxford University Press (1st edn, 1981).

Kember, D., Hong, C., Ho, A. and Ho, A. (2011) 'More can mean less motivation: applying a motivational orientation framework to the expanded entry into higher education in Hong Kong', *Studies in Higher Education*, 36(2): 209–225.

Keogh, P. and Wang, Z. (2010) 'Clickers in institutions: one campus, multiple perspectives,' *Library Hi Tech*, 28(1): 8–21.

Khan, Z. and Jarvenpaa, S. L. (2010) 'Exploring temporal coordination of events with Facebook.com', *Journal of Information Technology*, 25(2): 137–151.

King, N. and Horrocks, C. (2010) *Interviews in Qualitative Research*. London: Sage.

Kramer, A. (2011) 'Kinship, affinity and connectedness: exploring the role of genealogy in personal lives,' *Sociology* 45(3): 379.

Krueger, R. A. (1998a) *Developing Questions for Focus Groups*. London: Sage.

Krueger, R. A. (1998b) *Analysing and Reporting Focus Group Results*. London: Sage.

Kuh, G. D. and Ewell, P. T. (2010) 'The state of learning outcomes assessment in the United States', *Higher Education Management and Policy*, 22(1): 1–20.

Lawson, L. (2003) 'Becoming a success story: how boys who have molested children talk about treatment', *Journal of Psychiatric and Mental Health Nursing*, 10: 259–268.

Legard, R., Keegan, J. and Ward, K. (2003) 'In-depth interviews' in Ritchie, J. and Lewis, J. (eds) *Qualitative Research Practice: a Guide for Social Science Students and Researchers*. London: Sage.

Lester, J. D. and Lester, J. D. Jr. (2006) *Writing Research Papers in the Social Sciences*. New York: Pearson Longman.

Lewis, S. (2006) 'Minority ethnic experiences of probation supervision and programmes' in Lewis, S., Raynor, P., Smith, D. and Wardak, A. (eds) *Race and Probation*, Cullompton: Willan Publishing.

Liamputtong, P. (2011) *Focus Group Methodology*. London: Sage.

Lopes, A. (2006) 'Participatory action research' in Jupp, V. (ed.) *The Sage Dictionary of Social Research Methods*. London: Sage.

Macdonald, K. (2008) 'Using documents' in Gilbert, N. (ed.) *Researching Social Life* 3rd edn. London: Sage (1st edn, 1993).

Mackie, S. E. (2001) 'Jumping the hurdles – undergraduate student withdrawal behaviour,' *Innovations in Education and Teaching International*, 38(3): 265–276.

Martel, J., Brassard, R. and Jaccoud, M. (2011) 'When two worlds collide: Aboriginal risk management in Canadian corrections,' *British Journal of Criminology*, 51(2): 235–255.

Mathews, S., Jewkes, R. and Abrahams, N. (2011) '"I had a hard life": exploring childhood adversity in the shaping of masculinities among men who killed an intimate partner in South Africa', *British Journal of Criminology*, 51(6): 960–977.

Matthews, B. and Ross, L. (2010) *Research Methods: A Practical Guide for the Social Sciences*. Harlow: Pearson Education Limited.

Mautner, G. (2008) 'Analysing newspapers, magazines and other print media' in Wodak, R. and Krzyzanowski, M. (eds) *Qualitative Discourse Analysis in the Social Sciences*. Basingstoke: Palgrave Macmillan.

May, J. (2000) 'Housing histories and homeless careers: a biographical approach,' *Housing Studies*, 15(4): 613–638.

Mayock, P. and Sheridan, S. (2011) 'Women and homelessness in Ireland: a biographical pathways analysis', *European Journal of Homelessness*, 5(2): 215–216.

McMullen, L. M. (2011) 'A discursive analysis of Teresa's protocol' in Wertz, F. J. Charmaz, K., McMullen, L. M., Josselson, R., Anderson, R. and McSpadden, E. *Five Ways of Doing Qualitative Analysis*. New York: The Guilford Press.

Mead, M. (1943) *Coming of Age in Samoa: a Study of Adolescence and Sex in Primitive Societies*. Harmondsworth: Penguin.

Miles, M. B. and Huberman, M. (1994) *Qualitative Data Analysis*, 2nd edn. London: Sage (1st edn, 1984).

Miller, J. and Glassner, B. (2011) 'The "insider" and the "outsider": finding reality in interviews' in Silverman, D. (ed.) *Doing Qualitative Research*, 3rd edn. London: Sage (1st edn, 1997).

Mok, D. Wellman, B. and Carrasco, J. A. (2010) 'Does distance still matter in the age of the internet?' *Urban Studies*, 47(13): 2743–2783.

Morgan, D. L. (2010) 'Reconsidering the role of interaction in analyzing and reporting focus group data,' *Qualitative Health Research*, 20(5): 718–722.

Moses, J. M. and Knutsen, T. L. (2007) *Ways of Knowing: Competing Methodologies in Social and Political Research*. Basingstoke: Palgrave Macmillan.

Muncie, J. (2006) 'Discourse analysis' in Jupp, V. (ed.) *The Sage Dictionary of Social Research Methods*. London: Sage.

Murdie, R. and Teixeira, C. (2011) 'The impact of gentrification on ethnic neighbourhoods in Toronto: a case study of Little Portugal', *Urban Studies*, 48(1): 61–83.

Murthy, D. (2008) 'Digital ethnography: an examination of new technologies for social research', *Sociology*, 45(5): 837–855.

National Audit Office (2002) *Improving Student Achievement in English Higher Education. Report by the Comptroller and Auditor General*. HC 486 Session 2001–2002: 18 January 2002. Available online at: http://www.nao.org.uk/publications/0102/improving_student_achievement.aspx, (accessed 23 May 2009).

Nare, L. (2011) 'The moral economy of domestic care and labour: migrant workers in Naples, Italy', *Sociology*, 45(3): 396–412.

Neuman, W. L. (2006) *Social Research Methods: Qualitative and Quantitative Approaches*. Boston: Pearson Education.

Newburn, T. (2007) *Criminology*. Cullompton: Willan Publishing.

Newman-Ford, L. Fitzgibbon, K., Lloyd, S. and Thomas, S. (2008) 'A large-scale investigation into the relationship between attendance and attainment: a study using an innovative, electronic attendance monitoring system', *Studies in Higher Education*, 33(6): 699–717.

Oates, C. (2000) 'The use of focus groups in social science research' in Burton, D. (ed.) *Research Training for Social Scientists*. London: Sage.

Onifade, D. (2002) *The Experience of Black/Minority Ethnic Police Officers, Support Staff, Special Constables and Resigners in Scotland*. Edinburgh: Scottish Executive Central Research Unit. Available online at: http://www.scotland.gov.uk/Publications/2002/06/14841/5304 (accessed 23 May 2012)

Onwuegbuzie, A. J., Dickinson, W. B., Leech, N. L. and Zoran, A. G. (2009) 'A qualitative framework for collecting and analyzing data in focus group research', *International Journal of Qualitative Methods*, 8(3): 1–21.

Oppenheim, A. N. (1992) *Questionnaire Design, Interviewing and Attitude Measurement*, 2nd edn. London: Continuum (1st edn, 1996).

Pain, R. and Francis, P. (2004) 'Living with crime: spaces of risk for homeless people', *Children's Geographies*, 2(1): 95–110.

Parish, J. (2011) 'West African witchcraft, wealth and moral decline in New York city', *Ethnography*, 12(2): 247–265.

Patton, M. Q. (2002) *Qualitative Research and Evaluation Methods*. London: Sage.

Pells, K. (2011) 'Keep going despite everything: legacies of genocide for Rwanda's children and youth', *International Journal of Sociology and Social Policy*, 31(9/10): 594–606.

Plummer, K. (2001) *Documents of Life 2: An Invitation to Critical Humanism*. London: Sage.

Pryke, S. (2004) '"Some of our people can be the most difficult". Reflections on difficult interviews', *Sociological Research Online,* 9(1).

Radwin, L. E., Farquhar, S. L., Knowles, M. N. and Virchick, B. G. (2005) 'Cancer patients' description of their nursing care', *Journal of Advanced Nursing,* 50(2): 162–169.

Rager, K. (2004) 'A thematic analysis of the self-directed experiences of 13 breast cancer patients', *International Journal of Lifelong Education,* 23(1): 95–109.

Rapley, T. (2011) 'Some pragmatics of qualitative data analysis' in Silverman, D. (ed.) *Qualitative Research,* 3rd edn. London: Sage (1st edn, 1997).

Ray, L., Smith, D. and Wastell, L. (2004) 'Shame, rage and racist violence', *British Journal of Criminology,* 44(3): 350–368.

Reason, P. and Bradbury, H. (2006) 'Introduction: inquiry and participation in search of a world worthy of human aspiration' in Reason, P. and Bradbury, H. (eds) *Handbook of Action Research,* 2nd edn. London: Sage (1st edn, 2001).

Reay, D., Davies, J., David, M. and Ball, S. J. (2001) 'Choices of degree or degrees of choice? Class, "race" and the Higher Education choice process', *Sociology,* 35(4): 855–874.

Richards, L. (2009) *Handling Qualitative Data,* 2nd edn. London: Sage (1st edn, 2005).

Riessman, C. K. (2006) 'Narrative analysis' in Jupp, V. (ed.) *The Sage Dictionary of Social Research Methods.* London: Sage.

Robotham, D. and Julian, C. 2006. 'Stress and the higher education student: a critical review of the literature', *Journal of Further and Higher Education,* 30(2): 107–117.

Robson, C. (2011) *Real World Research.* Chichester: John Wiley and Sons Limited.

Rosenthal, G. (2004) 'Biographical research' in Seale, C. Gobo, G. Gubrium, J. F. and Silverman, D. (eds) *Qualitative Research Practice.* London: Sage.

Roulston, K. (2010) *Reflective Interviewing: A Guide to Theory and Practice.* London: Sage.

Rudestam, K. E. and Newton, R. R. (2007) *Surviving Your Dissertation: A Comprehensive Guide to Content and Process.* London: Sage.

Saldana, J. (2009) *The Coding Manual for Qualitative Researchers.* London: Sage.

Sapsford, R. (2006) 'Methodology' in Jupp, V. (2006) *The Sage Dictionary of Social Research Methods.* London: Sage.

Schmidt, D. (2004) 'The analysis of semi-structured interviews' in Flick, U., Von Kardoff, E. and Steinke, I. *A Companion to Qualitative Research.* London: Sage.

Schon, D. A. (1987) *Educating the Reflective Practitioner.* San Francisco: Jossey-Bass.

Scott, J. (2006) 'Content analysis' in Jupp, V. (ed.) *The Sage Dictionary of Social Research Methods.* London: Sage.

Semmens, N. (2011) 'Methodological approaches to Criminological research' in Davies, P., Francis, P. and Jupp, V. (eds) *Doing Criminological Research,* 2nd edn. London: Sage (1st edn, 2000).

Sheard, L. (2011) '"Anything could have happened": women, the night-time economy, alcohol and drink spiking', *Sociology* 45(4): 619–633.

Sheikhattari, P., Burke, J. G., O'Keefe, A. M. and Bazargan-Hejazi, S. (2012) 'Sustaining relationships between communities and local health systems: two Iranian villages', *Journal of International Development,* 24: 433–447.

Silverman, D. (2006) *Interpreting Qualitative Data,* 3rd edn. London: Sage (1st edn, 1993).

Silverman, D. (2007) *A Very Short, Fairly Interesting and Reasonably Cheap Book About Qualitative Research.* London: Sage.

Skovdal, M. and Andreouli, E. (2010) 'Using identity and recognition as a framework to understand and promote the resilience of caregiving children in Western Kenya', *Journal of Social Policy,* 40(3): 613–630.

Spicer, N. (2012) 'Combining qualitative and quantitative methods' in Seale, C. (ed.) *Researching Society and Culture*. London: Sage.

Steinke, I. (2004) 'Quality criteria in qualitative research' in Flick, U., von Kardoff E. and Steinke, I. (eds) *A Companion to Qualitative Research*. London: Sage.

Tierney, J. (2010) *Criminology: Theory and Context*, 3rd edn. Harlow: Pearson Education Limited (1st edn: 1996).

Tones, M., Fraser, J., Elder, R. and White, K. M. (2009) 'Supporting mature-age students from a low socioeconomic background', *Higher Education,* 58(4): 505–529.

Tonkiss, F. (2012) 'Focus groups' in Seale, C. (ed.) *Researching Society and Culture*. London: Sage.

Valentova, M. and Zhelyazkova, N. (2011) 'Women's perceptions of consequences of career interruptions due to childcare in Central and Eastern Europe', *Journal of Social Policy,* 40(1): 89–112.

Wang, X., Xu, L., Shan, X. and Guo, P. (2010) 'Extra costs for older people with disabilities in Northern China', *Social Policy and Society,* 10(1): 79–91.

Wertz, F. J. (2011) 'A phenomenological psychological approach to trauma and resilience' in Wertz, F. J., Charmaz, K., McMullen, L. M., Josselson, R., Anderson, R. and McSpadden, E. (2011) *Five Ways of Doing Qualitative Analysis*. New York: The Guilford Press.

Wharton, C. (2006) 'Document analysis' in Jupp, V. (ed.) (2006) *The Sage Dictionary of Social Research Methods*. London: Sage.

Wilkinson, S. (2011) 'Analysing focus group data' in Silverman, D. (ed.) *Qualitative Research*. London: Sage.

Wimshurst, K. (2011) 'Applying threshold concept theory to an unsettled field: an exploratory study in criminal justice education', *Studies in Higher Education,* 36(3): 301–314.

Winchester, H. P. M. (1999) 'Interviews and questionnaires as mixed methods in population geography: the case of lone fathers in Newcastle, Australia', *The Professional Geographer*, 51(1): 60–67.

Woodfield, R., Jessop, D. and McMillan, L. (2006) 'Gender differences in undergraduate attendance rates', *Studies in Higher Education,* 31(1): 1–22.

Wooffitt, R. (2005) *Conversation Analysis and Discourse Analysis: A Comparative and Critical Introduction*. London: Sage.

Yin, R. K. (2003) *Case Study Research*, 3rd edn. London: Sage (1st edn, 1989).

Yin, R. K. (2011) *Qualitative Research From Start to Finish*, New York: The Guilford Press.

Young, M. and Willmott, P. (1957) *Family and Kinship in East London*, London: Routledge and Kegan Paul.

Index